IN THE
SHADOW OF
BEN
NEVIS

IN THE SHADOW OF
BEN NEVIS

IAN SYKES

Foreword by Hamish MacInnes

**bâton
wicks**

Bâton Wicks, Sheffield
www.v-publishing.co.uk/batonwicks

To the members of RAF Kinloss Mountain Rescue Team
and Lochaber Mountain Rescue Team past and present
for years of friendship, camaraderie and glorious fun.
To Gay who is my constant support and puts up with
a continually vanishing climber, and Jane Cooper whose
enthusiasm and help made this book possible.

In the Shadow of Ben Nevis
Ian Sykes

First published in 2016 by Bâton Wicks.

BÂTON WICKS
Crescent House, 228 Psalter Lane, Sheffield S11 8UT.
www.v-publishing.co.uk/batonwicks

ISBN: 978-1-898573-98-2 (Paperback)
ISBN: 978-1-898573-99-9 (Ebook)

Design and production by Jane Beagley.

Vertebrate Publishing.
www.v-publishing.co.uk

Bâton Wicks is committed to printing on paper from sustainable sources.

Printed and bound in Scotland by Bell & Bain Ltd.

Contents

Foreword | Hamish MacInnes

My association with Ian Sykes (Spike) goes back over fifty years to when he was a young lad on the RAF Mountain Rescue Team based out of Kinloss. One might find it anomalous (after half a century) that I could possibly remember the circumstances of our first meeting. But remember I do with crystalline clarity: New Year, the Cuillin, Isle of Skye, 1963. What should have been a festive evening turned ever more grim by the hour: climbers missing, many hours overdue, conditions hellishly icy and Arctic.

So began the now legendary Skye New Year call-out – the longest and most protracted rescue ever enacted in Scotland. I was there – as was Spike (with the Kinloss Team). He presents here the RAF version of the rescue for the first time.

There is an immediacy and accessibility in his telling of this heart-wrenching, compelling story – as if he were an old friend recounting the tale to you before a smoldering peat fire in some Highland pub on a winter night. It's all here: the pathos of dead bodies, undaunted bravery and courage, holiday merrymakers enlisted as ill-equipped rescuers with primitive equipment. Days without sleep culminating in numbed reactions and sheer exhaustion. In the end there are weeping survivors and broken hearts as well as broken stretchers.

Many friends of mine were involved in this epic and, in Spike's telling, the tale takes on an almost cinematic breadth and sweep – except one must keep reminding oneself: it really happened! I will never forget the culminating boat journey home with dead bodies lashed to the deck and bottles of whisky circulating among the fifty or so rescuers jammed in the hold below singing, '*It was sad when the great ship went down*'. It was a sobering experience that none of us will ever forget.

For many, an epic like the rescue on Skye might be thought of as a 'high point' in a lifetime – but not Spike – he was just getting started and he recounts here a good many further lively tales of explorations, adventures, mishaps but, as well, and of equal importance to him, the enduring bonds of friendship and camaraderie, be it with man or beast.

An example of this is Antarctica, which occupied a considerable chunk of Spike's life. Spike gives us a deep insight into what it is like living day to day with a dog team. He captures the harsh realities of life at the edge and the end of the world and so brilliantly expounds the tremendous bond between the huskies and their handler – each relying on the other for survival. By sheer coincidence, Spike's posting to Antarctica with the British Antarctic Survey highlights the end of the era where dogs were the main form of Antarctic travel, replaced – if you can imagine – by the combustion engine, as being far more eco-friendly! Spike captures it all beautifully, as if taking you by the hand, as if bringing you along on the journey to the end of the world.

For myself, oddly enough one of the highlights of the book is Spike's tale of re-imagining himself as a visionary outdoor entrepreneur and, no doubt, one of the first eco-adventure capitalists in all of Scotland – never mind the Highlands. His animated recounting of setting up Nevisport, which he and his friend Ian Sutherland built into a national chain of mountaineering shops, and then the construction of the Nevis Range – a world-class ski resort and mountain-bike centre, is both awe inspiring and side-splittingly funny at times – can you imagine in this day and age your shop being picketed by protesters because they want you 'closed on the Sabbath', which just happens to be your busiest trading day of the week? As a testament to Spike's inspiring and wonderful spirit, he not only won the day, but soon most of the town converted to Sunday opening. When you consider that much of what you see today about Fort William and its environs – even the moniker the 'Outdoor Capital of the UK' – is directly due to Spike's life-long commitment and love affair with the people and wild places of the West Highlands, one can only be inspired by what he has accomplished.

In the Shadow of Ben Nevis is Spike's life story – it brims with passion, resilience, honesty, patience, courage, adaptability, and a fair amount of intrigue. To this day he remains remarkably self-effacing and kindhearted to one and all for all his success and achievements. To that end I shall call it quits here – if I carry on any further it would be most embarrassing!

1 | Fort William Station

The ticket inspector eyed me suspiciously as he clipped my RAF pass. He clearly mistrusted servicemen.

'Which is the London train?' I asked, looking down the platform. Trains were waiting on both sides, their long dirty carriages with doors hanging open devoid of passengers. A gentle hissing from the engines built up steam.

He nodded to the right. 'Plenty of room until Glasgow, then you'll be lucky to get a seat,' he said malevolently.

I walked to the end of the platform feeling uncomfortably smart in my best blue uniform. It was a cold morning in Fort William, my breath mingling with the smoke from the engines. I dumped my bag in an empty compartment then wandered back down the corridor and stuck my head out of the window. There was no sign of Tony. A few passengers arrived, doors slammed, the whistle blew and slowly the train began to rumble out of the station. Where the hell was he?

As the train moved off I saw him leaning out of the window of a carriage on the opposite platform. Our eyes met in shock!

'My God, I'm on the wrong train!' Not for one second did it occur to me that Tony might be the one in the wrong.

I hurled myself down the corridor and flung open the compartment door. A small lady was now sitting in the window seat.

'Is this the London train?' I gasped.

'I don't know, son, I'm just going to Spean Bridge,' she said.

By now the carriage was fully off the platform, still moving slowly. There wasn't a second for hesitation. I flung open the carriage door, slung out my bag and dived after it. It's a long drop without a platform. I bounced down the bank and landed in a tangle of brambles, unhurt but ripping my

1

trousers from knee to backside. A sea of startled grinning faces stared down as the train trundled passed. Shouts were coming from the platform as an angry guard screamed obscenities. I extracted myself from the thorn bush, grabbed my bag and limped back along the line to the platform holding my trousers together at the backside and trying to look dignified.

Tony was leaning out of his carriage window grinning from ear to ear.

'What was that all about, Spike?' he asked, looking perplexed, as I scrambled into the train.

At that precise moment there came a jolt. The carriage I had jumped from had stopped, points had changed and it had shunted back up the line and linked us together into a single train. I couldn't believe it!

Cringing with embarrassment, I made my way along the now familiar corridor to make my apologies to the lady from Spean Bridge. She was very nice about it and, laughing, gave me a safety pin to hold my trousers together.

Thus started my ill-fated journey to the Admiralty in London, where I failed the interview to become the RAF's representative to go on the Joint Services Expedition to South Georgia.

I know that this is a strange place to begin a story but it seems somewhat appropriate considering the way things have panned out. I have never kept a diary so forgive any discrepancies with dates and names and perhaps the odd exaggeration. I'll tell the tale as I remember it and maybe change the occasional name to save embarrassment and perhaps protect myself from libel.

At the time of the train incident it was 1962 and I was nineteen-year-old Leading Aircraftman Ian Sykes, best known to my friends as Spike, as I still am, for no other reason than it half rhymes with Sykes. I was stationed at RAF Kinloss on the Moray Firth coast of Scotland and a member of the Mountain Rescue team. It was the height of the cold war, of which I was oblivious.

The chance to go to South Georgia had come my way through the kindness of my squadron leader, John Sims, who had recommended me. In those days few of the RAF Mountain Rescue team members were serious climbers; they were much more interested in long hill walks and Munro bagging. I'd been climbing for years in the Yorkshire Dales and was quite experienced for my age and this was to be my big chance. To cut a long story short, I blew it.

I arrived late at the Admiralty, my trousers still held together by a safety pin, and was ushered into an interview room, where three fully uniformed admirals sat with what looked like old scrambled egg on their hat visors and their chests weighed down with medal ribbons.

'Sit down, Sykes. At ease.'

My knees were shaking.

'I understand that you're a bit of a climber?' one of these exalted ones asked.

That's a stupid thing to ask any mountaineer, especially one as young and naïve as I was. False modesty is the order of the day when climbers talk.

I shook my head with embarrassment. 'Oh no sir, I'm really pretty useless,' I stammered. He looked at me strangely.

'Why do you want to go on this expedition?' the second sailor asked through gritted teeth.

I couldn't think of a single reason why an idiot like me should go on such a jaunt. The interview became a horrible blur and I finally staggered out of the room knowing full well I would not be going.

What really irked was that when I chatted later with some of the other candidates, I discovered that almost all of them had exaggerated their ability to get on to the expedition; bullshit I call it. Tony Back, my flight lieutenant companion on the train, got to go. A well-deserving case. I'm pleased to say that the expedition turned out to be a bit of a shambles. When I finally did get to go to South Georgia it was under much better circumstances. I returned to Kinloss a wiser man, determined to bullshit for all I was worth in my next interview.

I spent three years on the Kinloss Rescue team – a time of great happiness. It was the end of an era: National Service was coming to an end. When I joined the team about half the members were National Servicemen. I'd signed on for five years and was paid the princely sum of £6 a week, about twice their pay. By the time I left, the RAF had become a professional air force with no more conscription; a smaller and supposedly more efficient service but it had lost some of its character.

The team leader was Chief Technician John Hinde. He had just taken over as the boss and was still feeling his way. It was a rough and ready set-up of thirty-six volunteers, bored and penniless on an isolated RAF station and pleased for the chance of free weekends walking the Scottish mountains. I had taken up climbing much younger than the rest of them and as luck had it the chief needed a full-time store man and offered me a job on his permanent staff. It meant dropping out of my career in air movements for a while and I jumped at the chance.

The RAF was, until the late sixties, virtually the only rescue service in Scotland. Small fledgling civilian teams were starting up and there was no shortage of volunteers, but they were badly equipped and the services had the advantage of radio communications. Not that they worked very well. The old ex-wartime no. 38 radio set was heavy and cumbersome; they weighed about twenty pounds and one man operated while another pedalled a small generator. The radios didn't work very well either. The trick was to accidently leave them in the Land Rover or dump them under a convenient bush to be picked up on return from the hill and claim that you couldn't make contact. We had an old Bedford signals truck for communications, operated in my time by Leading Aircraftman Peter Myers – 'Sweet' to his friends – who to my certain knowledge never contacted a soul on the mountains in the three years I was there.

Sweet and I shared a room in the old sick quarters, which had become the mountain rescue HQ. This was wonderfully divorced from the rest of the station where the enlisted men lived in old wooden Nissen huts. Here we had a private bathroom and a comfortable common room with a coal fire. On one wall was a one-inch scale map, roughly thirty feet long, covering the whole of the north of Scotland from Glen Coe in the south to Cape Wrath in the north, and from the Cairngorms to the Outer Hebrides.

This represented 20,000 square miles of the wildest country in Britain; the map was speckled in pins marking the sites of crashed aircraft and old rescues. The number of aircraft was horrific; dozens of planes had crashed returning from operations during the war and it was part of our job to keep an eye on the wrecks.

Our equipment was basic, consisting of Robert Lawrie boots, sea-boot socks, RAF working blue trousers (very itchy), string vests (all the rage in the sixties), a navy sweater and an aircrew issue cold-wet jacket. The last item is worthy of description. Made from a rough canvas it had a tail that hung over the backside down to the backs of the knees, and a woolly lining that absorbed water like blotting paper. In the rain it weighed a ton and in the winter it would freeze solid like a suit of armour. Some of our boots still had old-fashioned Tricouni nails, as worn by hill shepherds, although most of us preferred commando soles. Vibram rubber soles had not yet appeared.

Wearing Tricounis in winter was a bitter experience; the iron nails would freeze terribly and we had constant frost blisters on the soles of our feet. We had War Department crampons, the points of which bent with ease. I remember jumping down the path on Ben Nevis once and the entire points of my crampons splayed out flat. We were also issued an Austrian Aschenbrenner long-shafted ice axe; mine still hangs on the wall, an heirloom of the past.

Two well-known climbers had just left the team when I arrived; Terry Sullivan, a Geordie and terrific rock climber, and Ian Clough ('Dangle' to his friends), a fine all-rounder whom I knew slightly as he came from Keighley near my home in Leeds. We both learned to climb at Almscliff Crag near Harrogate. Surprisingly, although 'demobbed', Ian was living quietly in the morgue at the back of our sick quarters, eating happily in the airman's mess and travelling with the team on weekend exercises. This seemed quite normal and nobody took a blind bit of notice.

There were some strange characters. Corporal Yorky Watson had a pedal organ at the side of his bunk with bundles of black German sausages dangling alongside. The place stank of garlic but was worth a visit. During inspections, thankfully rare, the inspecting officer would usually stare at Yorky's strange set-up in consternation, shrug and move on. I guess it was too much bother to deal with him.

Another character was Leading Aircraftman Barry Halpin. 'Dirty Lonnie', as he was known, came from Liverpool. He was a fine banjo player with an amazing repertoire of Irish rebel songs, Scottish ballads and bawdy folk songs. Not so long ago a book was written about sightings of Lord Lucan in Goa, India. To my amazement, there grinning back at the camera on the cover was a long-haired Dirty Lonnie. How anybody could mistake him for Lord Lucan I'll never know. More of Lonnie later.

There were more rescues than I had expected. Most call-outs were for lost walkers, many of whom were badly equipped and inexperienced, and these often involved long multi-day searches. The RAF had helicopters but in the sixties these were not readily available other than for sea searches or for lost aircraft. Actual mountaineering accidents involving technical climbing were rare, but things were about to change.

My first mountain rescue taught me a lesson I have always remembered. The Cairngorm ski centre at Aviemore was still under construction, the White Lady ski lift was operating and the Shieling refuge in the middle of the ski field was half complete and a family called Carter were living in it as custodians.

We had been exercising in Glen Nevis that day and had just returned to Kinloss when a call came through that a skier called Billy Garland had failed to return when the ski lifts closed. As we left Kinloss it was snowing heavily and the road was lethal. Just outside Aviemore, at a narrow railway bridge, a BBC van slid into our leading truck. The rest of our vehicles coming down the hill concertinaed gracefully into the backs of each other. There were a lot of bumped heads, wounded pride and twisted bumpers, but fortunately nobody was hurt. By the time we reached Aviemore the roads were virtually impassable and high winds were blasting off the Cairngorm plateau.

Johnny Hinde had an amazing knack of knowing where to search. He assumed that Billy had probably skied off in the wrong direction and reasoned that if he was uninjured he would end up somewhere in the region of Loch Avon. He split us up into search parties and in appalling conditions we set out over Cairn Gorm.

I was to search the Hell's Lum crags, but in the high winds and drifting snow visibility was absolute zero. By the time daylight arrived we were wallowing around the foot of the crags but there was nothing to see. It took us all day in waist-deep drifts to make our way back to the Shieling where Mrs Carter hovered over us with tea and kindness. We were dead on our feet.

The following morning we went out again, searching over the top of Cairn Gorm to The Saddle and down Glen Strath Nethy. If anything the wind had increased and the drifts made progress agonisingly slow. Nobody could survive in these conditions and the search for Billy had become a search for his body. It was dark when my party reached Bynack Stable bothy, where we sheltered before walking along the snow-blocked track to Glenmore Lodge, the Scottish National Outdoor Training Centre. The instructors from the Lodge were all out searching with us. Other rescue parties were struggling back exhausted.

We spent a glum night drying out soaking wet clothes and poring over maps. There was nothing left to do but start to cover the same ground again, yet finding a body in this snow would be almost impossible. Many of the civilian searchers were beginning to leave, having done more than their best.

Day three and the wind was still blasting the Cairngorms, but the sun was shining and the mountains were gleaming, spindrift dancing along the surface in beautiful plumes. The northern corries were vividly stark with huge snow cornices hanging out over the cliffs, a white wilderness of mountains as far as the eye could see. Loch Morlich was frozen solid and snowploughs were attempting to open the old A9 road at the Drumochter and Slochd passes. The little town of Aviemore was cut off from the world.

That day my party searched Lurcher's Crag and the old Jean's Hut in Coire an Lochain which had been checked and rechecked but was worth another look. While we were fruitlessly covering old ground on the other side of Cairn Gorm a miracle happened. John Hinde had taken a party back down to the head of Loch Avon. As they made their way down through the drifts, a strange figure loomed out of the mist wearing a huge gas-cape that had become plastered in snow. He looked like a walking tent. Incredibly it turned out to be Billy Garland.

Throughout this incredible storm he had wandered about, blown along by the wind, and although slightly frostbitten he still was able, with help, to make his way back over the mountain to the ski centre. He was dressed in very basic ski clothing but fortunately had the old gas-cape with him; as this became plastered in snow it gave him good insulation and undoubtedly saved his life. He was an extremely fit man, athletic and a weightlifter. He told us later that in his misery he had lain down to sleep with a polythene bag over his head with the idea of asphyxiating himself, but this had warmed him sufficiently to give him the strength to keep going.

So this extraordinary search had a happy ending. In the many rescues I have been involved with during the last forty years such an escape has proved all too rare. Even experienced and well-equipped mountaineers rapidly succumb to exhaustion and hypothermia when caught out in far less desperate conditions than these. As a young and inexperienced member of the rescue team I found it incredible that Billy had survived. He did everything wrong. He was on his own with no map or compass and was poorly clothed. The best thing to do in his predicament would have been to find shelter and dig in. He did none of these things and still survived.

It's not the job of the rescue service to criticise, but to do everything possible to save life and not give up too soon. I know people who have fallen thousands of feet and come out with hardly a scratch, wandered lost for weeks or been buried in avalanches and lived to tell the tale. Life is a great blessing and in many people the will to live is a driving force. I vowed never again to take it for granted that we were looking for a body.

2 | Garforth

My family lived in Garforth, a country village about ten miles from Leeds where my grandparents ran the Miner's Arms, the local pub, which sat across the green from an old farm. Most of the locals were either coal miners or worked on the land. The village has now become part of the suburbs and urban sprawl of the city. The farm is the site of a supermarket and the fields have become housing estates.

In his day my father was the biggest bookie in Leeds. He had offices in York Road and Upper Fountain Street and, as I remember it, most of our family friends were in the racing business, from professional backers of horses to bookies, runners and policemen.

He had been in the Royal Naval Air Service in the First World War before it became the Fleet Air Arm, and had flown Shorts biplanes. There is a family story that he was on the first flight of aircraft to land on a modified battleship. I have his old album with pictures of biplanes, many in various wrecked states; aerial shots of massed shipping, which I reckon are taken on reconnaissance flights. There are a number of photographs taken in a pigeon loft; I assume pigeons were his method of communication, and there are young men grinning at the camera, many of whose names are underlined and there is an ominous note saying 'deceased'. How he made the transition from airman to bookmaker I'll never know. He always said that the day that betting on horses became legal in England his business would be ruined.

My mother, Nancy, was born in Headingley in 1914. My grandfather was fighting in Nancy in France at the time – hence the name. He was in the Seaforth Highlanders and my grandmother spent much of the First World War in Musselburgh near Edinburgh where his regiment was based. When he was wounded out of the fighting they rented the Miner's Arms. He died of his wounds just before I was born.

My mother worked behind the bar. She had wanted to go to art school but the war intervened and she had been sent to Pitman College in Liverpool. She trained as a secretary and learned to type at a phenomenal speed, probably in anger. She was a very beautiful woman and did some modelling work. A great swimmer, I can see her now plunging into the sea and crashing through enormous waves without a care for life or limb.

I entered the world on 10 January 1943 in Wetherby. Apparently my mother was taken by taxi to a nursing home during a heavy snowstorm. Most of the roads were blocked and petrol was rationed, so my father didn't manage to see us for over a week. I can't imagine the petrol being much of a problem because as well as his betting business he seems to have been a major player on the Leeds black market.

There was an Italian POW camp outside Garforth and they must have been free to wander and visit the pub. I can just remember them taking me around the village in my pushchair. Each morning at 6 a.m. I could hear all the street doors open and the tramp, tramp, tramp of hundreds of pairs of clogs as the miners went on the first shift at Temple Newsam pit. I have a very vague memory of seeing barrage balloons over Leeds.

The pub was an exciting place to grow up in. It was a rambling old building, and upstairs was the Lodge of the Grand Order of Buffaloes with great horned heads of beasts and spears and flags on the walls. The tap-room was a cheery place with a big log fire surrounded by the miners' dogs. It reeked from a heavy fog of pipe and cigarette smoke; a place of darts and dominoes and an escape from the reality of what must have been a very austere time. There was a ramp where the barrels were lowered by rope into the damp and whitewashed cellar.

On a ledge behind the barrels lived a huge old toad. At some time in the distant past a barrel must have run over him as he had only three legs. Grandma said that he had lived there before the previous owners of the pub and that he was thought to be over eighty years old. I would slip down to the cellar to watch him. He never moved but sat staring out over the barrels, an occasional blink his only sign of life.

My great friend was Mr Lyons, a wonderful old man who must have been in his seventies. He had a weather-beaten round face with a walrus moustache, a toy that he twiddled constantly. We scoured the country-side. He seemed to know everybody and I remember sitting with him behind two giant carthorses as he ploughed the fields that are now housing estates.

One day he took me to the farm across the road from the pub and I wandered into a shed where a tractor was driving a turnip-chopping machine. As children do, I reached out into the cogwheels and my fingers were dragged through and mangled along with the turnips. The old man had a terrible fright, grabbed me and ran across to the pub yelling for help.

I was rushed to St James's Hospital in Leeds where surgeons did a mar-vellous job of saving my hand. I lost my right middle finger and a couple of joints in the others but my hand was saved. I was young enough to com-pensate easily and the loss has never been a problem. There are in fact several advantages: I can tell the most incredible stories about the daring deeds that caused the loss of my finger. Young climbers have been sent up to look in the crack where I fell off, to see if the bone is still sticking out, and I have a great one about being tied to a railway line and escaping not quite in the nick of time.

The men began to return from the war. Grandma celebrated my Uncle Andrew's homecoming with a party in the pub by opening a tin of ham, which she had kept hidden throughout the war. She had only seen her son once in the entire conflict when he got a few days leave after escaping from the beaches of Dunkirk. He was an armourer in the RAF and had watched his entire squadron of aircraft wiped out by dive bombers:

'My squadron was in a place called Vitry-en-Artois. We had twenty-two Hurricanes which were all lined up ready when a flight of Heinkels screamed down from nowhere and got the whole bloody lot with one burst. The Germans turned up almost immediately and we were strafed all the way down the street. We were ordered to leave everything and make for the coast. A stupid sergeant took it literally and we left rifles and food and personal effects and spent the next few days running through the fields dodging the Germans. I gave my last cigarettes to a Belgian refugee.'

After Dunkirk he went to North Africa and was chased up and down the desert by Rommel. He was then posted to Italy where he was bombed to blazes, and from there to Malta where the same thing happened. At the end of the war in Europe he was loaded on to a boat bound for Japan and was at sea when the atom bombs were dropped on Hiroshima and Nagasaki and hostilities ceased. Thus, Andrew wholeheartedly approved of atomic bombs. He arrived home a changed man from the boy who had left Garforth.

About this time my father tried to become the landlord of the Miner's Arms but was refused a licence by Tetley's, the owners, because of his bookmaking activities, so Grandma kept the licence and my parents helped out. In the summer we went to Blackpool. This was a working holiday as my father spent the days running a book at Blackpool racecourse. Two of his best friends there were Gordon Richards, the jockey, and Charlie Cairoli the famous clown at the Tower Circus.

In 1948 my father bought a bungalow in Temple Newsam and we moved out of the pub. He must have been doing well because we were beginning to have the trappings of affluence. He acquired an American Railton car and we bought a Bush television, the first in our street. All the early programmes were interspaced with 'Normal Service will be resumed as soon as possible,' and 'Test card C'. Many goods were still rationed but I have no recollection of hardship. At weekends we would run out into the Dales or North Yorkshire, often it was to Ripon, Thirsk or York where the race meetings were held.

We had a burglar one night. He had actually tiptoed into my parents' bedroom and I was wakened by yells from my mother and the sound of my father chasing him down the street. Nothing much was taken, apart from some clothes but the *Yorkshire Post* had a field day with the headline 'Well-known Leeds bookmaker loses his shirt'.

At the bottom of our road was a high steel fence, on the other side of which sprawled the massive Halton Moor housing estate. Recently built, it was considered a no-go area by my parents. There lurked danger. The Moor and Quarry Hill flats were considered the roughest parts of Leeds and the boys there were different from my friends. 'They're rough and common, you'll be murdered if you go in there,' I was told. I did, of course, sneak in occasionally but always kept well clear of the gangs of youngsters who roamed there. Mostly we went the other way, scouring the woods and fields between Garforth and Colton and fishing for sticklebacks in the lawn pond in Temple Newsam park.

It was possible to take the tram from Temple Newsam right across Leeds to Ilkley. My Aunt Agnes took me there often and we would swim in the open-air swimming pool and walk up to the Cow and Calf rocks. The Calf is a huge boulder with a line of ancient holds cut into its smooth side, which have worn down over the years. I remember the excitement of scrambling up those sloping holds and Agnes screaming in horror at me as I tried to reverse back down. My first climb! The Cow and Calf would be a great training ground in the future.

Sometime in 1949 my father asked me if I would like to go to boarding school. This sounded very grown up and exciting. 'Yes,' I said without having a clue about what he was asking. Thinking about it now, I can't imagine what possessed my parents to send me away at this early age. The realisation of my impending doom did not occur to me in the exciting weeks of preparation. I was taken to Horne Brothers in Leeds and fitted into the smallest Marlborough suit they had ever made; pinstriped trousers and jacket for Sundays and a blazer and shorts for the rest of the week, along with a wooden tuck-box and trunk for my worldly possessions.

I was to go to Fulneck, a boys' boarding school run by Moravians in a religious settlement near Pudsey. Moravians are similar to Quakers; they had been persecuted in Germany in the Middle Ages, escaped and settled in one or two communities in England where they founded schools. Most of the masters were either ministers or brethren. Their good intentions knew no bounds but I was to find that 'spare the rod' was categorically not one of their doctrines. I reckon that persecuting us little boys was their revenge for the torment of their ancestors in Bohemia.

On the evening of 10 January 1950, my seventh birthday, my parents drove me sobbing with fear to Fulneck and I was handed over to an austere woman called Matron Watson who grasped my hand and marched me quickly away. My mother must have been as shocked as I was. Life as I knew it had come to a sudden and terrifying end.

3 | Fulneck

January 1949 marked China's invasion of Tibet, the beginning of the Korean War, but more importantly to me as a frightened seven-year-old, my arrival at Fulneck School. I had plenty to be afraid of. It was a violent place, run during the day by a bunch of disinterested old men, who had avoided the war by age, along with some younger, recently demobilised, disillusioned survivors.

At night prefects kept control by the use of the gym-shoe – lines of us little boys would stand shaking outside the common room awaiting our turn for six of the best and listening to the screams of those ahead. To build up tension they would keep us waiting while slapping a gym-shoe against the wall with a loud and terrifying crack. During that time my entire life was spent with a bruised bottom. Had I realised that my next ten years would be spent here I think I would have died.

By the age of eight I had wised up. By then, like all the others, I was smoking like a chimney. We could buy Woodbines illicitly in the tuck shop for a penny each and these were normal currency in the school. We got nine pence a week pocket money, but I was better off than most as my father posted the *Eagle* comic to me every week and now and then there would be a half crown coin hidden in the packet.

Twice daily we were subjected to prayers and on Sundays we donned our pinstriped Marlborough suits and were inflicted to two long services in the Moravian church. This would have been utterly unbearable but for the fact that on one side of the chapel we sat, the boys, and on the other side sat the girls. My only contact with this alien species was longing looks from below the pews and the occasional tossed note 'sealed with a loving kiss'. In my ten years at Fulneck I learned dirty words to every hymn in the book and a lot of nonsensical fantasies about women.

In the beginning I was useless at games. This was considered bad form as Fulneck was in the heartland of cricket and the school prided itself on providing the world with stalwart men who might ultimately play for Yorkshire. I loathed the game and still do. The same went for hockey and football, although as I stretched out I finally made the rugby team. I was small and podgy and frightened of being hurt and found it better to try and sink into the background. I did, however, join the Cubs and then the Scouts.

There were exceptions: Taffy Jones was an exceptional music master and I enjoyed being in the choir and had an unsuccessful go at a number of musical instruments. The scoutmaster, Billy Biggs, was an excellent English teacher with a liking for hiking and camping and I began to take a keen interest in hillwalking.

In 1953 the king died and the country went into ecstasy about the forthcoming coronation of Princess Elizabeth. Just before the great day, the news that Edmund Hillary and Tenzing Norgay had reached the summit of Everest flashed round the world. I was spellbound; the papers were full of it and I devoured every word. This was something that I could associate myself with; Hillary and Tenzing became supermen. Years later when I met Edmund Hillary I was so overcome that I had difficulty speaking to him.

From then onwards most of my school holidays were spent trying to go climbing. Mostly I went camping at Malham Cove with my friend Terry (Toby) Ford. Toby was at Leeds Grammar School, a place I was desperate to go to. He was small and tough with dark, sharp eyes and a wicked sense of humour and he seemed to know all the lads that were keen on climbing. Sometimes we would cycle to Almscliff Crag near Harrogate and try to get the older boys to top-rope us up the climbs. Some of these have become legends in their own right: Arthur Dolphin, Allan Austin and Dennis Gray are well-known names in the climbing world.

In the summer of 1954 tragedy struck our family. My father was run over and killed while crossing York Road. My mother sheltered me from much of the agony that she must have gone through and I have never been certain as to exactly what happened. I was eleven years old and since going to boarding school had seen little of him as he had become a figurehead of the family to whom I seldom spoke. I suspect that my lack of sporting prowess was a disappointment to him.

As a bookmaker he had little regard for tax, and the Inland Revenue raided his offices immediately on the announcement of his death. My mother, who was in great distress and had little knowledge of the business, handed over the books. There followed a long court case in which my mother lost almost everything, with the exception of money that had been left in a trust for my education. I was packed off back to school unaware of what was happening, apart from gibes from older boys who were following the case in the newspapers. I pleaded with my mother to allow me to leave the school, but to no avail.

I have found it hard to feel any emotion when writing about my father's death. It was such a long time ago and he seems such a distant character whom I thought had long ago faded from my memory. However in the year 2000, when I was in my late fifties, a strange thing happened: that year I became ill and had an operation on my throat and finished up in intensive care. I was in a lot of pain, taking morphine, and things were not looking very hopeful. My partner, Gay, was sitting at my bedside reading a book when suddenly there was my father sitting talking to her. This was no dream; he was as large as life and just as I knew him. I tried frantically to speak to them but they took no notice of me and were deep in conversation. I remember thinking how young he looked, almost as if he was the same age as me. When he left I had the distinct feeling that he had been watching over me. Gay remembers nothing about the conversation. It seems a dreadful thing that he died so young – he was only fifty-seven when the accident happened, just as his business was flourishing, the same age as I was when I had the operation.

The year after my father's death, Toby, a friend called Martin Dickinson (Dicko) and I had our first camping trip to the Lake District. These days it would be unheard of for three twelve-year-olds to go off alone on such a trip, but times were different. The Lakes were quiet and empty of tourists and the farmers were friendly and let us sleep in their barns.

We took the train to Windermere and walked to Rydal Water where we camped in a beautiful spot on the lakeside. All our stuff was ex-army – boots, rucksack and blanket. We had an ex-US Army bivvy tent, which unbuttoned down the ridge and turned into two trench coats. It had wooden poles and weighed a ton. With our pots and pans and food we were hopelessly overloaded. The next day we flung away anything extra that we didn't need and amongst this I ditched the tent poles.

That day we plodded through Grasmere and over Dunmail Raise along the side of Helvellyn to Thirlmere. It started to rain as we left the road and followed the track up the hill onto Watendlath Fell. It was a long, nine-mile walk for three twelve-year-olds. We all had blisters from our ill-fitting army boots, and by the time we left Blea Tarn we were soaked and miserable. Once we got on to the fell we lost the track altogether and began to wander about without a clue where we were going.

'I think we should camp here,' Toby said.

The enormity of the situation flooded over me. 'I've thrown away the tent poles,' I confessed, sobbing. 'I thought we could tie the ends of the tent to a tree.'

We stood there in the pouring rain looking at each other hopelessly. There was nothing for it, we sheltered behind some rocks and wrapped the canvas tent around us and shivered through the night, drenched to the skin, three very miserable and frightened small boys. We couldn't have been more than a mile from Watendlath Tarn where there was a farm with outbuildings, but where was it?

At first light it was still raining and we were in thick mist. The logical thing to do was head downhill and we splashed our way down the fell side until we saw Thirlmere way below us – we had been walking in a circle. There was nothing for it but try to make our way back. Late that afternoon we arrived at a farm outside Grasmere, soaked to the skin and starving. A kind lady took us in and dried us out and we were allowed to sleep in the barn. Our fortunes were taking a real turn for the better – the place was full of eggs and we feasted on them for a couple of days.

Dicko had terrible, festering blisters on both heels and was very home-sick and unexpectedly announced that he was going home and off he went. That day Toby and I had spotted a sign saying 'Langdale Pikes'. It had a magical and enticing ring about it and we set out on the path over Lang How and dropped into the village of Chapel Stile in Great Langdale. We were mesmerised – the valley was gorgeous with its fertile, stone-walled fields and scattered farms. The Pikes rose vertically up the sides of the valley, great rocky buttresses leading up to Harrison Stickle, Pavey Ark, Gimmer Crag and Crinkle Crags. The names alone were exciting, though neither of us realised at the time that this beautiful place would become the centre of our teenage world. Even now, every time I visit Langdale I feel that I'm coming home.

On this first visit we walked up Dungeon Ghyll through fields filled with cows and the fell sides speckled with sheep, up the track past Side Pike into Little Langdale and then through Tilberthwaite, where in those days the slate quarries were still operating and the quarrymen shouted cheerfully to us as we plodded past. Almost everywhere we went people fed us and sent us on our way. The grand finale of our adventure was the ascent of 'Coniston Old Man', one of the better-known Lakeland Mountains; it was cold and misty on the summit but our first real mountain. We returned home in triumph and I didn't tell my mother about the night out on the fells for many years; she would have had hysterics.

And so the years passed. Bill Haley launched rock 'n' roll. Elvis and Cliff topped the charts. Under the dormitory floorboards our crystal sets were tuned to Radio Luxemburg and we listened weekly to *Journey into Space* and *Dick Barton, Special Agent*.

By the end of 1957 Toby and I were regular weekenders. Much of our time was spent in Langdale doing odd jobs for Ike and Zeek Myers at

Wall End Farm to pay for our accommodation in their barn. We had begun to climb on a regular basis. Our first rope was eighty feet of Italian hemp bought from Pools in Leeds and was surreptitiously stashed in Toby's garage. We would hitch to Ambleside and doss in the bus station and then travel on up to Langdale in the morning. There was a habitual bunch of us Langdaleites: Stewart Baird, Peter Tait, Mick Burke, Roger Marshall, Ginger Warburton and Stu Gallagher to name a few.

The Creag Dubh club from Glasgow were regular attendees and the barn was a dangerous place when they returned from the pub – a lot of noise and the odd scrap, so it was better to keep quietly rolled up in your sleeping bag out of the way. Slowly we learned to climb, mainly on the easier crags. *Holly Tree Wall* on Raven Crag, *Centipede* and *Savernake* and then the easier climbs on White Ghyll and Gimmer Crag. By the end of the decade we were on to steeper stuff and itching for new horizons.

North Wales was another popular place. Getting lifts was easy and the roads were full of hitchhikers. We stayed in Mrs Williams's barn below the road at Ogwen. That barn was always full of climbers. The same crowd seemed to tag around and we knew almost everybody. The Idwal Slabs and east face of Tryfan were the order of the day, with the occasional excursion to the Llanberis Pass.

At Easter in 1959 we hitched up to Scotland and spent some time at the youth hostel at Ardgartan where we climbed The Cobbler, before heading north to Fort William. On this holiday we plodded up the Ben in its winter coat, but chickened out of any of the climbs – they seemed too big for us.

Fort William's narrow High Street, that a century earlier had been a double row of crofts in front of the original Fort, or 'The Garrison' as it was called, was a busy road filled with shops and jammed with traffic. The main trunk road to the Western Isles passed through what is now a pedestrian precinct. The town centred at the west end, where the railway station with its platforms on the waterfront led on to the jetty where ferries docked. This was the shopping centre for the Western Isles and, at that time, the true capital of the Highlands. There were regular visits from naval ships, which anchored offshore and crowds of cheery sailors enjoyed the pubs and chased the girls. The town hall in Cameron Square was the venue for a hectic social life with fantastic ceilidhs and dances. Tweed, plus fours and fore-and-aft stalking hats were the standard dress of the locals.

Sitting on the pier one day we watched a fisherman catch a large sea trout. It was about three feet long, and to our delight he gave it to us. Having no means to cook it we went to the local fish and chip shop and the friendly owner, Colin Neilson, dumped it in batter, fried it up and slapped it in a bag of chips. We sat with our legs dangling over the pier munching the best fish and chips we had ever tasted. In later years Colin became a close friend, and one without whom the Nevis Range ski centre would not have happened. He was elected convener of the Fort William Council, the Scottish equivalent of the mayor, and was one of those unsung heroes who work endlessly to improve the lot of the local people. However, all this was in the future.

At the end of that school year I insisted that I should leave Fulneck. I was sixteen and hadn't a clue what would become of me. I turned my back and marched away, never intending to look round. I had lived there for ten years and didn't feel that I could stand it a day longer. I had hardly stayed at home and found that I was so institutionalised that it was almost impossible to live there. Mum and I were not getting on very well. She, very rightly, thought that I was a bit of a waster, and after a few weeks I moved out and lived in the YMCA in Leeds. It was similar to school where a bunch of us lads lived in dormitories and this was much more to my liking.

With my mother's help I managed to get a job working for the Geological Survey at their offices in Crossgates while doing a sandwich course at Leeds University. The geology department at Leeds was a lively place. My manager was David Thomas, a well-known Welsh mountaineer and pal of Joe Brown who had been on a number of expeditions to the Arctic. David in later years approached Karrimor, a small company manufacturing bicycle saddlebags, and managed to persuade them to make him a rucksack. This was the prototype that ultimately became the 'Chamonix', which for years was the standard English climber's pack and transformed Karrimor into a world-class rucksack manufacturer.

Another climber there was Barry Page who had been to the Towers of Paine in South America. Barry had a pet chameleon that wandered freely around the department feeding on flies. It had the most amazing ability to change colour and blend into the background and we were constantly searching for it. I actually saw it with a check coat as it blended into the office carpet.

On the way up Woodhouse Lane to the university I walked past the RAF recruiting office and one day casually ambled in to pick up a pamphlet. I had no aspirations to go into the services but got into conversation with a recruiting sergeant who quickly picked up that I was a keen climber.

'I bet we could get you on to one of the mountain rescue teams,' he said.

This sounded like manna from heaven. 'Where do I sign?' I said.

A couple of weeks later, still in a state of shock, I was boarding a troop train to RAF Bridgnorth.

4 | Kinloss Mountain Rescue

I should have known better; there was no mention in my enlistment papers about the promise of mountain rescue if I signed up. RAF stations tend to be in flat places. I did my training in air movements at RAF Kirton in Lindsey in Lincolnshire where it's almost as flat as you can get, and was then posted to RAF Marham, a V-bomber station in Norfolk. From my billet window it was possible to see forty miles of cabbages with not a hill in sight. For the next six months I pestered and pleaded and finally succeeded, and was sent for a month's trial on the rescue team at RAF Kinloss in northern Scotland. John Hinde had just taken over as team leader and offered me the full-time job. I was saved. Within a few weeks I was back in the mountains.

My spare time at Kinloss was spent climbing. Morayshire has the highest sunshine record in Britain and has the advantage of long hours of daylight. This far north the summer sun sets at around 10 p.m. and rises at 3 a.m. It never gets really dark. Long evenings were spent on crags at Loch Duntelchaig and other local outcrops around Inverness, and at week-ends we plodded the Scottish hills: Applecross, Glen Affric, Ben Hope and Ben Loyal, and the Fannichs. It was the chance of a lifetime to travel and climb anywhere with free food, lodgings and transport.

The rescue team was imperceptibly split into two factions, the Munro baggers and the climbers, and there were always battles as to where we would go for the weekends. Some of the walkers were very prolific. Jim Patterson, Plug Suttle, Ross McKerron and Ken 'G.B.' Shaw were the big padders whom I tried unsuccessfully to avoid, knowing that with them there would be long, gruelling Munro-bagging ridge walks ahead. We climbers were in a minority and stuck together, preferring Skye, Fort William, Torridon and the Cairngorms. I climbed mostly with Chief

John Hinde, Robin 'Dinger' Bell, Martin Mackie and Gordon Ballantine, and we were fiercely competitive.

John Hinde was one of the finest mountaineers I have met. He must have had a hell of a time keeping this motley crew in order. Bursting with enthusiasm he would walk the hills all day and then go rock climbing in the evening while the rest of us were soaking it up in the pub. He would drag me off in the dark to some obscure outcrop and we would climb by torchlight. Another of his passions was climbing summer rock routes in crampons. I realise now that this was a fantastic apprenticeship.

Almost all rescues in the sixties involved long searches and much of the emphasis was on navigation and search techniques. There were few call-outs for climbing accidents; most mountaineers looked after their own. We did wonder how we would fare if there was a winter accident on one of the bigger mountains; climbers were in the minority, none of us were experienced and we were woefully equipped. Our moment was about to come on a scale larger than any of us had anticipated.

On 3 March 1963 the team camped by Loch Maree and, in glorious, bitterly cold weather, Martin Mackie and I climbed A' Mhaighdean, reputedly the most isolated of the Munros. It was a long walk but we saved a few miles by crossing the frozen Lochan Fada. The scenery was spectacular in the snow and from the summit we could see the huge cliffs of Beinn Lair and right down the Fionn Loch to Poolewe. We were late returning, the long drive back to Kinloss was exhausting.

At the time that we set out, a hundred miles to the south two climbers from Fort William started up the North-East Buttress of Ben Nevis. One was Keith Stanley, team leader of the newly formed Lochaber Mountain Rescue Team, and the other, eighteen-year-old Ian Sutherland. I didn't know it at the time but Ian would one day become both my climbing and business partner. This was to be his first big climb. 'Suds', as he was known, was working as an apprentice cobbler in a local shoe shop at the time but was soon to quit and take up instructing at an outdoor activities centre on the Applecross Peninsula. The cobbling was to become very useful in our future.

These days the North-East Buttress is a serious undertaking, but back in the sixties it was a real tour de force and ascents were few. The buttress, which profiles the skyline of Ben Nevis, rises 2,000 feet in three giant steps split by two ledges known as the first and second platforms. Above this and only a couple of hundred feet below the summit is a short, steep rock step known as the Mantrap. This is the crux of the climb. It can be desperate in winter and has stopped many an able climber. The problem being that you arrive there late in the day, tired and possibly in the dark, and are then faced with either getting up it or a 2,000-foot retreat. Not a pleasant place to be caught in unpredictable Scottish weather.

To their surprise Keith and Ian were not alone, two other climbers were ahead of them and had already reached the First Platform. The weather was perfect and they quickly overtook the two who were climbing slowly but seemed in good cheer; they chatted and discovered that they were members of the Dundee Mountaineering Club. During the afternoon conditions began to deteriorate and darkness had fallen by the time Keith and Ian reached the Mantrap.

'It was snowing and getting windy. We failed to climb the Mantrap but I managed to traverse to the right over the Orion Face and, with a rubber torch in my teeth, climbed the Forty-Foot Corner,' Ian remembers.

'The Dundee lads were a long way below and we couldn't help them. We reached the summit in a gale and headed off down as quickly as we could.'

As the two men descended the storm increased. They realised that in these conditions the two slower climbers would have great difficulty at the Mantrap. In the early hours of the morning, as they struggled down the Allt a' Mhuilinn in ever deepening snow, Keith and Ian met members of the rescue team and to their relief found that the alarm had already been raised by anxious friends in the Dundee club.

It was after midnight at Kinloss when the call-out was sounded. We had just got back from Loch Maree and were refuelling the vehicles. Martin and I took turns driving the Land Rover ambulance the hundred miles to Fort William and catnapping on a stretcher in the back. Four of us, Gordon Ballantine, Dinger Bell, Martin and I, set off across the everglades from the Long John distillery and up the Allt a' Mhuilinn, the long valley to the CIC hut, the mountaineers' refuge hut below the cliffs of Ben Nevis.

As we reached the hut it was snowing lightly and visibility was poor, but it was beginning to get light. Just then the clouds parted and for a few moments the North-East Buttress appeared. It was absolutely plastered in snow and looked enormous. About halfway between the Second Platform and the Mantrap were two tiny dots, which had to be the Dundee boys. My heart fell into my boots, they were miles up, spindrift avalanches were coming down all over the Ben and the thought of going there up in these conditions was not appealing.

In the hut we met two climbers unaware of the impending rescue; they were Paul Seddon and Spider Penman. Without hesitation they both offered to come and help and we readily accepted. Spider is a well-known Lakeland mountaineer. Paul, who ultimately became one of the founders of Troll mountain hardware, was a real innovator of climbing equipment, but these were the days long before drooped ice tools and clever nut protection and the kit they had was no better than ours.

The six of us left the CIC hut and started up the summer rock climb of *Raeburn's 18 Minute Route*, up to the First Platform. First ascended in 1895, it's interesting to note that the old boys' exaggeration was much the same then as it is now – nobody takes less than an hour to climb this route and in winter it can be quite desperate. In these conditions it was slow and painful. It was snowing steadily and virtually impossible to stay on route, and the rock was glazed in ice and powder snow was pouring down the gullies and obscuring our vision. At times we were wallowing up a deep trench in the powder as we struggled up to reach the crest of the buttress at the First Platform. We then traversed back round on to the face where steep twin gullies lead up to the Second Platform about halfway up the climb where the two men were stranded.

Meanwhile, high on the mountain, another situation was unfolding. John Hinde had first gone to Fort William police station and then taken a party of three up the path to the summit. They were Ross McKerron, Andy Anderson and Ron Lowe – all fit lads, but none of them were climbers.

It was just getting light when they reached the top, it was snowing and the wind blasting over the cornice made it difficult to find the true summit. There was no sign of the ruined observatory or the emergency shelter, which were buried deep under the snow. They managed to find the top of Zero Gully and look down but couldn't see a thing.

John had carried a 500-foot spool of Terylene rope on a pack-frame and they crawled out on to the crest of the North-East Buttress and rigged up an abseil. He was extremely concerned for his men in the high wind and sent Andy and Ron back down the mountain.

'You come with me, Ross,' he shouted.

I questioned Ross recently on what happened next. In 1963 we didn't have harnesses but used a hemp waistline and a sit sling. He was dressed in a RAF cold-wet jacket with a cheap nylon cagoule over the top. John was equipped much the same.

Ross described the situation: 'The Chief set off abseiling over the edge with a great tangle of rope which he was throwing out as he went, and I just about crapped myself as he vanished into the storm. When the rope finally went slack I decided I'd better get going. I made a sit sling and the rope went through a karabiner at my crutch and over my shoulder, I took a deep breath and went over the edge. Once I got down a bit I was out of the wind but the rope was cutting into my shoulder and as I slid down it burned through my cagoule and jacket. I still have the scar of the burns on my back to prove it. I dropped down over the Mantrap and the Chief pulled down the rope. It felt as though our lifeline was being pulled away. We abseiled on down the buttress and suddenly there they were.

'Both guys were like bits of frozen meat. They were all in and very cold and couldn't speak properly. It was windy and snowing. We had tins of Heinz self-heating soup which we fed them and they revived a little. It must have been early afternoon as the first of the climbers arrived from below. We rigged another abseil and then discovered that, unbelievably, neither of them appeared to know how to abseil. What the hell were they doing up here?

'The Chief and Spider Penman began giving them an urgent lesson in abseiling as the rest of the guys were rigging the ropes. We made it down to the Second Platform in a terrible tangle and the 500-foot rope jammed so we abandoned it as booty for future climbers.'

Without the 500-foot rope that John and Ross brought it would have been a much slower job getting everybody down. The two Dundee men were Gordon Joy and Andy Gracie. All together there were now ten of us climbing down the buttress. There was a lot of spindrift falling and visibility was almost zero, probably a good thing as the drop below was awesome. There was no point in worrying about what you couldn't see, but we were all moving with great care and anxiously watching each other for the slightest slip.

We reached the First Platform as it got dark. Spider now led a difficult traverse across steep ice to avoid the long descent to the foot of the face. We were all strung out together and there were no adequate belays. Anyone falling here would, I'm sure, have pulled the whole group off in what could have been the worst Scottish climbing accident in history.

One by one we edged our way across the ice. The concentration was intense and we were very concerned for Gordon and Andy who were not in good shape. I crossed last, feeling very frightened and conscious that any slip I made would pull the entire party off the mountain. The final, easier pitches to the bottom were done by torchlight.

Once back on terra firma tiredness kicked in. Martin and I had now been on the go for thirty-six hours and we were exhausted. We walked down to the CIC hut to discover that it was full of climbers who had come up to help – there was no room at the inn. We were yearning for our sleeping bags and so set off on the long walk back to Cameron's barn in Glen Nevis.

It was the first time in my life that I fell asleep while walking along. We crossed the Halfway Lochan and headed down the Ben path, both of us repeatedly keeling over in the snow. We reached the barn in the early hours of Tuesday morning. I tried to drink some soup but couldn't hold it down so dropped into my sleeping bag and slept for a solid twelve hours.

Ross told me later that when he and John Hinde got to the CIC hut, to their embarrassment Andy Gracie and Gordon Joy got on their knees and offered them their ice axes in gratitude. I think that Ross McKerron was the hero of that day. The rest of us were all keen climbers and knew exactly what we were getting into, but when Ross went over the edge it must have taken real courage – he should have got a medal.

During my three years at Kinloss there were a lot of call-outs, but we also went to a number of aircraft crashes, the worst of which was an RAF Vulcan which hit the summit of a hill quite close to Aberdeen. This was one of the V-bombers that, as part of Britain's commitment to NATO, kept an atomic bomb in the air all the time during the cold war. I had actually helped to load atom bombs on to Vulcans at RAF Marham on my previous posting and was very nervous that there might be one of these horrors lying about in the wreckage spread over about five miles of Aberdeenshire hillside. Air Ministry, as was their way, neither admitted nor denied that there was a bomb on board.

Martin Mackie and I were in the Cairngorms when the call came and were not among the group that found the wreck. By the time we got there it was pouring with rain and difficult to see much. By then and to our relief it was known that there wasn't a bomb on board. It was dark and the entire hillside was covered in knee-deep silver tinsel. The plane must have been loaded to the gunwales with bales of 'window', the RAF's code name for radar-blocking chaff (tinsel), which had burst open on impact. Sadly the eight-man crew had all perished and the team were searching fruitlessly through the tinsel for their remains. This was a grizzly business and hopeless in the dark; the search was called off until morning.

As Martin and I were the last to arrive, the Chief left us on the site to act as crash guards. It was a wet and miserable night and this seemed futile as it was hard to imagine that anybody else would be daft enough to be out on a night like this. We sheltered in part of the tail wreckage until it got too cold and then went for a wander around. This was when our luck changed; we found a whole area that was scattered with hundreds of cartons of cigarettes. The aircrew must have been returning from a foreign detachment and doing a spot of smuggling on the way. This was a gift from the gods and we spent the rest of the night stashing the booty. Over the next few days we had the unpleasant task of sifting through the wreckage. The cigarettes vanished back to Kinloss with us when the search ended and for a short time Martin and I were wealthy men.

A strange incident started with a phone call from some farmers in the Easter Ross-shire village of Ardgay who had found some odd-looking wreckage on the hills. We assumed that it was an old wartime aircraft wreck, and the station doctor, Flight Lieutenant Hamish Barber, and I went up to investigate. What we found was absolutely startling and at first we thought it must be a hoax.

Lying in a peat bog was a large capsule approximately six feet square with a small, thick glass porthole. It had a solid, angle-iron bar fixed to its side with the remains of some parachute webbing attached. It was covered in layers of asbestos cloth and was badly damaged. It must have weighed at least half a ton and there was nothing inside it. It seemed to have been there for some time and had clearly been visited by someone else before we got to it. To our astonishment we had found the remains of a Russian Sputnik.

The first Sputnik had orbited the world only three years earlier and most of us imagined a tiny ball about a foot in diameter going bleep,

bleep, bleep. Everybody was shocked when a few months later the Russians had sent into orbit a small capsule containing a dog called Laika, but this thing was on a different scale. Here was a half-ton monster that must have taken one hell of a rocket to launch into space.

Then, there was the most almighty flap. The team was called out immediately and we began a huge and systematic search of the moor above Ardgay. Experts appeared from Farnborough and the Air Ministry and the whole thing was 'D-noticed' (i.e. made top secret), and to my knowledge has never been mentioned in anything that I have seen since.

Some distance away we found some plastic bottles that had been buried and a sheet of metal engraved on which was a cartoon showing some turban-clad men pointing at the thing coming down on a parachute and a picture of a big bag of shekels. The obvious inference was that whoever found it would get a reward. All the bits were taken back to Kinloss and were spread out in the mountain rescue common room. The inner layer below the asbestos cover was a sort of metal honeycomb and I remember one of the Farnborough men muttering angrily, 'that's a British invention!'

After a week's unproductive searching, the whole lot of junk was taken away and that was that. A few months later Yuri Gagarin became the first man in space. I guess that somewhere in the bowels of Farnborough the remains of our Sputnik are still rotting. The Doc and I never did get to claim the bag of shekels.

The cold war was at its height, Khrushchev and Kennedy were squaring up to what was to become the Cuban Missile Crisis and the RAF was preparing for nuclear war. As well as our normal training we underwent GDT – Ground Defence Training against nuclear attack. We were pretty sceptical, especially when our trainer, a Flight Lieutenant Ellingham told us that the whole of the British Isles could be covered in fireballs from just two hydrogen bombs. We looked at each other in consternation.

'Don't worry,' he said, 'the RAF is getting brand new firefighting equipment.'

He looked bemused as we fell about laughing.

At the time of the Cuban crisis, Barry (Lonnie) Halpin and another team member, Ray (Soapy) Surf, had completed their National Service and, after hanging around the station for a while, took a job tree planting at the end of Glen Etive. In the sixties this glen was even more isolated than it is now. The famous Trilleachan Slabs had yet to be discovered and their accommodation, a small hut, was twelve miles down the glen from the Kings House Hotel on Rannoch Moor. The other planters were Poles, most of whom had escaped the Nazis during the invasion. They were a tough crew who spoke no English but were good company, drank a lot and bashed each other over the head with a spade every now and then. It was winter, cold, with snow on the ground and hard manual work with virtually no contact with the outside world except for a twice-weekly visit by a psychotic postman who kept them in touch with events. The Poles hated the Russians and as the Soviet fleet approached Cuba and the crisis developed they were convinced that Khrushchev would not back down.

One afternoon the postman arrived with the news that Kennedy had issued his final ultimatum.

'This is it,' he said. 'There's going to be a nuclear war!'

A very worried and isolated bunch of tree planters went to their beds that night convinced that it may be their last.

The following morning Lonnie ambled out of the hut to stretch his legs. To the south a blood red dawn was rising, beautiful columns of light, streaks of red and orange the likes of which he had never seen before. He stood admiring the view when a horrible thought struck him and he called Soapy and the Poles out of the hut. They stood in awe watching the spectacular sunrise from the direction of Glasgow, about sixty miles to the south. Great swirls of colour in one of those spectacular displays that only Scotland can produce.

'Christ,' Soapy murmured. 'They've gone and done it.'

Work ceased that day. By lunchtime the postman had not appeared and they decided that something had to be done so the whole bunch set out to walk the nine miles to the Clachaig Inn in Glen Coe, wallowing through deep snow over the high saddle of Gleann Fhaolain.

Of course they staggered into the bar to discover a bunch of locals quietly sipping their pints.

'Don't be bloody stupid,' they were told. 'Khrushchev backed down and Kennedy promised never to attack Cuba again. It's all over!'

So, that was that. A few weeks later the boys packed in the job and got a lift with the postman to the Kings House Hotel where they parted company, hitching in opposite directions – Lonnie for Liverpool and Soapy back to Kinloss – and they never saw each other again. Lonnie ended up in Goa, India, where he lived the life of a hippy.

In 2003, a book written by Duncan MacLaughlin and William Hall, two investigative reporters attempting to track down Lord Lucan, showed some extraordinary photographs of a man who they claimed to be the missing lord. There, staring out of the front cover, was Barry Halpin, large as life. How anybody in their right mind could mistake Lonnie, the gifted banjo player and raconteur of bawdy songs, for the missing cousin of the Queen beggars belief. However the book, *Dead Lucky*, is a good read. Ray Surf lives in Canada. The trees they planted in Glen Etive in 1962 are currently in the process of being harvested …

The road to Skye was dreadful, especially alongside Loch Cluanie and through Kintail where it was a single track, narrow and winding with shaky narrow wooden bridges. Our three-ton trucks struggled and it was a lengthy wait at the Kyle ferry, a long journey but worth it. We went regularly to Glen Brittle where Hugh MacRae let us use his barn for accommodation. It was an idyllic place not far from the beach with an easy walk up to Coire Lagan and the great cliffs of Sron na Ciche, the heart of the Cuillin, and the most perfect climbing in Britain.

The social life on Skye was terrific in the sixties. We went to the dances at Carbost, Broadford and Portree. Local people were very friendly, television had not yet reached the islands and they made their own entertainment. When we turned up there would often be spontaneous ceilidhs and we were made welcome everywhere. These were warm, friendly people living in isolated places who impulsively invited us into their homes.

I became very friendly with one of Hugh MacRae's shepherds, John Finlay McInnis, and went out with him on a number of occasions bringing in the sheep from the Cuillin. John could control dogs by arm signals from well over a mile away. We would stand in the lower corries and his dogs could move sheep down from the Skye Ridge, 1,500 to 2,000 feet above, bringing them down the most spectacular mountainsides, where a man would have great difficulty finding a way. This experience with dogs would stand me in good stead in later years in Antarctica.

A wonderful character in Glen Brittle was Ronald MacDonald, who lived in a tiny croft on the north side of the bay. The croft acted as the post office, although I can't remember Ronald ever receiving or delivering mail. He was a real Skye boatman, small and unshaven and permanently dressed in a blue seaman's jacket and a sailor's peaked cap. He was a Gaelic speaker with a broad Highland accent, a real twinkle in his eye and a host of tall stories.

In the summer his small and very unseaworthy boat became a pleasure cruiser for unsuspecting tourists. Loaded well over capacity he would sail out of Loch Brittle round to the islands of Soay and Rum on sightseeing and fishing trips. The police were constantly trying to catch him as he had no licence to carry passengers. His wife had a signalling system with a line of washing that she would hang out if the police were lurking. Ronald would promptly turn back round the point and unceremoniously dump his unsuspecting passengers on the shore leaving them faced with a five-mile walk back along the muddy coastal path, while he sailed innocently back into Glen Brittle.

Cleaning out the Land Rover one morning I found a pair of false teeth, which I assumed to be Ronald's, as I had given him a lift back from a ceilidh the previous night. I wrapped them in newspaper and took them round to the post office. After much banging on the door, a toothless and very hungover boatman staggered out. A look of delight crossed his face as he spotted the teeth. He grabbed them, wiped them on his sleeve and stuck them straight in!

'Och, thank you, you'll be coming in for a dram,' he said enthusiastically.

It was eight o'clock in the morning.

5 | The Alps

I arrived in Chamonix in pouring rain after a ghastly train journey from Scotland at the end of my first year at Kinloss. Somewhere between Paris and Chamonix I'd had my wallet stolen and my companion, Reg Middleton, a member of Leuchars Mountain Rescue Team, was ill. I was eighteen years old, excited and nervous at the prospect of climbing these bigger mountains.

Chamonix in the early sixties was still a large village and a shadow of the world's large tourist attraction that it would become. It was and is the holy grail for mountaineers; nowhere on earth has such a concentration of mixed rock and ice climbs with relatively easy access from an amazing system of cable cars. So much has changed. The golden age of mountaineering was over and modern alpinism as we now know it had begun. Walter Bonatti had climbed the South-West Pillar of the Dru six years earlier, and a new breed of well-equipped young climbers was invading the valley and opening up new and exciting routes.

The main attraction in town was the Bar National, where a wonderfully friendly Frenchman, Maurice, blinked at us through bottle-thick lenses, served huge steins of grande bière, passed on messages and rescued drunks from the fountain, even though he had not the slightest interest in mountaineering.

As the weather cleared I got my first view of the Aiguille du Dru soaring high above the clouds and plastered in snow. Its knife-blade peak looked massive and desperately out of my league. Toby and a few of the Langdale lads had arrived and while Reg recovered I had a climbing partner.

Our first climb was the Menegaux route on the Aiguille de l'M; so called for its M shape it is perhaps the most popular climbers' peak in the Chamonix Aiguilles because of its easy access from the top of the

Montenvers funicular railway. Unfortunately, we had no money for the railway so we had a gruelling approach march. We managed the climb, which was steep and exciting, but were caught in a thunderstorm on the descent – the first of many over the years. The Alps are notorious for afternoon storms (I have the feeling that I attract them). Soaked but triumphant we arrived back to Chamonix.

Reg had recovered and the next day we repeated the long plod up the railway track and walked across the Mer de Glace glacier, which at the time was almost at the level of Montenvers station. (These days there is a cable car up from the glacier which is now 800 feet below the station, an alarming sign of the speed with which the glacier has receded.)

We clambered up steel cables and over the moraines to the Couvercle hut where I bivouacked outside. I had only a small amount of borrowed money and was unable to pay for either lifts or huts, and was living on courgettes, the cheapest vegetables in the supermarket.

We failed to complete a traverse of Les Courtes, a relatively easy snow plod. Both of us suffered from the altitude and were moving far too slowly. As the sun hit the face, small avalanches kept triggering off around us and we were lucky to escape unscathed. The following day we climbed the Aiguille de Triolet and got sunburned and dehydrated. It was all experience. I realised that we had to move faster and with less protection than we were used to in Scotland. The grand finale was the Mayer-Dibona ridge on the Dent du Requin where we followed the famous guide Gaston Rébuffat and his client. He was very friendly and didn't seem to mind us using him to find the way. All told it was not a bad effort for the first trip. I returned to Kinloss determined to return as soon as possible.

The following summer, 1962, was much more successful, Dinger Bell and I went to the Dolomites in northern Italy. This beautiful area, known as the Sud Tyrol, was annexed from Austria after the war. Most of the local people spoke either German or Ladin, a form of Romance, and seemed resentful of their situation – the odd bridge was still being blown up by dissidents. It was a popular climbing area for the British, being relatively cheap, and had fierce rock climbing that suited us, without the long approach marches and early starts required in the Western Alps.

Our first port of call was the Catinaccio in the Val di Fassa. This must be one of the most stunning places in the Alps. In German it's called 'Der Rosengarten', the Rose Garden, and is a peaceful area overlooked by the massive vertical face of the Catinaccio and the impressive Vajolet Towers. Below the faces the tranquillity was slightly disturbed as every boulder seemed to be claimed as a bivvy site by the impoverished British. The pinnacles echoed with Scottish voices: the Creagh Dhu club was here in force.

Dinger and I started, as many young climbers do, with a traverse of the Vajolet Towers. The climb was plumb vertical, much steeper than we were used to and the exposure, as we inched our way up the yellow rock on the edge of the first tower, was extraordinary. We had a few engineering nuts threaded on to bits of rope for runners, but the only real protection was pitons that were in place, and these were few and widely spaced. The top of the towers was very airy. We rigged up the long, free-hanging abseils and nervously slid back down to terra firma. This steep Dolomite climbing was going to take some getting used to.

That evening we met up with Terry Sullivan and his friend who talked us into an attempt on the Via Steger, a grade-VI on the east face of the Catinaccio. This was a step too far for us; Terry vanished upwards into the yellow overhangs and Dinger and I struggled up behind, frantically pulling on every available piton. We finally chickened out after four or five pitches, not realising that we had done the hard part. We had a desperate time abseiling back down through the overhangs, trying to swing back into contact with the rock. Discretion was the better part of valour that day but I did manage to complete the climb a few years later.

From the Catinaccio it was a short hitch-hike to the Sella Towers. This popular place was very isolated at the time but is now in the centre of a vast ski area, the Sella Ronda – great skiing but the presence of the infrastructure has rather spoiled the gorgeous remote valley for climbers.

To our amazement the Alpini, the Italian Alpine troops, were on exercise in the area and, surprisingly, shelled the Sassolungo with a field gun. This beautiful peak that overlooks the Sella Pass is one of the most popular climbers' mountains in the Dolomites. They seemed unconcerned that there were climbers on the mountain at the time and it must have been exciting to be on that huge face with shells bursting all around, giving a whole new dimension to the sport of climbing.

That night the bar in the Sella Pass hut was full of Alpini. Dinger began to argue with them. They were a fierce-looking lot, small, tough and wiry, so to protect him, Terry and I threw him into a horse trough outside the hut. Terry cleared off and left me to face Dinger who, quite rightly, got very stroppy with me before being violently sick in the tent. The following day was one of those difficult days when the best of friends are not speaking. We hitchhiked separately to Misurina, where we got in tow with a film crew who were celebrating the completion of an Italian version of *Lawrence of Arabia*, filmed in the Dolomites, complete with camels. One of their crew drank the oil from a gallon jar of olives, a spectacular feat that must have spoiled the rest of his day.

Late that afternoon we started the long 4,000-foot slog up to the Tre Cime, possibly the most famous peaks in the Dolomites. I tried not to gaze at the appallingly vertical walls. I always have a sense of fear before any Alpine climb but the Dolomite faces looked so outrageously steep that I just couldn't bear to look. We had heavy packs and hangovers so arrived wearily at the Lavaredo hut, put up the tent and went in for something to eat: jam omelettes, the Italian climbers' speciality, delicious! Here we discovered that the hut did not sell cigarettes. This was catastrophic as without these neither of us would be willing or able to go climbing and so we drew straws for who should go back down to Misurina on a shopping trip. I lost. I'm sure Dinger cheated but off I went into the evening, plodding wearily back down the mountain.

The Italian film crew were still drinking in the bar when I got to the village so I joined them and it was well after midnight when I staggered out and headed back up the nightmare 4,000-foot path clutching the cigarettes. There was no water on the trail and I tottered upwards through the night with a terrible thirst. I finally reached the tent at 5 a.m. Dinger was just waking up.

'This is it, Spike. The weather's perfect, let's have a go at the Yellow Edge.'

To this day I marvel that I didn't refuse to go. Zombie-like, I sorted out my climbing gear and stumbled after him up the screes to the Cima Piccola, and thus started one of the never-to-be-forgotten climbs of a lifetime.

In 1962, Emilio Comici's classic *Spigolo Gallo* – Yellow Edge – on the Cima Piccola, was one of the most sought-after rock climbs in the Dolomites, and although its first ascent was in 1933, it had at that time had very few British ascents.

Comici's description of his climb in the Italian guide was the stuff of legends:

> The most exposed climb one can imagine ... two days of raging battle we experienced on this route, clinging astride it to micro-scopic holds, while she defended herself with torrents of falling stones.

We found that most of the stones had long fallen to the valley floor and the microscopic holds had grown but were well polished. What we had, though, was breathtaking exposure and the fantastic feeling that comes with climbing the perfect line.

These glorious days without a cloud in the sky and the entire mountain to ourselves are never to be forgotten. It was still the era of the hemp waistline and Tarbuck knot, we were dressed in miners' pit helmets, mole-skin breeches, red socks and Pierre Allain rock boots, and had a small selection of slings and karabiners and a few pegs. Our rope was 120 feet of Viking hawser-laid nylon. The stunning vertical climbing was much steeper than we were used to but the holds were good on the beautiful yellow limestone. We were getting used to the awesome exposure.

A thousand feet vertically below was the Lavaredo hut and we watched walkers, tiny black specs plodding up the white limestone path from the gorgeous Marzon valley. Comici's audacity in finding a route up this seemingly impregnable fortress was astounding. For Dinger and me, it was the breakthrough into the harder Dolomite climbs. For once we made good time and, surprisingly, I have no recollection of fatigue from the previous night.

Relaxing on the summit of the Cima Piccola we had a profile view of the north face of the Cima Grande. It looked barely credible; it's first 600 feet gently overhung, before another 1,500 feet of vertical face above. We watched two climbers who had broken out above the overhangs and were moving slowly up the seemingly unassailable wall. This was the Via Comici, one of the six great north faces of the Alps.

Instantly all thoughts of our success were forgotten, all I could think about was that I must have a go at it. Such is the drug of mountaineering. We have these high ambitions and become fixated, only to find that our obsession is incomplete, the goal is not enough. It seems that we must keep driving forward on these totally futile enterprises. Lionel Terrey summed it up nicely in the title of his book, *Conquistadors of the Useless*.

We descended the ordinary route, where easily spaced fixed abseil rings allowed a quick escape. Exhausted, I reached the scree and walked down to the tent in darkness, thankful to be on solid ground. Unbelievably, some of the Italian film crew had walked up from Misurina and were staying in the hut.

'We ought to be sociable,' Dinger said.

Easily led and too tired to argue I followed him into the hut.

Today, a spectacular mountain highway goes up the mountain to the Auronzo and Lavaredo huts where there is a huge car park and spectacular viewing point. Recently I watched a party of Japanese tourists walking along the track to the Lavaredo hut. A little man kept blowing a whistle at the places where they were to stop to take photographs. The isolation of the place is long gone but the road must make life a lot easier for climbers.

I lay a wager they don't make the wonderful jam omelettes in the Lavaredo hut anymore and I bet they sell cigarettes now.

The following summer I was off once again on what had become my annual pilgrimage to the Alps. The Profumo affair had just hit the headlines and the French newspapers were far less restrained than the British. They ran great pictures of Randy Mice Davies and Christine Keeler and we spent happy hours in the Bar National translating the scandal.

In the bar I met an American climber, Eugene (Mac) MacMillan, a GI stationed in Stuttgart in Germany. Mac was more experienced than me and very keen and talked me into having a go at the Mer de Glace face of the Grépon. This classic climb was a very popular target in those days but is now somewhat neglected for the short, harder climbs on the Chamonix side of the Aiguille.

We slept in the Envers hut and started out in darkness the following morning, leaving our bivvy gear at the hut. So began another of those series of coincidences that make mountaineering the outrageous sport that it is.

It was great climbing, and lovely weather in the most beautiful situation with the spectacular Mer de Glace, that huge river of ice, curving round below us. It's a long route, about 2,500 feet of steep clean rock that had once been considered technically the hardest in the range. We passed a very decrepit wooden hut balanced on a tiny ledge, the Tour Rouge, where a couple of Scottish climbers were just emerging. One was Bugs McKeith, from Edinburgh, who I knew slightly, and the four of us joined up together. (Bugs joined the British Antarctic Survey with me a few years later.)

All went well until we climbed past the spectacular Aiguille de Roc just as the sky began to darken and heavy clouds rolled in. We were high on the mountain and, rather than retreat, thought it would be quicker to go over the top and descend the easier Chamonix side.

We reached the summit just as a thunderstorm hit. None of us knew the way down. It was blasting hail and lightning was flashing all over the place with sparks flickering off our iron climbing gear. I distinctly re-member a humming noise like an angry bee as I watched a yellow spark buzzing around the tip of my ice axe.

There was a gigantic flash and an explosion of thunder and all of us felt the electric shock as lightning struck the summit blocks. It was truly terri-fying. I'd never been in an electrical storm like this and the top of the Grepon was a gigantic lightning conductor. We frantically rigged abseil after abseil and slid slowly down the ropes on the Chamonix side of the mountain. We were hopelessly off route with nowhere to hide but anx-ious to keep off the exposed ridge, which was flashing and banging, alive with electricity.

By now it was pitch dark and snowing heavily. What is normally a short and easy descent took hours. We were soaked to the skin and the sodden ropes kept jamming. We reached the Nantillons glacier, missed the easy way down, and had to abseil dangerously down the ice front and then splashed our way down the track to a small shed, the Chalet Austria, which we reached at around midnight, soaked to the skin. The tiny shack was jammed with climbers. As we tried to get in an unmistakable bearded face emerged from its sleeping bag. It was Joe Brown, Britain's most famous mountaineer.

'Bugger off,' he growled. 'There's not enough room here.'

To anyone else we may have put up a stronger argument but there wasn't much point in a dispute with a living legend, and we buggered meekly off into the pouring rain. Sometime in the early hours we reached Montenvers where we climbed into a shed at the back of the railway station and slept on a heap of drying animal skins. At first light we awoke, crawling with lice and faced with the long walk back up to the Envers hut to recover our bivvy gear. Oh that we had taken it with us.

After a long lice-picking walk we reached the hut where a group of climbers were sorting out the biggest pile of equipment I had ever seen. One was a Scott, Stewart Fulton, a Creagh Dhu member, whom I knew. The other three were Americans who Mac knew by reputation and he was highly impressed. They were John Harlin, Gary Hemming and Tom Frost, three of the best-known American mountaineers. John had just started the International School of Mountaineering (ISM) at Leysin in Switzerland. He was already famous, having been in the US Air Force flying team and was a well-known American football forward. Gary was a Yosemite climber who became celebrated in France for a remarkable rescue on the Aiguille du Dru, which brought him almost film star status. Tom was the quiet man of the group and possibly the best climber.

Their plan was to climb the south face of the Aiguille du Fou, a route that they expected to be the hardest rock climb of its time in the Alps. The idea was to siege the face using similar tactics to the big wall climbs in the Yosemite valley in the States. Modern rock protection was not very advanced, and pitons were the order of the day. Stewart had been taken on as a bold free climber and he and Tom Frost were to be let loose on the hard, unprotected pitches.

Mac and I were press-ganged into helping to hump the climbing gear up to the foot of the face. The rock stars went ahead leaving the two mugs to bring up the heavy stuff. In compensation we were joined by Marilyn, John Harlin's wife, and the beautiful French girlfriend of Gary Hemming, who had decided to go to the bivvy site to see what was happening.

To reach the foot of the south face of the Fou we had to climb a short distance up the south-east ridge of the Aiguille de Blaitière, a hard climb in its own right, and then traverse left along a series of ramps to a bivouac ledge below the Fou. The view of the face from here was awesome and my first realisation of the sheer size and steepness of this wall. The team was already established on the lower section of the face and their situation looked very precarious. Stewart was leading a diagonal crack and seemed to be in big trouble when he took a short fall just after we arrived.

It was frustrating watching the others on the wall so we left the women at the bivouac site and set off to climb the south-east ridge of the Blaitière. We hadn't got far when the sky blackened and another thunderstorm rolled in, the second in twenty-four hours, and we set off frantically abseiling back down to the ledge. Lightning was flashing all around and it must have been a terrifying situation for the climbers dangling exposed on the wall of the Fou.

There wasn't anything we could do to help. It was pouring with rain, so we joined up with the women and decided to try to get back to the Envers hut. We reached the glacier at the foot of the ridge in darkness and I promptly fell into the bergschrund, the crevasse that often surrounds the foot of a rock face. It was still pouring rain with the odd flash of lightning and my predicament down the hole seemed safer than that of those on the top trying to fish me out. We reached the Envers hut just as a rescue party was setting off – they had seen our torches descending the ridge and realised that something had happened.

Stewart and the Americans bailed off the Fou the following day having spent a miserable night on the open face. They dried out and completed the climb a few days later. It's still considered one of the most formidable rock climbs in the Mont Blanc range.

At the end of the holiday Mac and I parted company and I headed back to life in the air force. I never met him again but am sure that he will have continued to climb when he was demobbed from the US Army.

6 | A New Year on Skye, 1963

All told, I spent almost forty years in the rescue teams – they were a fantastic club with great camaraderie. Mostly we enjoyed the call-outs; they could be very exciting and we rarely got involved personally with the casualties. It was a great way to keep fit. Call-outs had a habit of happening at awkward times, during holidays or just as one was sitting down to dinner with friends. The accident on Skye, at New Year 1963, stands out as one of the most memorable in that it gives a flavour of how much things have changed in both ability and attitudes. Many of the characters involved have become personal friends.

Travel in the Highlands was slow, mainly single track winding roads and the Ballachulish, Kessock and Kylesku bridges were only dreams in the architects' minds. The RAF had yet to make helicopters available for rescue, and walkie-talkies and mobile phones didn't exist. Additionally, drunken driving was not considered a crime in the Highlands, the New Year celebration lasted for a week and the last man to fall was considered something of a hero. It was a miracle that a large-scale rescue ever managed to be mounted in the festive season.

The Kinloss team planned to spend Christmas and the New Year in Fort William. Conditions for mountaineering were possibly the best that I can remember; snow lay on the ground to sea level and the weather was perfect, bitterly cold with clear skies.

We were based in Hugh Cameron's barn in Glen Nevis and had great plans for the break. I had a date with a lovely nurse from the Belford hospital. On Christmas Eve, Dinger and I climbed Moonlight Gully on Ben Nevis and were on our way down when we met a rescue party heading up to what turned out to be a fatal accident on Green Gully. The bodies were already on the old Thomas stretchers and we joined in the long haul down. The path was a sheet of ice and unfortunately one of our team, Hector Macleod, slipped and fell into the Red Burn breaking a leg, so that we had a third casualty to carry off. Poor Hector, lying on the stretcher, was taking quite a ribbing and not getting much sympathy.

Back in Glen Nevis we were called out to another accident in Glen Coe where Hamish MacInnes had asked for all the help he could get. We crossed the Ballachulish ferry to help them carry off yet more casualties from Buachaille Etive Mor. It had been a long day and a night. I'd missed my date with the nurse who didn't give me much sympathy.

That afternoon we were called out to yet another accident 150 miles to the north, at Kinlochewe. Off we went again. Christmas had been a shambles but the worst was yet to come. Trouble was brewing with vengeance on the Isle of Skye.

In the heart of the Black Cuillin of Skye, totally surrounded by mountains, lies Loch Coruisk where there is a solitary mountaineers' hut. The best way to get there is by boat, otherwise it is a long, complicated walk over various difficult passes. Many of the streams flash flood and it is possible to be stranded for days in this beautiful but very isolated place. This New Year the island was plastered in snow and the mountains were truly alpine.

A party from Glasgow University Mountaineering Club was staying at the Coruisk hut for the New Year. There were fourteen in all, seven men and seven women, who had been dropped in by boat from Arisaig and were looking forward to a cheerful holiday celebrating Hogmanay. Mostly they were hillwalkers, planning to spend their time wandering around Loch Coruisk, but there were some climbers among them keen to get on to the tops and enjoy the perfect conditions.

On New Year's Eve, three of the men, John Roycroft, John Methven and Tom Reid, set out from the hut to traverse a complicated offshoot of the Cuillin called the Dubhs Ridge, an excitingly narrow and exposed place that requires an abseil between its two summits.

All three were experienced and capable of making the traverse, but John Methven, at nineteen the youngest member of the party, had no crampons. Although most of the climbing was relatively easy, to protect Methven they remained roped throughout the day and must have been rather slow. Conditions were perfect – the rock-hard windblown snow crunching under their feet, and the mountains sparkling in sunshine with breathtaking views of the islands of Rum and Eigg covered in snow.

They were late and it was almost dark when they reached the col between the Dubhs: no one in the party was carrying a head torch. They decided to descend a tempting little snow-filled gully which led down towards the Coruisk hut. It was steep enough that they had to turn inwards and kick steps into the snow and they moved cautiously together. As the angle steepened, it is likely that John Methven, without crampons, lost his footing and slid rapidly down the slope dragging Roycroft and Reid with him, and the three men catapulted down the gully into darkness.

The New Year festivities fizzled out at the Coruisk hut that night when the three men failed to return. As the rest of Scotland celebrated in the usual way, an anxious group waited through the night hoping their friends would return. Two experienced mountaineers in the hut were Colin Stead, one of the Glasgow University club members, and Cammy MacLeay of Inverness Mountaineering Club.

Cammy and his friend, Alan Laird, set out before dawn to follow the route the three men had taken, while Colin Stead, Robert Russell and George Wallace climbed directly up to the ridge to the Thearlaich Dubh Gap from where they could see Cammy and Alan moving up the ridge of the Dubhs. They were in shouting distance and Cammy's cheerful call gave Colin the impression that they had found the men and everything was okay. In a more positive mood they set off down the tempting little gully leading down from the Dubhs into Garbh Coire. They had not gone far when they found an ice axe lying in the snow and as they kicked steps down the gully they began to see blood spots. Four hundred feet down, on a terrace, they found the men.

John Roycroft was dead, lying face down on the step. Tom Reid was also dead; he seemed to have moved and was sitting with his back to the rock with his arms folded over his chest. John Methven was still alive but was in a terrible state; he was moving his head slightly and mumbling. Colin did what he could but was afraid to move him.

It was an appalling situation. They were in a most isolated place and Colin knew that it would take some hours to get help. George Wallace had the best knowledge of the Cuillin and they decided that he should climb over to Glen Brittle and raise the alarm. Robert Russell headed down to the hut to get blankets and some kind of shelter and Colin stayed with John Methven.

It was 2 p.m., still fine and cold but a sharp wind was blowing. Colin sat, shattered and lonely, frustrated that there was nothing that he could do and was shocked at the hopelessness of the situation. John died quietly about a quarter of an hour after the others had left. It was Colin's first experience of death. He had been up most of the night and climbing since the early morning and was worn out and miserable.

Sometime later he heard Cammy and Alan crossing the col above and attracted their attention with his whistle, and much to his relief they kicked steps down the gully and joined him. Cammy confirmed that all three men were dead. There seemed little point in staying in that wretched place and they left their friends as they were and set off down to the Coruisk hut with the dreadful news.

Hamish MacInnes had spent most of Christmas involved in rescues in Glen Coe. It had been a hectic time and he was shattered. He and his wife, Catherine, decided to get away and spend the New Year quietly with friends at Glen Brittle. He'd spent New Year's Day helping them lopping trees when, just as darkness was falling, he spotted a lone climber running down the path from Coire Lagan and from bitter experience knew that something was amiss.

George Wallace had made fast time over the ridge. He gasped out his story, 'Three climbers have fallen on the Dubhs. One is still alive. Colin Stead is with them.'

Over a bowl of soup George filled in the story. Hamish had already phoned the police at Portree. 'Can you get the RAF boys here as quickly as possible; I think they're in Fort William? Also call Norman Tennant at Kintail Lodge Hotel, I need all the hands I can get.'

With a seriously injured climber out on the mountain, time was of the essence. Hamish had his rescue equipment with him and his wife Catherine was a doctor.

'How do you feel about coming back up with us, George?' he asked. 'We'll need your help to find them.' George didn't hesitate. He had been on the go since before dawn but within half an hour he, Hamish and Catherine set out for the Dubhs.

While all this was happening we in the RAF team had completed the rescue in Kinlochewe and driven back to Fort William. The police had the monumental task of pulling us out of the bars around the town. Within the hour the majority of us were setting out along the Road to the Isles to Skye. Most of the boys had been out all night celebrating and were much the worse for wear. They climbed into their sleeping bags in the back of the trucks and tried to get some sleep. I was driving the Land Rover ambulance and would have been arrested under today's law for drunken driving. The roads were sheeted with ice and treacherous.

We reached Kyle where a special ferry had been laid on by the police. The ferrymen were all drunk and celebratory bottles were merrily handed round. As the trucks trundled aboard, a Mini Cooper S screamed up behind and bumped up the ramp. It was Norman Tennant from Kintail with a bunch of mountaineers crammed in the back.

Norman was a well-known mountaineer of his day, an ex-wartime submarine commander and a climber in the mould of Tilman and Shipton. He had already written off two Mini Coopers and as the trucks trundled off the ferry the Mini hurtled off, reportedly to twice spin a full 360 degrees on the icy road, as they rocketed through the night.

We reached Glen Brittle sometime after midnight; Norman's party had already set off for the ridge. By the time we set up base in Hugh MacRae's barn the weather had deteriorated slightly and there were occasional snow flurries. A makeshift police rescue team from Portree had also set off for the Dubhs.

Luckily, just as we were setting out to follow, two tired-looking climbers arrived at the barn; it was Colin Stead and Cammy McLeay who had walked round the coast to let us know what had happened. Their terrible news that all three men were dead changed our plans.

A few hours earlier Hamish and Catherine MacInnes with George Wallace made fast time cutting up the path below Sron na Ciche round into Coire a' Ghrunnda. They cut large bucket steps up a steep ice pitch knowing that other rescuers were likely to be following. A sharp icy wind was rushing over the rim of the Skye ridge as they crossed and skirted on to the slopes of the Dubhs. George was shouting to Colin and struggled to find the spot where he assumed his friend must be sitting with John Methven. They were spread out and unroped, searching the broken, ice-covered mountainside. A nerve-wracking predicament as their head torches scanned the steep snow and boulder slope in vain.

'I think we're wasting our time. We've searched for well over an hour. Let's face it, if Colin was here we would have a reply from him,' Hamish said.

Hamish knew that Colin Stead was a competent mountaineer and wouldn't do anything foolish. He had told the police that he would have someone with a light on the ridge to indicate where they were but now decided that it would be better to climb down to the hut, find out the situation, and try to get somebody over to Glen Brittle as quickly as possible. They descended a long way down the mountain but ended up above a steep cliff. Far below they could see the lights of the Coruisk hut but there was nothing for it but to climb back up to the main ridge to find a safer descent route. They finally found a hard-packed snow and rubble gully into the Garbh Coire and reached the hut at 2 a.m. George was first through the door, anxious for news.

The atmosphere as they entered was terrible and people were talking in monosyllables. From Colin Stead they learned that John Methven had died soon after George had left for Glen Brittle.

Hamish was still worried about the rescue parties whom he guessed must now be making their way up to the Dubhs. 'Someone will have to go to Glen Brittle right away to advise the other rescue groups of the situation, otherwise they'll be searching the Cuillin all night. Any volunteers?' Hamish asked.

'I think Cammy and I are the only two who fit the bill. We'll go.' Colin said.

Both men had done enough that day but Colin was right, very few in the hut were in a fit state for the long trek. It was up to them. They decided to take the coastal path.

'Let them know that George and I will take some of the party up at first light and start getting the bodies down.' Hamish said. 'Tell the police that a boat will be the best way to evacuate them.'

The two men left a few minutes later, their head torches bobbing along the slabs as they crossed the ice-encrusted Mad Burn and skirted the steep rocky shore of Loch Scavaig. Neither of them knew the route, but they managed the long hike in just under four and a half hours, arriving just as the Kinloss team were about to set off.

John Hinde realised immediately that there was little point in heading for the Dubhs. Now that they knew that John Methven was dead, getting to him was not quite so urgent. Hamish's idea of a boat to Coruisk seemed the most logical. It would be much easier to get three bodies down the other side, rather than up and over the ridge. The police sergeant from Portree phoned Brucy Watt, the skipper of a local fishing boat, the *Western Isles*, which acted as a passenger and ferry service from Malaig to the islands of Rum, Eigg and Muck.

'I'll be off right away,' Brucy said cheerfully. 'I can't get there before eleven o'clock.' He was wondering where he would be able to get a crew and what sort of a state they were going to be in with the Hogmanay celebrations still going on.

'Okay chaps, you can get a couple of hours' shut-eye,' John said, much to my relief. The long drive had sobered me up somewhat and I thankfully climbed into my sleeping bag in my hill clothes.

Just after 11 a.m. the *Western Isles* rounded the point into Loch Brittle. As we backed one of the Bedford three-ton trucks down the beach to load our equipment, it sank to the axles in the shingle. It had all the aspects of a Brian Rix farce as we loaded kit on to the boat while trying to rig up a winch to pull the truck out before the tide enveloped it. The day was eventually saved by dragging the truck out by tractor. Soaking wet, I finally scrambled on board.

We sailed through the Soay Sound, passing the island where Tex Geddes and Gavin Maxwell ran their shark fishing business, and into Loch Scavaig. There were about thirty of us crammed on board including some police and members of Norman's New Year dinner party. The *Western Isles* was bucking like a bronco in the heavy sea. It was my first time in the astonishing channel into the heart of the Cuillin and on this day, with the snow covered mountainsides coming right down into the sea, it was positively arctic and incredibly beautiful.

We reached Coruisk mid-afternoon. By then Hamish and George had already taken a small party back up the gully to the bodies. There was a dreadful atmosphere among those remaining in the hut. Catherine Mac-Innes had left on foot taking some of the women back round the coast to Glen Brittle. A worried woman, she knew she had plenty of stamina for the long icy walk around the coast but was extremely concerned for the girls who were physically and emotionally shattered and inadequately equipped.

As the team sorted out the equipment, John Hinde asked a small group of us to go straight up to the accident site.

'You go ahead Spike, with Jack Baines and Nev Colingham. We'll bring up the stretchers and some rope, if you can find a route.' It was a relief to get away.

'I'll show you the way up,' said a rough Highland voice. It was Cammy MacLeay, still going strong after almost two days of non-stop effort.

He led the way up the 2,000 feet of steep slabs into the Garbh Coire at breakneck pace. As we finally scrambled up into the gully it was getting dark, a dangerous place with a lot of debris lying about.

'Sorry it's taken us so long Hamish,' I said. 'The boat took a bit of organising.'

It was a dangerous situation; Hamish had already moved two of the bodies down a small cliff. There was a lot of loose stuff about and rocks were trundling all over the place.

'The team will never find us here. How about letting off a flare?' Jack suggested.

I had a Swedish Rocket in my pack. I'd never actually fired one and I gingerly unscrewed the cap, held the thing at arm's length, and pulled the cord. There was a tremendous whoosh and the missile flashed 600 feet into the air and exploded in a red light that lit the whole coire. The rocket had drifted in the wind and this proved very confusing for the rest of the rescuers who had no idea where the flare had come from. It turned out to be more of a hindrance than a help and lost half an hour while the boys searched for us.

Leaving Hamish dealing with the two bodies below the cliff, the four of us clambered up and set about moving the third man. It was an unpleasant job. We lowered him down on a rope on to the snow and then made a series of long lowers down the steep snow slope below.

So began one of the worst and most exhausting descents that I have experienced. Hamish and John Hinde organised the two lower bodies. My party was struggling behind and it took some time before somebody arrived with an old Thomas stretcher. Jack acted as guide and was lowered with the stretcher. Foolishly we had put the body on head first, which was a mistake as it made the stretcher front heavy. We had about 2000 feet of snow and ice-covered rock slabs to get down. Under normal circumstances this would have been an easy descent, but with our unpleasant load and our crampons scraping off sheets of brittle ice that tinkled down the slabs it was becoming a nightmare.

At one point the wooden runners of the stretcher jammed in a chimney. Jack was pulling frantically to free it, as I paid out more rope to him. The stretcher suddenly broke loose and dropped with a sharp jerk. Jack was thrown backwards and the body broke loose from its straps and smashed into him. He managed to hold on to it while he was lowered on to easier ground. He told me later that for a horrible moment he thought that the body had woken up.

The descent seemed to take hours. We finally reached the edge of Loch Coruisk and staggered along the icy slabs to reach the hut. The place was mobbed and there wasn't room to get inside. The women had prepared a large meal from their own food and some of the RAF rations. One was the girlfriend of one of the dead men and she was in a very distressed state. Somebody had fainted at the sight of the bodies. Nobody was particularly hungry but there was plenty of drink being passed around.

The three stretchers were loaded on to the *Western Isles* and lashed to the deck and we clambered aboard. Colin, Cammy and George stayed behind with their friends; a boat would come to take them to Mallaig later. Their effort had been magnificent.

A strong swell was throwing the boat about as we put out into Loch Scavaig. There were thirty or so in the cabin and I discovered that it was the 3rd of January. It was a strange place to be sitting with three bodies above us on the deck.

Somebody started to sing. It may seem callous but rescuers have a way of making light of death; this is not through any disrespect but is partly a release from a very grim situation. If we took the thing too seriously we would never be able to do the job.

As the *Western Isles* sailed through the night an unlikely sing-song took place below deck. Bottles of whisky seemed to have materialised out of thin air and were being passed around. I particularly remember the singing of *Titanic*, full of embellishments and harmonies:

The lifeboats they set sail
Across the dark and stormy sea,
And the band struck up
With 'Hail my lord to thee.'
Little children sobbed and sighed as the waves went o'er the side.
It was sad when the great ship went down.

We were all shattered, but considering the uncomfortable and macabre situation there was an air of camaraderie and festivity among the rescuers as the voices rang out over the Minch.

At Armadale, the New Year's party was still in full fling. Although it was the middle of the night, the pub was open for us and drinks were on the house. That should have been the end of the call-out, but for Hamish and me there was more to come.

Corporal George Patterson had driven one of the three-ton trucks the fifty miles or so from Glen Brittle. Arriving early in the evening, he had waited fruitlessly for the boat. Finally he was taken to the policeman's house overlooking the Minch, where he would be able to see the lights of the incoming *Western Isles*.

'They won't be long,' the constable assured him. They were joined by a cheery bunch of reporters from the *Daily Express*. Six hours later, with no sign of the boat, they were enjoying the police hospitality. George, a broad Aberdonian, was standing on a chair, reciting 'The Buchan Bobby' to the delight of his police hosts.

As he said later, 'In Skye, you know, they don't use glasses at New Year, they serve whisky in buckets.'

When we were finally dragged from the pub Hamish and I acted as shotgun in the truck while the rest of the troops climbed into sleeping bags in the back. George the driver was singing his heart out and careering drunkenly all over the snow-covered road. All went well until we reached the steep winding hill heading down to Glen Brittle. Here George fell asleep at the wheel and we slithered to a halt in a drift at the side of the road.

Hamish and I grabbed our ice axes and started to dig out the wheels. George, coming round, started the truck and somehow backed out of the drift and roared off into the night. Hamish and I were left standing there appalled as the tail lights vanished into the night.

'For crying out loud,' Hamish gasped. 'How did he do that?'

We plodded down the road faced with a five-mile walk to Glen Brittle. I was dead on my feet and Hamish, who had been going for twenty-four hours longer than me, must have been absolutely all-in. We found the truck a mile or so further on, it had slid off the road again and the boys were digging it out. George staggered over to me looking contrite and swore blind that he thought we were in the back. We reached MacRae's barn at four in the morning.

These days a call-out like this would be very different. It's unlikely that the outcome would have changed, but had John Methven been able to use a mobile phone, a helicopter would have been with him within the hour and possibly both he and Tom Reid may have survived. Colin Stead would certainly have been able to call for help immediately and a small team could have been mobilised and taken in by helicopter. The whole rescue would have been completed on the first afternoon. Such is the change in the last fifty years.

The rescue teams had been in action over the entire Christmas and New Year's break. Hugh MacRae's barn at Glen Brittle seemed like a luxury hotel when at last we were able to change out of our wet clothing and relax.

'Next time you want a quiet New Year go anywhere but Skye, Hamish!' I said as I crawled into my sleeping bag.

Life at Kinloss was, for the next year, as hectic as ever. In August the Great Train Robbery happened. People were finding mail sacks full of banknotes all over the place, stashed in telephone boxes and the oddest places. A few days after the robbery John Hinde and I were climbing *Hallelujah Staircase*, one of Tom Patey's routes on the sea cliffs at Peterhead, when we spotted a heap of sacks on a ledge above us. Both of us were convinced that we had found a stash of the loot. The climbing was slow and difficult and we took well over an hour to reach the ledge.

'What do we do with the money, Chief? Keep it or ask for a reward?' I asked.

'There's probably enough to retire on, Spike. What do you think?'

By the time we reached the ledge with the sacks we were arguing what to do. Sadly they turned out to be rubbish and we never did find out what we would have done.

That November I was playing darts in the Altnaharra Inn in Wester Ross when somebody ran into the bar to say that President John F. Kennedy had been shot. It seemed so unlikely that none of us took it seriously. Yorky Watson's dart hit the wall and he muttered, 'He could have picked a more convenient time.'

It was only later when we heard that the president was dead that I realised the enormity of the situation. We had been living in dangerous times with the constant fear of nuclear war. It was a time of optimism and the cold war seemed to be defrosting. Kennedy was incredibly popular and the whole world went into shock. How could this have happened?

I arrived back at Kinloss to a bolt from the blue to discover that I had been posted to Queen's Flight at RAF Benson, in the flatlands between Reading and Oxford. I anxiously phoned my squadron leader, John Sims, the inspector of mountain rescue at Air Ministry.

'Can you get me out of this, John?' I pleaded.

'There's a post coming up on the Kai Tak rescue team in Hong Kong if you can stick it out there for a bit,' he said.

And so began an interminable wait. The high-pitched scream of the Rolls-Royce Dart engines on the Argosy transport aircraft was excruciating and the smart little Andovers of Queen's Flight, for flying the royal family, weren't much better. There wasn't much to do on the station and I managed to get a part-time job working for the *Reading Evening Post*.

There was a newspaper war going on at the time. The *Post* had just been launched and was Britain's first all-colour news-sheet. The other local papers had ganged up and were trying to put it out of business. It was a real eye opener to see the tenacious way that a fledgling company had to fight for its survival, and it turned out to be good experience for what would happen to me in the future.

With the extra cash and my RAF pay I managed to buy a brand new Minivan for the then princely sum of £500. I lined this with some blue carpet engraved with 'ER' – half-inched from one of Her Majesty's aeroplanes. It looked very smart and I'm sure she would have approved.

There were no other climbers on the base and the nearest serious rock was in North Wales. I occasionally hitched to Bristol and climbed in the Avon and Cheddar gorges, but they were a hundred miles away and I was desperate. Outside Oxford there were some very loose chalk cliffs and I would fix a top rope and solo up the crumbly rock.

One evening I had completed one of these climbs and was scrambling down a ledge that I had already descended a number of times before. Suddenly the side of the cliff sheared off and collapsed under my weight. The whole thing seemed to happen in slow motion as I and three or four tons of chalk crashed down the hillside. I lay in the rubble for a while without moving, I could hardly breathe and almost everything was hurting. There was nobody about and I knew that I would have to get help and set off crawling down the field to the road. Most of the pain was in my chest, one leg was in a bad way and I had very obviously broken my wrist. It seemed to take forever to get to the roadside and I waved frantically at the lines of cars that streamed by without stopping. Who could blame them? I must have looked a mess.

An obliging man finally did stop and drove me to the local hospital where I blissfully passed out as they were examining me. I came round full of painkillers and tucked up in bed, very glad to be alive. I'd cracked a number of ribs and my arm and leg were in plaster. My climbing was curtailed for a few weeks and I've had a very healthy respect for chalk since then.

That was the end of my chance to get to the Alps that summer in 1964, but I managed to get sick leave and once my leg had repaired I went to North Wales with Dave Voisey, one of the Kinloss team who had just been demobbed. I still had a plaster on my arm but managed to climb okay. The thought of going back to RAF Benson was appalling. It was glorious weather and I went absent without leave and Dave and I had a splendid time climbing on Cloggy and in the Llanberis Pass. The week spent in the Guardhouse at RAF Benson cutting the lawn with a pair of scissors was well worth it.

While at Kinloss, three of us, Jack Baines, Robin Wilkinson and I, had discussed the possibility of opening a climbing shop in Fort William. It was a bit of a pipe dream. At the time there were less than a dozen such shops in Britain. We made a pact that the first of us to be demobbed should go and do a recce. I had never taken it very seriously, assuming that I would be the last to leave. All of a sudden the idea seemed very promising.

Life on a normal RAF base wasn't for me. The chance of a posting to Hong Kong seemed remote and my five years' service was almost finished. I decided not to take the option to extend my engagement. It was a spontaneous decision, almost in the same manner as I had joined the RAF. The speed of my demob was alarming: one minute I was a serviceman and the next I was walking down the road with my bag, and without a bed or a job. I hadn't a clue what I was going to do in the future, the only training I had was working on aeroplanes and I had absolutely no intention of doing that.

The *Reading Evening Post* kept me on for a while; they were having a tough time getting readers and I knew I wouldn't be there for long. Winston Churchill died while I was working there, he had been ill for some time and the front page had been set for days in an attempt to be first out with the news. It was interesting to see how the newspaper tried every trick in the book to get a different angle on the story.

I finally gave my notice and packed my rucksack and headed up to Fort William where I stayed with Ingrid Feany at the youth hostel in Glen Coe. Big Ingrid was a great character who ran the hostel with her husband Jim and their daughter Britta. Born in Berlin she had married Jim soon after the war and they had first run the youth hostel on Loch Lomond and then moved up to Glen Coe where she became 'Big Mama' to all of us waifs and strays. She loved boozy parties and singsongs and the hostel was always full of interesting characters passing through.

My luck was in – a new outdoor centre had just opened on the banks of Loch Eil, just outside Fort William, and they were advertising for a sailing instructor. I forgot all about the shop project and I went to the interview and remembered to exaggerate. The person interviewing me seemed very pleased that I had some mountaineering qualifications and fortunately didn't ask much about sailing and I got the job. I'd never sailed a boat in my life!

The two weeks prior to starting the job were spent reading everything I could on the subject, but by the time I started at the Locheil Centre, the only boats I had been in were my Uncle Harry's rowing boat at Robin Hood's Bay and a paddle boat at Blackpool.

7 | Locheil

1964 was some year! The United States crash-landed a rocket on to the moon, sending back the first ever close-up pictures of its surface; Nelson Mandela was sentenced to life imprisonment; Cassius Clay defeated Sonny Liston to become heavyweight champion of the world, and I got a job as an instructor at the Locheil Centre.

Sometime in the previous two years, Lord Tony Dulverton, who owned the shooting estate at Fassfern on the banks of Loch Eil, a few miles from Fort William, offered the use of some old forestry buildings for any takers who could use them for youth training. It was a fine gesture. Dulverton, who was heir to the Imperial Tobacco and W.D. & H.O. Wills family fortune, was one of the ten richest men in the country, a baron in more ways than one.

The offer was taken up by Alan Hill on behalf of Toc H, a charity set up during the First World War by an army Chaplin, the Reverend Philip 'Tubby' Clayton. Talbert House, or Toc H as it was called in trench signal code, was a refuge and club for soldiers resting behind the trenches at Ypres. Over the door of the chapel was the motto 'All rank abandon, ye who enter here'. This front line soldiers club gave birth to the Toc H movement. After the war Toc H became a gathering of men who sought to rebuild a broken world. As the old comrades died away the charity turned its attention to helping young people create a better life. Nowadays, the organisation is still active in the UK, Australia, South Africa, Germany and Belgium. Tubby Clayton was still alive when I started work at Locheil; he died in 1972 aged eighty-seven.

Alan Hill was a small man bursting with energy and possessing that rare gift of persuasion that makes people think they had come up with the idea themselves. He had given up a well-paid job with Littlewoods to organise the Toc H youth programme and while undertaking a week-end land improvement project had met Dulverton whom he befriended. Tony Dulverton told him about the sheds at Locheil and Alan instantly realised their potential.

The old buildings stood alongside the grounds of Achdalieu Hotel, a converted shooting lodge. Alan, never one to take the easy option, persuaded Lord Dulverton to buy the hotel and convert it and the farm buildings into a training school for underprivileged children. It's a lovely house standing on a rise overlooking Loch Eil, with a spectacular view of the Ardgour mountains. Here is some of Scotland's most beautiful and isolated country, and the perfect place for outdoor activities.

Achdalieu hotel was bought and converted with no expense spared. Alan visited a number of existing training schools, Eskdale Outward Bound and Brathay Hall in the Lake District, and the Moray Sea School near Elgin, and then set about putting his own stamp on the kind of courses he wanted to run. Loch Eil was ideal for canoeing and sailing and the surrounding wild countryside perfect for walking expeditions.

The initial courses had already been run in the old farm buildings. I arrived in the early days of the newly converted hotel. I was twenty-two, wet around the ears and very nervous and not much older than some of the boys I was expected to instruct. I still felt awkward in civilian clothes and had no experience in teaching. All the instructors looked extremely fit and very confident while I felt tongue tied and uneasy.

Another instructor, Jim Hunter, and I started on the same day. Jim was a Glaswegian whose parents ran a youth club for the children of workers at Stevens Shipyard on the Clyde. They ran weekend canoeing and sailing trips for the members and Jim was an expert canoeist and not a bad sailor, but he had done virtually no climbing and was as anxious about this as I was about the sailing. Both of us were very apprehensive as to how we were going to handle things.

The new centre had accommodation for sixty boys who were divided into groups of ten, which Alan called clans, named after the local

Scottish clans surrounding Fort William. I became the instructor for the McDonalds and Jim took on the McLeods. All the early courses were full; most of the boys were sent by the education authorities in Glasgow and Edinburgh and there were also some borstal boys.

The sailing boats were heavy, clinker-built 'Morags', with a dipping lug sail. This will mean nothing to non-sailors; all I can say is they were the most awkward, temperamental and uncontrollable boats imaginable. It soon became evident that I hadn't a clue how to sail. Fortunately, Alan was more amused than angry and I was given a crash course and became reasonably competent although sailing was never my forte.

In wild conditions, which happen often in Scotland, I would reef the sail in to pocket-handkerchief size and try to remain calm. I felt that I was only one step ahead of the boys I was supposed to be teaching. The month-long course was a terrific way to get to know the wild country of Moidart. This lovely remote part of Scotland between Loch Shiel, Loch Morar, Loch Nevis and Loch Horn is sprinkled with bothies, old disused houses and crofts that we were able to use.

There were no roads and once out in the mountains we barely saw a soul. It was a superb area for sea canoeing and the highlight of the course was a four-day hillwalking expedition which the boys organised themselves. It's marvellous how far some of the clans managed to travel on these journeys.

The chief instructor for most of my time at Locheil was John Ferguson, a fine artist and a great raconteur. Another was Alec Fulton, whose brother Stewart I had met climbing with the Americans in Chamonix. Alec was also a member of the Creagh Dhu, a small wiry man and an exceptionally good climber and excellent banjo player.

I soon discovered that I loved the work; I was doing what I enjoyed and at the same time found great pleasure in teaching young people. It was satisfying to see the change that came over a group of youngsters once they got the bit between their teeth. I was under no illusion that we made a life-changing difference to them, and I doubt if many will ever remember the rudiments of mountain navigation or handling a sailing boat or canoe. On the other hand it was amazing how a group of city boys, some of whom claimed never to have seen a hen, could blend together and help each other reach heights that they had never dreamed.

Alan had a different approach to education than that promoted by other outdoor centres of the time. He felt that the tough, high achievement philosophy advocated by Kurt Hahn in the Outward Bound movement was not appropriate to all youngsters, particularly those from the inner cities. He decided to add art, musical appreciation and discussion groups in which the boys would take an active part.

The accommodation was warm and comfortable; there were no cold showers or tough cross-country runs. Meals must have been a real shock to some of the Glasgow boys, many of whom were used to very basic living. At Locheil excellent food was served formally in a comfortable dining room and they were expected to behave with reasonable table manners, no easy task for a bunch of ravenous teenagers.

For me it was a grand awakening and in the first few months I probably learned more than the lads I was supposed to be teaching.

The mixture of outdoor and artistic activities seemed to be the ideal combination and I loved it. Jim took a great interest in the music and I often sat in at the back of his class as he played and discussed a mixture of modern pop mixed in with Rodrigo's Concierto de Aranjuez or Shostakovich's Leningrad Symphony blasting out gunfire in a way that fascinated his audience. In the atmosphere at Locheil this seemed to work perfectly.

There were some memorable days; one expedition with a group of Borstal boys stands out. They arrived at Locheil uncommunicative and full of resentment against authority but were a grand lot of lads, vital and full of energy, and once they got the idea that I wasn't trying to beat them down we had a great time. On the final expedition the weather was gorgeous and we made our way up into Coire Rath, a wild, high hanging valley at the south side of the Grey Corries ridge, part of the Ben Nevis range.

On the way up we swam in every pool in the river. I left the boys camping in the coire and walked up to the summit of Stob Ban and slept with

my back against the summit cairn. In the morning there was a temperature inversion and I found myself on a tiny island with a flat sea of cloud
below me. The Grey Corries, Aonachs and Ben Nevis were out of the
cloud and nothing else could be seen except the Cairngorms, some fifty
miles away. I sat on my island and watched the sun rise and listened to the
boys below in the cloud making breakfast.

We followed the Grey Corries ridge all day. It was raining in Fort William
but here we were in blue sky with a level carpet of cloud below with only
the highest peaks sticking out like islands in a foaming sea. Against all the
rules I promised the boys a pint in the pub at Spean Bridge if they got a
move on. Never have a bunch of lads sprinted along the Grey Corries
ridge at such a pace and I had a problem keeping up with them.

On the last day of the course they had a day out in Fort William and in
the evening they gave me a present of a couple of pairs of socks. I was quite
touched as I knew that they hadn't much money. Later that evening we
had a visit from the local police and it turned out that some of the boys
had been seen shoplifting in the town. Alan made a marvellous speech at
the evening meal; he was a great orator and extolled the virtues of honesty
and keeping up the high reputation of the centre.

'Okay lads,' he said, coming to the end, 'I promise that if the culprits
own up and return the goods no further action will be taken.'

To our astonishment the entire course of sixty boys put their hands up!
It was desperately hard to keep a straight face. They had just about emptied
every shop in the High Street. We collected basket loads of contraband:
socks, hats, knives; it was hard to believe that Woolworths and the Highland
Homespun had any stock left. Alan had a terrible time convincing the police
not to press charges. The stock was duly returned to its rightful owners but
that was the end of our letting the boys loose in town. I ruefully returned my
socks, but did say to the boys afterwards, 'It's the thought that counts!'

Occasionally, between courses, I went away with Jim Hunter's parents
on weekends with the Stevens Shipyard youth club. Canoe trips at
Dalguise on the Tay and camping around the Cobbler at Ardgartan. Ma

Hunter did the organising and kept a motherly eye on the girls and Jim Hunter senior fixed the transport and equipment. They were happy days and I was treated as one of the family.

Ma was a Glaswegian lady with a heart of gold and Jim was a retired shipyard worker. Both were tiny, typical of many Glasgow people; presumably their parents and grandparents before them had all suffered the hardships of poor diet and poverty. It's remarkable how a single city has spawned some of the smallest people in the country, and yet they were full of heart and laughter and ran a wonderful amenity in the centre of a very rough part of the city. The youth club was situated in some old buildings on the bank of the River Clyde near the entrance to the Clyde Tunnel. There were table tennis and snooker tables and the family had a small flat upstairs.

Tragedy struck very suddenly. The ship building industry in Glasgow was in decline and presumably Stevens Shipyard was in financial difficulties. Without any warning, a letter from the management closed the youth club and the Hunters were given seven days' notice to quit their flat. The shock was too much. In the horrific week that followed, Jim's father died of a heart attack and his mother was left without a home. With great difficulty, Jim eventually managed to get a council house for his mother but the events took their toll and he was never the same man that I knew when we first arrived at the Locheil Centre.

Outdoor education was in its infancy and there were none of the qualifications and safeguards that exist today. With my background in mountain rescue I had the uneasy feeling that we sometimes skated on very thin ice, an accident waiting to happen. The weather on the west coast of Scotland can be very unpredictable and we were often a long way from help.

At Glenmore Lodge, the national outdoor centre in the Cairngorms, Eric Langmuir was trying to create a standard qualification for our kind of work, the Mountaineering Instructor Certificate (MIC). Alec Fulton and I were sent on the first of these courses to be run at the lodge. Alec was at the time one of the best rock climbers in the country.

Both of us were sceptical and resentful that instructors at another centre, who had no qualifications themselves, had the right to examine us. Eric was very diplomatic and the course turned out to be terrific and I learned a lot. He was well ahead of his time and the MIC has now become the national standard and is much harder to achieve than it was in my day.

One very close shave sticks out in my mind and shows how a series of events can turn the best-laid plans into a nightmare. During the winter the four-day expeditions kept to the valleys and stayed within easy reach of each other in case of an emergency. In November the weather was miserable. Snow was falling on the summits and it was raining and sleeting in the glens.

On this occasion my clan were following another instructor, Charlie Pollock, and his group over a low col between Loch Eilt and Loch Shiel. Charlie stopped his clan in the shelter of an old wall for lunch and my lot caught them up. I wasn't keen to stop as it was a cold and miserable place so we kept going in the hope of reaching Glenaladale bothy on the side of Loch Shiel.

When I got near the bothy I found that the Aladale burn was in a spate and we couldn't get across, so we sheltered under the riverbank to eat our lunch. A few minutes later I heard a whistle blowing and two of Charlie's clan ran up to say that one of his boys had collapsed. Charlie had put up a tent and the boy was alright, but could I come up and give him some help.

I decided the best thing to do was get my group into the bothy, so I got out a rope and waded across the river, then took each of the boys across one at a time. It was waist deep, freezing cold and fast flowing, but we got across to the bothy okay and into dry clothes and I went up and gave Charlie a hand to bring the rest of the boys down.

The sick boy had recovered a little but Charlie was anxious about him. We decided to stay where we were for the night, and head back the following day. A few minutes later one of my boys trod on a nail which went right through his foot. I patched him up but it was clear that he would not be able to walk far.

At this point John Ferguson and Alec Fulton turned up with their clans so in all we were there with forty boys sheltering in the very small bothy. It was a nasty situation and after some discussion it was decided that Charlie and I would stay with the boys and John and Alec would walk out to Glenfinnan and bring down a boat to take out the two casualties. The rest of us would walk out the following day.

It was six miles of rough ground with no path along the side of Loch Shiel, and we weren't expecting John and Alec to get back with the boat until sometime the following morning. Anyone who has taught Glasgow schoolchildren will realise that keeping forty 12- to 14-year-old boys occupied in an old deserted house for a night was no picnic, but we got them organised and settled and all was seemingly okay. We awoke the following morning to one of those storms that happens in the Highlands. A foot of snow had fallen and a blizzard was in progress.

It cleared a little around midday and the mail boat that plied the Loch tried to get in to us. We could see John and Alec waving from the deck but it was far too windy to land and the boat pulled away. In the afternoon it cleared for a while but the wind was still blasting with no chance of a boat so we arranged an outdoor game to keep the boys occupied.

What happened next is almost unbelievable. From where we were it was possible to see the railway viaduct at Glenfinnan. Anyone who has seen the Harry Potter movies will recognise the beautiful curving structure used by the Hogwarts Express. Just below this lies the Stage House Inn. Unbeknown to us, three of the boys had a whip-round and decided that they would walk out to get cigarettes, in the clear light the viaduct looked only a stone's throw away. The rest were to say nothing and cover for them while they were gone. They set off at 3 p.m. along the snow-covered hillside.

Sometime later Charlie and I were sorting out the evening meal and I sensed that something was amiss; the boys were behaving strangely and there was funny atmosphere. It had started to snow heavily again and the wind was rattling the old building. I sat down with my clan and asked them what was going on. There was a silence. Nobody was willing to admit anything and it took some time to pull out the full story. Three of the boys were missing. Charlie and I were horror-struck.

We left the group sorting out the meal, with threats on pain of death about any tomfoolery, and set out along the loch side. It was pitch dark, snowing and blowing and our head torches wouldn't penetrate more than a few feet. Deep drifts filled every hollow. After a couple of hours of shouting we realised that it was hopeless, in these conditions there was no chance of finding them. There was nothing that we could do and we headed back to the bothy which we reached about midnight.

I think that was the worst night of my life. I was certain that the boys had perished and that it was my fault. I had visions of them lying frozen, covered in snow. How the hell were we going to explain how we had lost them? Should we have left the rest of the boys in the bothy and gone on to raise the alarm? What would we do in the morning; we still had two boys not capable of walking? What if the weather stayed the same and we couldn't move for another day?

Charlie was in the same state as I was, utterly devastated. We sat through the night taking turns to go outside shouting. It was snowing steadily with no sign of abating. Both of us were convinced that the boys must be dead. It was almost certain that there would be a public enquiry. What little sleep we had was filled with nightmares and both of us were playing mind games. I couldn't get out of my head the thought of the boys lying unprotected somewhere along the hillside. Charlie, like me, was making a career of outdoor education, and we sat in the bothy smoking countless cigarettes, and wondering what tomorrow would bring.

By morning it had calmed down, a thick blanket of snow covered the ground but it was going to be a fine day. We were up before dawn, Charlie was going to head straight up the loch side to Glenfinnan and raise the alarm, and I set about organising the boys to walk out. I knew that Alec and John would be down sometime with the mail boat to pick up the two casualties. Just as it got light we saw the boat heading towards us down the loch and there on the deck was Alan Hill waving urgently.

As the boat got nearer I could see Alec and John with our three abscond-ers. Oh blessed reprieve, I thanked all my gods at once! But how the hell had Alan got them? I had never been so relieved to see anybody in my life.

Alan jumped ashore with the boys in tow. They were noticeably very dejected.

'Take these three back and make them walk with the rest of the group,' Alan said, indicating the runaways. 'Sorry I couldn't get here earlier, I knew that you would be worried,' he said. Worried was an understatement.

'How on earth did you find them?' I gasped with relief.

The boys had gone off during the lull in the storm and had got much further than we believed they would. As night fell and the storm increased they were only a couple of miles from Glenfinnan and they reached the Stage House Inn at about 8 p.m., almost the same time that the storm increased, and Charlie and I went out looking for them.

They were tired and frightened when they went into the pub. The bar-man, Angus MacDonald, looked at them suspiciously, recognised the clothing as Locheil boys, and phoned Alan Hill. Angus the Gate, as he was known, was a lovely man and a great character at Glenfinnan and to him I'm eternally grateful.

Alan drove down immediately and picked them up. Once he got the story out of the boys he realised what a state Charlie and I would be in but there was nothing he could do that night. He gave the boys a tremen-dous ticking off and organised the boat for first light.

We got the walking wounded on board and from then on everything went okay. I spoke to Alan later and offered my resignation but thankfully he refused. I very much admired the calm way with which he handled the situation.

In the light of what happened we modified the way we were operating winter expeditions. A short time later a tragedy in the Cairngorms took place when six youngsters lost their lives in very similar circumstances. I knew Ben Beattie, the instructor involved, quite well and felt very sorry for him. There but for the grace of God.

Work at Locheil was very intense – long hours and only a two-day break between courses. I was feeling jaded and in need of a change. Alec Fulton and I took a well-earned holiday in the Alps. Alec's wife Kippy and Alan's secretary, Camilla Fagen, joined us. Camilla and I had become very close – she was a lovely girl, bouncing with energy and loved the life at the centre but she too was feeling the pressure.

We went first to my old haunts in the Dolomites and climbed the Piaz Crack on the Punta Emma, but the weather was poor. We tried the Wild Kaiser in Austria and then went to the Club Vagabond in Leysin where John Harlin had set up the International School of Mountaineering. John made us very welcome and we stayed and helped out as climbing instructors for a while.

At the time the Vagabond was a thriving community of mountaineers from all over the world. There was an American college in Leysin and many of John's customers came from there. Don Whillans was working there at the time and I got to know him quite well. He had a dry sense of humour, which I loved. In later years he often stayed with me in Fort William, and during a very bad time, which I will come to later, Don showed me great kindness.

Alec and I climbed the Miroir and Cheval Blanc routes on the Argentine (in Switzerland) with John Harlin and Gary Hemming and students from the ISM. At the time John and Gary were planning the winter direct route on the Eiger and arranged a helicopter flight to photograph the face in an attempt to figure out the line. They spent hours poring over photographs and preparing for the climb in every detail, not at all the happy-go-lucky way that we British went about things. They were very strong but different personalities: John, big and powerful with the overwhelming confidence of the wealthy and successful American, and Gary, the long-haired and handsome waif, brooding and moody.

The weather was foul and the whole bunch of us packed in the Alps and drove down to the Calanques, a popular sea cliff climbing area near Marseilles. It was a wonderfully relaxing place with great climbing on white limestone cliffs above the warm Mediterranean Sea. This was just what we needed after the long dark Scottish winter.

I intended to go back to the Vagabond but tragically John Harlin died on the Eiger the following winter and Gary Hemming was killed in strange circumstances in the Grand Tetons. It was not to be.

On our return to Locheil we discovered that Alan Hill had decided it was time to move on and had taken a senior post at Toronto University. He felt that the centre was running smoothly now and was in need of a change. When he left I missed him terribly. Like John Hinde at Kinloss, he had been an inspiration and his free thinking on a better way to run outdoor activities was, I knew, going to be great loss to the whole way that outdoor education was developing.

I still very much enjoyed the life of an instructor and Peter Downs, who took over from Alan, was an excellent choice, but I felt that the place was changing and some of the earlier pioneer spirit had gone. It also affected my mountaineering activities. It was impossible to climb for one's own enjoyment while courses were in progress and by the end of the month it was hard to be enthusiastic about going into the mountains for personal pleasure.

I had become friends with a local climber, Ian (Suds) Sutherland, who was instructing at a small outdoor centre at Applecross on the west coast, north of Kyle. Suds was one of the two men who overtook the two Dundee boys on the North-East Buttress call-out. He'd gained some local notoriety when he and his friend, Alan Savage, were pictured on the front page of the local newspaper standing at the roundabout in Fort William setting out to hitch-hike round the world. They got as far as Manchester and blew all their money on a bit of high life and had to slink quietly home a few weeks later. A man after my own heart, I've never let him forget it!

Suds and I had a very successful Alps trip that year. We managed to climb the Via Steger on the Catinaccio, where Dinger and I had failed a few years earlier and, among other things, had an epic descent after climbing the Chamonix face of the Aiguille du Peigne in a storm. I'd been chatting to Don Whillans in the Bar National and he'd recommended an easier descent route than the one in the guidebook. Don had drunk a few glasses of *grande biére* and must have got his rights and lefts mixed up. We finished up bivouacking in the most horrendous gully and I just about died of cold.

In 1965 I joined the Lochaber Mountain Rescue Team and it was a way to get to know some of the local climbers. Locheil was quite insular and the instructors tended to stick together and had little to do with what went on in the town. There was a thriving community of keen mountaineers in Fort William. A man called Vic Quirie had started a youth club in the mid-fifties and this had developed into a nucleus of the Lochaber Mountaineering Club, which ultimately became the rescue team.

Donald Duff, the surgeon at Belford Hospital, had been the inspiration to really get the rescue team going. He reorganised the hospital to handle the growing number of mountain accidents and developed an early stretcher that split in two and was easy to carry. Until then rescues had been attempted by volunteers, shepherds, gillies and policemen, who did a stalwart job but relied on the RAF for anything major.

A strong association was beginning to develop which would ultimately become the busiest rescue team in the country. Doctor John Barclay, Ian Sutherland, Gus McLean, Bill Robertson, John and Richard Grieve and Ike Jones were a few of the stalwarts of those early days. To the south the same thing developed as Hamish MacInnes set up the Glencoe team.

I spent as much of my spare time as I could climbing on Ben Nevis. Suds and I managed a few of the harder rock climbs, *Bull Roar*, *Minus One Direct* and *Centurion*, but it was the winter climbs that thrilled us. It was still the days of step cutting, a slow and painstaking process, but the Ben was the place for ice and although I didn't know it, a great change was about to happen which would put Scotland at the forefront of world mountaineering.

I was getting itchy feet and felt it was time to move on. While at Glenmore Lodge I'd had a long talk with Johnny Cunningham who had just returned from Antarctica. He, Davey Todd and Jimmy Gardener, all Creagh Dhu members, had gone down as general assistants, working as dog drivers for the British Antarctic Survey (BAS).

'It's right up your street, Spike, you'd love it!' Johnny told me. He started talking about the great sledge journeys, unclimbed mountains as far as the eye could see, sea ice, storms, midnight sun and dark winters, and South Georgia. That did it – memories of my failure to get there flooded back and I was hooked.

I wasn't that confident that they would give me a job. I hadn't the slightest idea how to drive a dog team, but who had? Johnny gave me the address of Bill Sloman in Cambridge and I wrote to him offering my services, and off I went, full of bluff and exaggeration, to the BAS headquarters in Cambridge for the interview.

The meeting went surprisingly well. I met Sir Vivian Fuchs who was the overall chief and was impressed at how pleasant and approachable he was. He was another of those larger than life personalities who had been a dog driver in the early days of the Antarctic Survey and gained fame in crossing the continent with Edmund Hillary. He was to prove a tremendous boss. I didn't realise at the time that Bill Sloman had phoned all my referees and had long discussions with them about my ability to get on with others. To my surprise and pleasure I got the job.

I loved my work at Locheil, all my friends were there and I had serious qualms that I was making a mistake. During my last few courses I almost changed my mind. I expected to be away for the next four years and as I drove south from Fort William I did not expect to return, nor did I imagine that I would work for Locheil Centre again. I knew though, that going to Antarctica was the thing I most wanted to do in the world.

8 | Falkland Islands

The *Queen Elizabeth* was moored at dock fifteen in Southampton. The mighty liner dwarfed all other ships and buildings in the harbour. I walked past it to dock sixteen which appeared to be empty. Below the level of the stonework was a small boat which I took to be the ferry out to the *Shackleton*, the icebreaker that was to take me to the Antarctic. It wasn't until I clambered down the ladder on to the deck and one of the hands indicated where I'd find a cabin that I realised that this was in fact the *Shackleton* itself.

I stowed away my few personal possessions, my banjo and precious rucksack of climbing equipment, and wandered up on deck. Everything was in mayhem, forty-gallon oil drums were being lowered into the hold that was crammed to capacity with crates of all shapes and sizes, steel beams, wall panels, a tractor, sacks of potatoes, grain, whole carcasses of beef. A rough-looking crew swarmed over the ship, they were tattooed with rings in their ears, a rare sight in 1967, and spoke English with a strange dialect, which I discovered to be Falkland Island, a cross between Australian, South African and Island Scots. They were in the final throes of preparation for our journey south.

I discovered that I had become one of the 'Fids'. There were a dozen or so of us on board, all bound for various Antarctic bases. New boys, feeling slightly lost.

'How come we're called Fids,' I asked? It seemed a strange name.

'It stands for Falkland Island Dependency Survey, but we call you *Fuckin' Idiots Down South*,' the boson told me with a grin. Somehow the latter explanation seemed most appropriate.

I shared a tiny cabin with John Ball, a young doctor bound for the Argentine Islands, one of the northern bases on the Antarctic Peninsula.

He had just finished his hospital houseman training and this was his first job. Almost all of us were in our early twenties, the majority of scientists going south had just finished university and this was their first job.

At twenty-five it was hard to believe that I was one of the older and more experienced men. We were a mixed bunch going to different jobs: Ian Flavell Smith, geophysicist, cultured and very clever; Mike Holmes, doctor, fresh out of university, cocky and full of the myth of Antarctica; a bunch of builders going to construct an aircraft hangar on Deception Island; Ken Portwine, a youth hostel warden from Coniston going to the Argentine Islands as a cook; Mike Fielding, surveyor; Phil Wainwright, surveyor and boatman; and Jack Donaldson, a schoolmaster from Newcastle, going as a general assistant.

I began to realise the enormity of the job Bill Solomon had in putting together this mixed bag of talents; met men, biologists, seismologists, mechanics, radio operators – everything to keep the survey going. We even had a king! Ken Doyle was a few years older than the rest of us and was elected King Fid to act as our representative to the ship's officers. I had been reading everything I could about Antarctica and our little bunch of raw recruits seemed remarkably similar to those who answered Ernest Shackleton's famous advert in *The Times* in 1901:

> Men wanted for hazardous journey. Small wages. Bitter cold.
> Long months of complete darkness. Constant danger. Honour
> and recognition in case of success.

Ken had already done a year's stint on the Adelaide Island base as an explosives expert and was now going to Stonington with the same job as me, a GA (general assistant – gash hand, guide, dog driver). As the only man on board with experience of the bases, we must have driven him crackers with our never-ending questions. During the previous season at Adelaide Island he had been involved in building a new jetty and had blown up some rocks to clear the area, one of which had landed on his head. Some expert – he was never allowed to forget it.

We left Southampton that evening – Thursday 12 October 1967. It was raining and miserable. I immediately discovered that the old *Shackleton* had an unpleasant screwing pitch. As she lifted over one wave she would settle down the trough with a kind of twisting motion that churned the stomach. As we headed into the Bay of Biscay in a howling gale I became violently sick. The second day was terrible, the boat rolled violently in the heavy sea and I hung over the rail with nothing left to bring up.

Half of us Fids were recovering from appendix operations. In those days it was recommended that we had them removed before going south after a doctor at Halley Bay had to oversee the removal of his own appendix the previous winter. My doctor in Fort William, Doc Allison, had gleefully insisted on this and I had spent my last couple of weeks at home hobbling around in misery holding on to my side. My already weak stomach couldn't take this rolling sea.

'Come and look at this. The *Queen Elizabeth* is overtaking us!' One of the crew shouted. Apparently the mighty liner was steaming past like a speedboat on the other side of the *Shackleton*. The sight of a lifetime.

'Bugger it,' I mumbled, hardly lifting my head. I never saw her and sadly this was her final voyage. She was sold by Cunard and later caught fire and was wrecked in Hong Kong harbour.

The journey south to Montevideo took three weeks. We sailed down the coast of Africa to the Cape Verde islands then across the Atlantic with a sight of St Paul's Rock and down the coast of Brazil to Montevideo. The tropics were glorious and I rigged a hammock under one of the lifeboats and on a number of occasions flying fish flapped on to my bed during the night.

I soon realised that Stonington, where I was to be based, was the most coveted posting of all. It was the southerly station on the Antarctic Peninsula, the place the sledging expeditions started and where the dog drivers were heading. There was a snag however: the sea ice that far south did not break out until late autumn and until then we would be on board the *Shackleton*, possibly for a period of three or four months. In the meantime we would help with the annual changeovers at the other bases.

I was horrified at this, I couldn't imagine being stuck on the ship for so long, I'd go mad! Phil Wainwright and I went to see Captain Turnbull. Frosty, as he was known, was a sailor in the old tradition, bearded and tough with a rasping voice and a well-hidden sense of humour, he didn't suffer Fids gladly. To him the *Shackleton* was the only ship in the world. He had made dozens of journeys to Antarctica and was the most experienced of the survey's captains. As the voyage continued I began to realise what a master seaman he was.

'You Fids are all the same,' he growled. 'Every time something interesting happens you bugger off. I'm not having you in my crew.'

Phil and I assured him that we were prepared to do anything and would stand watch with the rest of the crew; he finally gave way. This was the best thing that we could have done. Although we had to stand watch when the ship was in port or on one of the bases, we got to know the crew very well, and as the summer programme developed we found that we were very much involved in what was happening.

The ship's youngest engineer was Ian Curphey. Curph and I became great friends; he had the wanderlust and had signed on as engineer to get to the Antarctic. He had a grey beard and smoked a pipe and looked like a real explorer. He and I were roughly the same age but his experience and travels made my own adventures seem insignificant. Curph was desperate to drive dogs and on his return to Britain that autumn he managed to sign on as a Fid and the following year came back as one of us. He and I sledged together in my second year.

Montevideo, our first port of call, was marvellous. Phil, Curph and I hit the high spots: Pocitos beach on the waterfront – sun, sand, palm trees and South American girls. We were about to go to Antarctica for two years where we would not see a woman for the entire time and here, in the scantiest bikinis imaginable, were the world's most beautiful women. I began to seriously wonder if I was doing the right thing. The docks on the River Plate estuary were a hive of high and low life bars, full of drunken sailors, the Falkland Islander crew ran wild …

It was a fascinating city full of life. In the far distance it was just possible to see Buenos Aires on the other side of the estuary and alongside our dock stood the huge anchor of the *Graf Spee*, salvaged as a memorial to the battle of the River Plate when the German pocket battleship was scuttled in 1939.

Phil and I went down to the market and bought ten 5-gallon flagons of cheap wine that went under the fine name of Boozy. We had to hire a trailer to transport it, and the flagons entirely filled our tiny cabin to such an extent that we had to spread our mattresses on top of the mountain of wine bottles. This seemed to be sufficient for our first year in Antarctica. The stuff tasted okay but we soon discovered that once opened, a flagon went sour if not drunk immediately. This proved no great problem as we drank rapidly through the entire fifty gallons long before any of it reached Antarctica.

Our next port of call was Port Stanley in the Falkland Islands. The 300-mile journey, normally a day's steam from Montevideo, took four days. We hit a force-12 hurricane and the *Shackleton* had to heave-to into the wind and ride out the storm. By now, thank God, most of us had gained our sea legs. Forty-foot waves were towering above the bridge and crashing over the deck. During this storm the radar picked up a small blip and Frosty edged the ship towards it. There, in this violent sea, was the smallest sailing boat imaginable.

At this time a spate of tiny yachts were crossing the Atlantic, sawing lumps off their sterns to get the shortest length. This little boat could not have been more than twelve feet long and had a pocket handkerchief of sail out to keep her head into the wind. There was no sign of life. We sounded the ships hooter and a face appeared at the hatch, waved and vanished. It seemed incredible that a boat could survive in such a sea. We learned later that he was an Australian yachtsman who, sadly, was never seen again.

Port Stanley was very primitive. In 1967 it bore a striking resemblance to Stornoway on the Isle of Lewis. The Falklands were similar to many of the Scottish islands – rolling, treeless hills dotted with sheep. Most of the buildings were constructed from corrugated iron and around the harbour lay the hulks of old sailing ships damaged and abandoned after rounding Cape Horn. On the far side of the bay, in Sparrow Cove, was the *Great Britain*, Brunel's iron-hulled ship, once the largest in the world, abandoned and rusting since 1937. (The *Great Britain* would later return to Bristol where she was built.)

There were an abundance of birds of all shapes and sizes, many of them with exquisite plumage, and for the first time we saw penguins. The islanders had remarkable names for the birds. All small ones were called sparrows and this included such exotics as Patagonian mocking-birds and long-tailed meadowlarks. Medium-sized birds were called clews, and big ones were vultures. Sea and water birds were known as quarks. All nice and simple, but I don't think our biologists were very impressed.

My pay was £500 a year but once on the Antarctic Continent there would be no way of spending it and I had never felt so wealthy. Actually, most of us were quite surprised to be paid anything. We had gone for the adventure and the money was a bonus. Stanley was a tax-free port and I bought a very upmarket Nikon camera and lenses at Ray Binnie's store.

Curph and I took a couple of days off and went climbing on Twin Sisters ridge and a fine rock escarpment a mile or two out of Stanley called Mount Tumbledown. Here, about sixty feet above the ground, was a huge over-hanging flake of rock, so thin that there was a hole through it, very similar to the Great Flake on the *Central Buttress* of Scafell in the Lake District.

I made several unsuccessful attempts to get up this, so I went back to the ship and pinched a steel wire strop. I climbed back up to my high point and threw the wire through the hole, tied it off and managed to swarm up and complete the climb. Sixteen years later as the British Marines yomped into Stanley after the Argentine invasion, I watched on television as they passed under Tumbledown Ridge, and there, for the entire world to see,

TOP LEFT Sweet (centre) sitting on his signals truck, Glen More, 1961.   TOP RIGHT Mr Lyons and me, 1948.
MIDDLE LEFT Cairn Gorm ski road, 1961.   BOTTOM The Wall End gang, Langdale, 1960. L–R: Bill Harper,
Hodge, Stewart Baird, Ginger Warburton, Toby Ford, Peter 'Spud' Tait, and Nodge.

TOP John Hinde, 'The Chief', in 1961.   BOTTOM Kinloss RAF Mountain Rescue Team after the Vulcan air crash call-out, 1963. *Back row (L–R):* MT Driver, MT Driver, Jim Stellings, John (The Chief) Hinde, Mull Russell, Dave Voisey, Robin (Dinger) Bell, Iain Doig, Jack Baines, Alan Ward, Bob Cook, Peter (Sweet) Myers, Fred Jackson. *Middle row (L–R):* Keith Charge, Michael (Jim Crow) Raven, Tuke Brewer, George Paterson, Ray (Sunshine) Sefton, Chick Rafferty, Harry Dick. *Front row (L–R):* Stevie MacDonald, Hamish Brown, Martin Mackie, Geordie Armstrong, Ian (Spike) Sykes, Dave Walklet, Ross McKerron.

LEFT The CIC hut, Ben Nevis. The North-East Buttress is on the skyline. The First Platform is the step in the ridge; *Raeburn's 18 Minute Route* goes directly up to this.   RIGHT Dinger on *Spigolo Giallo*, 'The Yellow Edge', in 1962. Note the Tarbuck knot, hemp waistline, red socks and miner's helmet. A well-dressed climber of his day!

TOP John Harlin and Gary Hemming on fixed ropes on the South-East Ridge of the Blaitière. The South Face of the Fou is sunlit in the background.   BOTTOM Suds and me at the Biolay campsite, Chamonix, 1965.
OPPOSITE PAGE, TOP Port Stanley Pier, 1966. Falkland Islander families welcoming the *Shackleton* crew home. A world of Land Rovers and the governor's London taxi: at the time there was only one mile of tarmac road.
OPPOSITE PAGE, BOTTOM Grytviken whaling station, South Georgia, with Mount Hodges in the background.

TOP Winching elephant seal carcasses on board the *RRS John Biscoe* at Grytviken, South Georgia. BOTTOM Unloading cargo in Deception Island's crater lake. The base can be seen on the beach and the window escape route was over the low central col. OPPOSITE PAGE When Deception Island erupted, we had no idea of the fate of the base, or its staff. I remember feeling calm and wondering if anyone would find my camera.

TOP The *RRS John Biscoe* discharged her cargo on to the sea ice two miles from Stonington and the dogs began to ferry the loads to the base. BOTTOM Stonington in 1966. Tractor garage accommodation on the roof, ruined America huts behind and the old Fuchs huts on the left. The distant mountains are on Adelaide Island, 100 miles away.

TOP Heim Glacier, midwinter 1967. The daily chore of digging out the dogs and tent. I thought this was normal!
BOTTOM A fully loaded Nansen sledge. A powerful nine-dog team pulling over half a ton.

TOP Horseshoe Island base with Pourquoi Pas Island and Mount Verne in the background. OPPOSITE PAGE, BOTTOM On our way to assist Flavell Smith and co., the dogs were marvellous and seemed to respond to the urgency. THIS PAGE, BOTTOM A frightening moment as the sledge breaks through the sea ice.

TOP LEFT The first Nevisport. On the right are the two phone boxes and the pier, now the Crannog restaurant, and left is the Fort William Wee Free Church.   TOP RIGHT Callop. We were never short of meat, the hills were alive with game.   BOTTOM LEFT Nevisport, 1971. (Sunday afternoon.)   BOTTOM RIGHT The Dead Man's Bogey. Lochaber Mountain Rescue Team at their very best. Suds in the foreground.   OPPOSITE PAGE John Beatty and me on the final part of our 1,500-foot lower down Zero Gully on Ben Nevis. This was the first time this kind of rescue was attempted on the Ben, and was the first of many such lowers over the years.

OPPOSITE PAGE, TOP The Scottish Mount Kenya team, 1973. *L–R:* Bruce Barclay, Mike C, Ronnie Richards, me.
OPPOSITE PAGE, BOTTOM Traversing into the Diamond Couloir, Mount Kenya, 1973. THIS PAGE, TOP Gordon
Smith topping out on *Route II*, Ben Nevis, 1978. BOTTOM Gordon Smith on *Route II*, Ben Nevis, 1978.

TOP Mostly in mountain rescue situations we try to remain detached from casualties.   BOTTOM Don Whillans astride the Triumph Bonneville on the summit of Ben Nevis. Don proceeded to swig the bottle of champagne in its entirety while the rest of us looked thirstily on!

was my wire strop, still hanging from its hole in the flake.

A hilarious incident took place in Stanley Harbour. Frosty insisted that it was possible for the entire ship's company to escape on one of the lifeboats and held a practice to prove his theory. We all scrambled on to one of the boats and were lowered into the sea, packed like sardines in a can. As we drifted up the cove we were so tightly packed that it was almost impossible to use the oars.

Suddenly someone shouted in horror: 'Somebody's left the bungs out of the bilges!'

Sure enough, two spouts of water were welling up into the crowded lifeboat. The oarsmen were frantically pulling in all directions and the boat was zigzagging erratically about. By the time we got alongside the *Shackleton* there was a foot of water in the lifeboat and we were all drenched. Frosty Turnbull was leaning over the side in stitches and I knew instantly who had removed the bungs.

We were kitted out with our Antarctic clothing in Stanley. We sledgers had really excellent equipment – Ventile anoraks with a wolverine fur visor (wolverine fibres are hollow and don't freeze), a whole wardrobe of clothing, gloves and goggles, and a fabulous Fairydown double sleeping bag. I had lived for years on very generous tick from George Fisher's shop in Keswick and here I was getting everything I had dreamed of for free.

Our working time in the Falklands was spent surveying the tiny airstrip. The islanders were determined that they would one day have a decent airport. For us it was an introduction to the work we would be doing in Antarctica and we felt it was a help to the island community. No one could have imagined that two decades later a strip would be built to accommodate jumbo jets and the area we were surveying would become a dangerous minefield.

There had been one or two curious incidents with the Argentinians. Much to the amusement of the islanders, a plane had flown over dropping leaflets to say that they were going to be liberated. Liberated from what, they wondered? On another occasion a bunch of Argentinian students landed a small aircraft on Stanley racecourse. It went up to its axles in the mud and when one of the Antarctic Survey men went over to see what was happening, he was taken in at gunpoint and held hostage. The plane was surrounded by a bunch of locals brandishing shotguns and the students ultimately surrendered and were repatriated to Argentina. Nobody took this very seriously and there was never any suggestion that Argentina would invade the islands.

A second Survey ship, the slightly larger RRS *John Biscoe*, joined us with bunch of new Fids. With them came the *Perla Dan*, a Danish ship that the Survey had chartered for a project to build a new base at Halley Bay, the most southerly British base on the Weddell Sea. This was the third station to be built at Halley Bay. As the ice shelf advanced and calved off into icebergs, the buildings eventually drifted off into the sea and had to be replaced. Halley Fids, unlike us, would spend most of their lives buried deep beneath the ice as it drifted slowly north. They were a thousand miles away from the peninsula and had little to do with our world of sledging and mountains.

There was no time to get to know these new people before the *Shackleton* left port. We went first to Punta Arenas in southern Chile, via the Beagle Channel where we had a brief view of the Towers of Paine. The ship did some seismic work off the coast of the Rio Grande and then in perfect cloudless skies and calm seas we rounded Cape Horn and headed south-east out into the Scotia Sea. Destination: South Georgia.

9 | Deception Island

The continent of Antarctica sits centrally over the South Pole and is roughly the size of the combined land mass of the United States and Western Europe. Surrounding this icy continent is the Southern Ocean, a thousand-mile-wide circle of freezing water which merges into the three great oceans of the world: the Pacific, the Atlantic and the Indian.

Where these waters meet is known as the Antarctic Convergence. On a map, there is no real line separating these oceans but anyone who has sailed south will tell you that once crossing the convergence, one enters into a different world. There is a distinct line: an instant drop in temperature and almost immediately the first icebergs are in sight, great towering cathedrals, flat tabular bergs from the ice shelves and smaller growlers spinning noisily in the waves with the ever-possible danger of pack ice. Life is abundant with shoals of penguins, killer whales, petrels, skuas and albatross.

Around Antarctica an immense area of low pressure circulates the continent drawing warm air from the north and katabatic winds from the ice cap. These act as a huge pump where almost ceaseless westerly gales drive giant waves in a great oscillation around the continent: the Roaring Forties. The one narrowing gap in this thousand-mile circle is Drake Passage, where the Antarctic Peninsula reaches north towards Cape Horn, the southernmost tip of South America. Enormous seas spill through this 500-mile gap – 'Cape Horn rollers', or 'greybeards', have terrified seamen since the first sailing ships rounded the Horn. Sightings by terrified sailors of 200-foot waves were regularly reported – 80 to 90 feet is more likely, but 100 feet is not unknown. Crest-to-crest they exceed a mile, huge rollers that are the height of six-storey buildings.

Having passed through Drake Passage, the storms spill out into the Scotia Sea where, 800 miles west on the fifty-fifth parallel, in line with this great westerly flow, is the tiny isolated island of South Georgia. Surrounded by enormous seas and blasted by wind, this sub-Antarctic island, sixty miles long by twelve miles wide, suffers from the worst weather in the world.

My first sight of South Georgia was no disappointment, it was larger than I had imagined, and the mountains looked spectacular. As we sailed into Cumberland Bay, Mount Paget, at 9,625 feet the highest peak on the island, was gleaming in the morning sunshine with a magnificent wave cloud curving over its peak, the herald of wind. The *Shackleton* anchored alongside the jetty of the old Grytviken whaling station which had recently closed, although in 1967 the Salvesen whaling company still kept a caretaker there to look after their property.

The BAS base, Shackleton House, was about half a mile along the shore from the whaling station. Unlike the huts on Antarctica it was a pleasant two-storey building with comfortable living quarters, a nice bar and common room and scientific laboratories. The beaches were alive with seal and penguins and birdlife.

We wandered along the shore to the whaling station, which was the size of a small town. Over a thousand men once lived and worked there. The flensing pens and buildings were still in good shape, the roads and alleys full of grunting and snorting elephant seals that reared up threateningly and then backed off when they were approached.

The work of unloading the ship was the first time that I saw 'Fid power'. With no specialised equipment, huge crates of cargo had to be manhandled ashore. In charge of this and all the building projects was Al Smith, the brother of Harvey Smith, the famous horseman. Big Al is the strongest man I have ever met and could heave forty-gallon oil drums over the rail of the boat with ease. On one occasion a steel H-beam had been dropped over the side into shallow water and six or eight of us waded out and grabbed one end, with Big Al at the other.

'Okay, two – six, hup!' Al shouted and his end lifted out of the water while the rest of us floundered about struggling and worrying about our backs. Incidentally, for a long time I wondered why he called 'Two – six' before a lift. Apparently in Elizabethan times this was the order of guns in a navel broadside.

In the sixties none of the bases had any heavy-lifting equipment and everything was done with manpower and small winches. Big Al had spent months designing and planning how he was going to move heavy building materials and machinery ashore and into position. South Georgia was the easiest base to restock as the ship was able to tie up alongside the whaling station jetty. Once we reached Antarctica the problems were much more serious.

While at Grytviken we had the job of shooting 200 elephant seals for dog food. These huge animals can grow up to twenty feet long and weigh four tons. In the sea they have the remarkable ability to make dives of several thousand feet and can stay under water for up to two hours. They achieve this feat by lowering their heart rate to as little as one beat per minute. They have few predators but on land are cumbersome and have difficulty in lifting their huge bodies to haul themselves along the beach.

The Falkland Island crew ran along the shore with rifles shooting the panicking beasts at point blank range, and we Fids moved along behind opening up and gutting the still-twitching monsters. I confess to becoming carried away in the bloodletting, the carnage on the beach was dreadful and I guess that this was what happened in the early days of the sealing trade. I can only say that in the scale of things, our effect on the seal population was miniscule. King Edward Cove ran red with blood and it is a memory that has stuck with me ever since. The carcasses had then to be winched aboard the ship and the deck became one grizzly pile of dog food.

Fifteen years later in 1982 this same beach was the scene of the first battle of the Falkland Island War when a small detachment of British Marines defended Shackleton House against the invading Argentineans. A lot of blood was spilled on that day too.

Curph and I managed to slip away and climb Mount Hodges, a small peak overlooking Grytviken. We had splendid views of the island and it was a pleasure to escape from the boat for a few hours. The following day we were off again, this time at last into the Southern Ocean bound for Deception Island base at the northern tip of the Antarctic Peninsula.

Deception Island was a supposedly extinct volcano and shaped like a South Sea atoll. It had an internal crater lake that it was possible to enter via a narrow channel called Neptune's Bellows. In the Bellows were a large pinnacle and the wreck of an old whaling boat. We crashed our way into the bay through thin pack-ice and moored a hundred yards or so from the base in the most protected harbour imaginable.

The crater lake was about seven miles long and in its shelter were two other bases, one Argentinean and one Chilean. All three countries claimed the island as national territory, but apart from the occasional political squabble, the occupants got on well together and visited each other during the long winter months and played the occasional football match on the sea ice. At the time that we arrived a Chilean ship, the *Yelcho*, was restocking its base a few miles across the bay.

The island is ideally situated for aircraft as its position is halfway between the Falkland Islands and the southern bases and a rough airstrip had been constructed on the ash in front of our base. Big Al had employed a party of builders who were there to construct a hanger for the Twin Otter, which at present had to be tied down in the open. We Fids were set on as labourers shifting several tons of cement and foundation materials, steel beams and corrugated iron from the ship to shore. It was cold and miserable work in waders, shifting the materials on a rubber raft through the brash-ice on to the beach and dragging it up to the site.

During this time there were a number of small earthquakes and the base commander told us that this had been going on throughout the winter. Chalmers Clapperton, a volcanologist, and Ian Flavell Smith, the geophysicist, going to Stonington with me, were at pains to reassure him.

'Don't worry, there's nothing to be concerned about, extinct volcanoes do have the odd tremor from time to time.'

That same evening I was climbing a snow gully on a cliff at the side of Neptune's Bellows when suddenly the whole mountainside started to shake. My immediate thought was that it was an avalanche and I hung on waiting for the inevitable deluge, but nothing happened and I bailed off rather shaken in more ways than one. Climbing during an earthquake was a whole new experience.

Things seemed to settle down and for the rest of the week we finished the unloading of the ship. The *Shackleton* left the base with the building party, and once more headed north, bound for Port Stanley. During the night she suddenly changed course and we could hear the increased throb of the engines as, at full speed, the ship spun round and headed back the way we had come.

That afternoon the island came into view. Gone was the beautiful, snow-covered atoll we had left the previous day. A huge mushroom cloud, much as one imagined an atomic bomb, was rising out of ash-covered hills, going right up into the stratosphere and the sky was black and raining ash and cinders on to the ship's deck.

There was so much static electricity that the radio wouldn't work and it was not possible to approach too close. We had no idea of the fate of the base and its staff or the builders.

The following morning the eruption had died down somewhat. Frosty didn't hesitate; he sailed directly through Neptune's Bellows into the crater lake. Three or four small eruptions were going off around the island's rim and a new island of ash had formed and was smoking at the western end of the lake. A group of us took the *Red Peril*, the ship's boat, and landed at the base that was in a dreadful state.

Some of the buildings had collapsed under the weight of ash and there was no sign of life. The ruined Twin Otter aircraft stood sadly besides the newly built, but now battered, hanger. The beach was lined with dead krill, seal and penguins. We heard later that the lake had become boiling hot and the water had risen and fallen like huge lungs. It must have been a terrifying sight for those stranded on the three bases.

On the opposite side of the bay a huge new eruption started and a thick, hot-looking cloud began to roll towards us. If this had been scorching hot it would have been the end. As there was nowhere to run we stood taking photographs awaiting our fate. Cinders were raining down and lightning flashed as the huge tower of ash hurled up into the stratosphere. I can remember feeling quite calm and wondering if anyone would find my camera.

Fortunately for us the cloud turned out to be steam from the boiling sea. We'd had enough and rushed back to the *Shackleton*. Frosty ran the ship up the bay for a quick look and then spun around and took her out through the bellows as fast as he could go. The massive cloud of steam and ash was hurling into the sky and flickering with lightning, the sight of a lifetime.

On board the ash-covered *Shackleton* the roar was drowned out by the clicking of camera shutters. Hilariously, the ship's rail was lined with a contingent of sheathbills, a white Antarctic bird about the size of a pigeon, which had sensibly decided to hitch a lift off the island. They huddled under the ships lifeboats to avoid the falling ash. Much to our relief we now knew that all the base personnel and the builders were safe. Their story, I heard from an Irishman called Henry Blakeley, is worth retelling. Henry was a new Fid who had just arrived on the island.

'All day Monday we were feeling constant movement in the ground, rather like a bus that just had its engine ticking over. By 3 p.m. the general movement was greater, punctuated every few minutes by violent tremors. Crockery was rattling. We discreetly began packing our personal things in case we needed to make a quick escape.

'A seismologist on the Chile base reassuringly said that as long as the tremors continued there was nothing to worry about. That evening there was a lot of nervous joking about what to do if the earth started to crack open. Someone suggested that we should all walk about on skis with our legs wide apart. Some wag put Tom Lehrer on the gramophone, "We'll all go together when we go". Before long we were all singing it.'

Henry had wandered outside when the first eruption took place. A column of black ash and vapour burst upwards through the sea-ice in Telefon Bay near the Chilean station and a second discharge sent cinders and ash blasting 8,000 feet into the air. We learned later that the ash had in fact reached 30,000 feet.

'That looks impressive,' Henry thought and dashed in to get his camera. 'There's a funny-looking cloud near the Chilean station – sort of atom-bomb shaped!'

He was nearly crushed in the rush by the rest of the base staff charging out to see what was happening. He grabbed his camera and was again almost trampled by the Fids running back in to get theirs. Having done the important stuff getting the photographs, they set about the secondary objectives like saving their skins and films. The radio operator was sending out SOS messages while everyone got into their warmest clothes and put on goggles and silk scarves to protect themselves from the ash.

Two rowing boats were launched with sleeping bags and safety equipment, at first with the intention of going to the aid of the Chileans and then for possible escape. Outside, walking had become difficult as snow was melting from below the ground and ash and hail were falling and settling deeply on the surface. Even though it was the Antarctic summer it was getting dark. Thunder and lightning was flashing around the hills and there were little flashes of lightning in the air at eye level, like sparkling silver tinsel.

Two of the men climbed a hill to see if there was any sign of the Chilean base, but couldn't make anything out. They later received a message that the base crew had evacuated and were making their way over to join them on foot, and that the Chilean ship *Piloto Pardo* was going to attempt a rescue as soon as it could.

At 12.27 a.m. the Chileans staggered into the hut, very frightened, weary and poorly clothed. The ash in their boots was so tight it was almost impossible to remove them; they were covered in it and had literally fled as they were. They were fed and clothed and everybody settled down to a singsong awaiting the *Piloto Pardo*. An hour later she tried to enter the bay but the water level was rising and falling and in the poor visibility the attempt was called off.

It was a long, nerve-racking night until at 8.20 a.m. they heard the sound of two helicopters arriving from the Chilean ship which immediately began taking the men off two at a time. At the same time the Argentinean ship *Bahia Aguirre* was also evacuating the men from their station and the *Shackleton* and Chilean ship *Yelcho* had arrived on the scene. By 10 a.m. everybody was safe on board ship after a great adventure.

So ended the first Deception Island eruption. The base was abandoned that season and Henry, along with the rest of the base personnel, was sent home without a job. Undeterred, he managed to sign on the following year as a builder and returned south to Adelaide Island base.

The powers that be in Cambridge decided that this was a one in a hundred year event and the base was reopened the following season with Dick Stocks, an experienced builder on the BAS staff, as base commander. In mid February 1969 the tremors started again and Dick decided to evacuate, but once again the eruption started before the men could be rescued. This time a hail of cinders rained among the ensuing storm of snow, ash and lightning.

The Fids were moving about holding corrugated-iron sheets over their heads. Once more the *Piloto Pardo*'s helicopters came to the rescue and the Chilean pilots took considerable risk flying in through falling snow, ash and cinders and landing the men safely back on deck in high winds and heavy seas. Another exciting episode.

Frosty Turnbull, watching from the bridge of the *Shackleton* and not one to hand out credit said, 'The evacuation was a superb example of skilful seamanship and flying'.

After this incident, BAS decided to abandon the Deception Island station permanently.

My journey south continued with a return to South Georgia where I swapped ships for a trip down the Weddell Sea to Halley Bay base on board the *Perla Dan* to help build a new ice station, before finally heading back down the west coast of the Antarctic Peninsula calling at most of the British bases on the way to Stonington Island, which would be my home for the next two years.

I visited Deception Island on my way home. It was deserted and looked nothing like the beautiful, snow-covered island I had entered through Neptune's Bellows two years earlier. Most of the buildings were wrecked – the aircraft hangar we had been building was partially standing with the remains of one of our Twin Otter aircraft standing alongside it. A new ash island had formed at the end of the bay and the hills and glaciers were covered in a layer of grey ash and cinders. I will always remember it as the most exciting spectacle of a lifetime, a view of the awesome power that our amazing world can produce.

10 | Stonington

My journey south was almost over. I had changed ships and was aboard the *RRS John Biscoe* as she smashed her way through thick sea ice into Neny Fjord. Captain Tom Woodfield had ordered one of the ship's lifeboats to be lifted on the derrick and was swinging it wildly from side to side in an attempt to rock the boat and break her further into the ice. She finally ground to a standstill a mile or so short of our destination, Stonington Island.

It was March, the Antarctic autumn, and at sixty-eight degrees south we were just about to lose the midnight sun. In brilliant sunshine, the mountains were rising almost vertically out of the water on either side of the ship. At the head of the fjord the massive ten-mile-wide North-East Glacier fed the frozen sea with icebergs as it flowed down from the polar plateau. The whole panorama was absolutely spellbinding. It was, and still is, the most beautiful place I'd ever seen.

It was going to be a difficult change over, there was no way to get the ship any closer to the island and all the stores would have to be transported across the ice by dog sledge. Within minutes the first of the teams came running out between the icebergs and trotted alongside the ship. I had seen huskies before on some of the northern bases where they were used for recreation but these dogs were magnificent. Extraordinarily healthy and bursting with energy, and with their tails up like curled radio antennae, they were much heftier than the dogs I had seen previously. These were working dogs, square-chested and rippling with muscles built from thousands of miles of sledge hauling.

The drivers picketed them alongside the *Biscoe* and clambered aboard grinning. It was a year since the ship's last call and they were dying for news and to see old friends. There was a lot of shaking hands and back slapping, but I noticed a certain reticence and tongue-tiedness in these men. They were difficult to talk to; worse than that they all smelled rather doggy. It was not until a year later when the tiny community who had been my only companions were confronted with the shock of the ship's arrival and a crowd of new faces that I discovered that I too had nothing to say.

While we were watching over the rail a dog fight broke out. Two of the teams had been parked close to each other and a picket had broken loose. The flaying mass of dogs looked like the worst rugby scrum imaginable, teeth gnashing and a tremendous barking and snarling. The friendly bunch of drivers suddenly went berserk and were transformed into raging mad-men. Within seconds they were overboard and wading into the melee, boots and fists thrashing, dogs sailing in all directions. Moments later it was all over and they scrambled back on board and continued as if nothing had happened.

Work started immediately transferring the cargo on to the sea ice and loading the sledges. Hundreds of boxes of man and dog food, crates of scientific equipment, tons of elephant seal carcasses. All had to be transported to the island. That evening I packed my small bag of belongings and had my first run with a dog team to the base that was to be my home for the next two years.

Stonington is a tiny island roughly 200 yards wide by 400 yards long. A tiny outcrop of rock with a huge glacier sweeping past. A refuge in the heart of a huge ice continent that was warm, comfortable and full of friends.

An ice ramp poured on to it from the North-East Glacier, giving an easy way up the ice cliffs and a possible approach to the polar plateau. Easy routes inland are rare on the peninsula and this is the main reason for the island's situation as a sledging base.

It had been an American station before the war and was named Stonington after the small port in Connecticut from where the US Antarctic research ships sailed. It was later occupied by the British, and for a time both countries shared separate bases on this minute island.

There wasn't much snow at this time of year and the island was covered in a greasy mess of seal blubber and dog dirt which had built up over years of dog feeding – the island had its own particular smell. There had always been dogs at Stonington and when I arrived there were about 120 huskies and about fifty pups. The teams were picketed out on the sea ice and the pups were running wild and free.

The base was an ugly wooden structure with a tractor garage bolted on the roof for extra accommodation. Behind it was a generator shed and a number of cages like small tennis courts, which were the pens where the pups were kept before training.

At one end of the island were the ruins of the original base, from where our boss, Doctor Bunny Fuchs, had sledged soon after the war. Down by the ice ramp were some old American huts, still in good condition, which we called Finn Ronne after the original US base commander. These we used as workshops to build up the Nansen sledges. Alongside this was the seal pile, a great heap of frozen dog food where one of our daily chores was to chainsaw a seal into logs and axe it into doggy-sized feeds.

Inside, the base was a small comfortable home, a single living room with a beautifully built stone fireplace, a work of art from an earlier resident, which acted as the corner piece to a bar that would have been the pride of any English pub. There were comfy leather chairs and the walls were shelved with a remarkably well-stocked library that had built up and improved over the years. Leading off this room was a well-equipped kitchen with a coal-fired Rayburn cooker and a large, abundant larder. The rest was pretty basic, a porch with a tank and stove to melt ice and dry out clothes and dog harnesses, and a radio shack and doctors surgery.

Upstairs the garage was converted into a bunkroom, and as usual on a Fid's base there wasn't much space for personal stuff. I was given a bunk and spread most of my things out under the mattress. It wasn't that comfortable but I was to find that we sledgers didn't spend much time on base anyway. In those days I could have slept on a bed of nails and it was a good place to go for a bit of privacy. Once the ship left, the eleven of us who remained were rarely there at any one time. In the summer months only the diesel mechanic, radio operator and a doctor (if we had one) lived there permanently. Even in winter the base was only partially full.

On the first afternoon on base, Ken Doyle, who had just taken over the 'Giants' dog team, took me for a ride up the ramp on to the North-East Glacier. Ken, although a competent driver, was struggling with his dogs which were not reacting well under new management. We drove for a mile or so to a line of oil drums that marked the landing strip for visiting aircraft. As we turned back I was sitting happily on the sledge enjoying the experience while the dogs hurled down the glacier at a breakneck pace.

'Slow down, Ken!' I shouted, thinking he was showing off.

As we approached the ramp down the ice cliff the dogs were running like wild things. I glanced over my shoulder and realised there was nobody on the back of the sledge. Ken was half a mile away running down the glacier waving his arms. We hurtled down the ramp totally out of control. I frantically started to try to climb over the back of the sledge to get at the large spike brake between the sledge runners, but it was too late, the team raced on, hit the island and dashed out across the tide crack on to the sea ice. I bounced off the sledge into the crack and was instantly submerged in frozen water and brash ice. I had joined the Antarctic Swimming Club!

As I clambered out I watched the dogs run on and park in their usual place and knew the whole team was laughing at me. The fracas had been watched by the entire base staff and half the crew of the *John Biscoe*. I staggered up to the base drenched and shivering to a grinning audience. Not a great start for a fledgling dog driver.

That night the Stonington crew held a 'Ching' party. The men were desperate for mail, news from home was scarce, and in 1967 we were allowed to radio home a hundred-word message per month, which was sent as a telex from the Falkland Islands. Inward messages were much less frequent. Quite a few of the men had left girlfriends at home and two and a half years is a long time to expect them to wait. While we Fids lived in our isolated cocoon, the rest of the world moved on, and so among the rest of the mail came the inevitable letter:

Dear John,

Please forgive me, I've met the most wonderful man, we were married last August. Here is a picture of little Cyril, he was born in September! I'm sure you will understand ...

We understood right enough, we'd been Chinged! So we had a Ching party. A beer bottle top was nailed alongside the dozens of others on the Ching stick and large quantities of alcohol, of which there was plenty, were consumed by recipients and sympathisers alike. The world moved on.

Our base commander, Ali MacArthur, was an Australian on his second season. (The two-year contract system with Antarctic Survey meant that half the base staff changed each year, leaving an expert team to teach us new boys the ropes.) Ali told me I would be taking over the 'Vikings' dog team from John Noble who was about to leave. I went down on to the sea ice to find John sitting dejectedly with his dogs.

He looked me over very carefully and I realised that after living for two years with this fine team it was going to be a great wrench for him to pass them over. It was not until two years later when I handed the Vikings over to Henry Blakeley, the cheerful Irishman I had met on Deception Island, that I fully realised what a terrible struggle John had been going through.

As it turned out I was only at Stonington for a week learning the rudiments of dog driving from George McLeod, a diminutive Scotsman whom I knew from Glenmore Lodge days. George was on his third Antarctic contract and had probably sledged more miles than any other Fid. We spent the week helping to unload the *John Biscoe* and then six of us were taken back on board and sailed about 100 miles north and dropped on to the Jones Ice Shelf on Blakelock Island.

Derek (Thwaits) Postlethwaite, a surveyor, was running the show, which was to survey the Heim Glacier and Blakelock Island and then head back to Stonington when the sea ice formed, in time for midwinter. It was supposed to be an easy trip to break the new boys in, but this was not to be.

It was a short autumn, and winter struck early with a vengeance. It was mild with a colossal amount of snow falling. Day after day we were pinned down by high winds and spent much of our time digging out the tents and the dogs. On this supposedly short journey we had two 11-day and one 16-day 'lie ups' (i.e. pinned down and unable to move.) The sea ice kept forming and then blowing out to sea with each incoming gale.

On midwinter's day we were still stranded on Blakelock Island unable to move and the weather was so warm that it actually rained. The sun had been gone for a month and although there was a false dawn each day, it was dark and dismal; one expected bad weather and bitter cold during this time but these mild temperatures were most unusual. Masses of snow kept falling and burying the tents and the sea was covering in a slush of snow but not forming as proper ice.

Our dogs were very short of food and we took every opportunity to hunt for seal to supplement their meagre rations. It was an anxious time, there was plenty of food for us but the dogs were losing weight without seal meat to supplement the meagre rations of dog pemmican we were carrying. Fortunately the seal were plentiful and, once we got the knack, they were reasonably easy to shoot.

As a new driver I didn't fully appreciate that this extreme weather was out of the ordinary. Thwaits was a careful teacher and it was a tremendous learning curve. Two weeks after midwinter the weather finally settled and the sea ice set solidly around the fjords. At last it was safe and we set off skipping from island to island on our journey home.

Having made one of my many attempts to stop smoking I had finished up as the only member of the party still at it, having found a supply of

Old Holborn pipe tobacco in the hut at Blakelock which I used to make bog-paper roll-ups. We stopped in at the old deserted base on Horseshoe Island where there was a depot of man and dog food and a vast supply of blessed cigarettes. Food we could do without, but shortage of fags was very serious. In glorious relief we actually lit up three at a time.

On the final day we left Horseshoe Island in darkness and followed the coast around the dangerous Camp Point, a place where the sea ice was well known to be fragile, and finally by moonlight reached Stonington late that night. Gone was the blubber-covered rocky islet we had left three months earlier. Now, half buried in deep snow with lights shining from the windows and the mountains gleaming in moonshine, it had transformed into a Shangri-La. Everybody on base turned out to help us picket the dogs and for the first time in three months we entered a warm base. I realised that I had become a real dog driver.

The following evening we celebrated a belated midwinter's party; we had missed 21 June, the Antarctic version of Christmas. It was the darkest time of the year without the sun, and a time when everybody was usually at home. As it happened I was away from Stonington on both the midwinters of my stay, but that was unusual.

Jack Donaldson and I had written a play during the 'lie up' times on Blakelock Island, and the rest of the party had learned their parts in the tents. We put it on after the dinner. The play was a disgusting and improbable tale set in the Globe Hotel in Port Stanley, with Sir Cosmo Haskard, the then governor of the Falklands, the villain of the piece. It was a masterpiece of Fids jokes. Unfortunately the entire cast were far too drunk to take it seriously and I vaguely remember being extremely angry when the audience attempted to grope the bearded heroin each time she staggered on stage.

The rest of the winter passed uneventfully. It was relatively relaxed and we attended to the normal chores of base life; taking turns as cook and gash (clearing up) and daily seal feed and dog training. I built a new Nansen sledge and spent my spare time constructing a kayak. I had brought a set of plans of the canoes we had used at Locheil which I modified to suit the ice. I managed to strip off wood framing from the old Fuchs hut and there was plenty of plywood about. The frame was then skinned with canvas and doped with paint. She finished up as a very respectable boat, which I used for sealing the following autumn.

The sun returned in late July; we had grown used to the dull light but as the first rays of sunshine caught the mountain tops and colour returned to our world a new sense of purpose filled the base and we began to plan the spring journeys.

In my time at Stonington we travelled at all times of the year. I've been told that our time stranded on Blakelock Island was followed with much concern back at Cambridge HQ, and was one of the reasons that a few years later BAS gave up using dogs altogether and went entirely mechanical. If this was the case then I'm truly sorry; our predicament must have seemed much worse to the people at home following our attempts to get back to base, than to our party stuck on the Jones Ice Shelf enjoying ourselves.

Dogs can travel in much more difficult terrain than machines, and without support they can cover longer distances. On the coast there were seals and penguins in abundance and food for survival is almost limitless. It's slower than mechanical transport but requires less backup and large quantities of fuel don't have to be moved forward by aircraft or tractor.

On long sledge journeys aircraft do have to lay depots of man and dog food but they require nothing of the maintenance and amount of fuel required by a tractor or skidoo. A dog team is roughly sixty feet long from leader to driver and the load is well spread for travelling on thin sea ice or up a crevassed glacier. Give me a dog team any day. One last horrible thought – you can't eat a tractor!

Winter sledge journeys were slow, painful affairs. We would wake up in the tent with a layer of frost on our sleeping bags. Temperatures varied anything between 5 °C Celsius and -45 °C in winter – I guess it averaged about -15–20 °C. In summer it was much more pleasant at around -5–10 °C.

The inside man would light the paraffin Tilley lamp and duck back into his bag until the tent warmed sufficiently, then light the Primus and make some tea. The outside man would drag himself into his clothes and scramble out, sometimes tunnelling up through the snow, and set about dismantling the campsite. His first job was to dig out the dogs that were usually curled in a ball in their snowy burrow, after that came the sledge and starting to load the boxes and dig out the tent.

Meanwhile the inside man cooked the breakfast and packed up the inside boxes – the radio, cooking stuff, personal things – and then let down the airbeds and rolled up the sleeping bags and sheepskins and lifted the ground sheet. After breakfast the man in the tent would have the honour of a sheltered toilet before it came down. This was pure luxury and as we took daily turns inside and out we tried to regulate our functions to alternate days.

Striking camp was easy, the big Antarctic pyramid tents had long bamboo poles; you just untied the guy lines, shifted any boxes or snow off the valances and lifted the tent out and pushed it into a long tubular bag that fitted neatly on to the top of the boxes on the sledge. Then it was just a case of unclipping the dogs from the wire night traces and putting on their harnesses, by which time they would be barking and bursting with excitement, frantic to be off.

This was a dangerous moment. We would spend hours training them not to start without a call, the first two or three hundred yards was always a helter-skelter charge, very scary if there were crevasses or cliffs around.

'Dogs, dogs, *Hup* dogs, *wheet!*' We were off.

A fully loaded Nansen sledge weighed about 1,200 pounds, over half a ton, and a good dog team could pull this through almost anything. On a good, hard, icy surface with a full load we occasionally covered fifty miles per day, but we averaged about thirty. On winter journeys, when dogs and driver wallowed through sometimes waist-deep snow, I've seen us pack it in after only a couple of miles.

Unlike drivers in the northern hemisphere, we never rode the sledge but walked alongside on skis – our loads were already far too heavy.

These distances are nothing compared with the hundred-miles-plus a day that Canadian huskies achieve on races such as the Alaskan Iditarod, but theirs are fast dogs, bred for speed and pulling light racing sledges. Our dogs were larger, almost square with enormous muscles in their hind legs, bred for pulling heavy loads through difficult terrain, and our journeys were of a much longer duration.

How far we travelled depended on what our scientist wanted to do. There were a number of ongoing science projects taking place, such as geology, glaciology and survey. During my first year I mostly worked on mapping and geology. With the geologists it was a case of moving from one rock outcrop to the next. Drivers like me mapped using a plane table and alidade and the geologist would put his geology on to the map.

In my second year I travelled with Ian Flavell Smith, a geophysicist. This was easier and much more interesting work – he was making a gravity and magnetic field map of part of the peninsula and all that was required was to take readings every five miles or so. This was pure heaven and we travelled hundreds of miles with a comfortable stop every five miles or so for Ian to take his instrument readings.

Setting up camp was a careful event. At night there would often be winds of over a hundred miles per hour and the thought of losing a tent was terrifying. We would pull up the sledges with enough room to pitch the tent close between them. We'd dig out an area three spade lengths square, removing snow blocks to create a nine by nine-foot hole using the blocks to build a wall around it. The pyramid tent pitched neatly in this with only the narrow point of the tent exposed to the wind.

All the spare man and dog food boxes were placed on the valences and in extreme conditions we would tie the whole thing down with a climbing rope. Our chances of survival if we lost the tent would be very low. Once the tent was up the inside man climbed in and set about organising home while the outside man sorted and fed the dogs.

Winter sledging was hard work; it was cold and dull with little or no colour. We lost the sun for around three months but a false dawn arrived in late morning and dulled away in the afternoon. Sometimes we sledged by moonlight, the sea ice stretching away into darkness and the mountains picked out in sharp relief in silver-trimmed shadows.

On occasions we would see nacreous clouds (of gases), high enough in the stratosphere to catch sunlight. While we were hidden in the earth's shadow, they gave glorious rippling colours across the sky. On rare nights we saw the Southern Lights, the Aurora Australis, beautiful dancing and shimmering curtains of light like gigantic cascading waterfalls with pulsating blues and reds flashing from horizon to horizon, great magnetic storms of untold power exploding over the pole.

Summer could be glorious, it sometimes became so warm that we were able to sledge in shorts, boots and little else. The sea ice developed large melt pools on its surface and it was difficult to travel during the heat of the day. With twenty-four-hour sunshine we could reverse our day and travel through the night when it was cooler with the sun at a lower angle.

We usually sledged for eight hours before pitching camp. Once settled down and fed we were often too tired to do much other than turn in and read a book. The scientist had to write up his notes and we drivers worked on our maps. Travelling with the same person for several months we got to know our companions very well, although after a few weeks you tended to run out of conversation. Our daily talk tended to be how the dogs were fairing.

'Gringo and Devon had another go at each other today, there's no love lost between those two! Perky's not pulling his weight; the lazy bastard had a slack trace all day!'

The love affair that we drivers had with our teams is almost indescribable. I would have gone mad without my dogs and to me the Vikings were the finest of all the twelve teams running out from Stonington. Considering the harshness of their lives their total loyalty to us was astonishing. They took any opportunity to fight among themselves and if they got loose would mercilessly attack any available seal or penguin.

As I became more understanding of their thinking it became much easier to pre-empt oncoming trouble and the fights became a rarity. A dog dragged angrily from a scrap would promptly roll on his back presenting his unprotected stomach to his master in an act of total submission, take his inevitable thumping, then jump up and lick his face as if nothing in the world could make him happier. For our part we became more doglike, I began to be able to smell the bitches coming on heat, always a difficult time, and anticipate the problems and jealousies of the males all trying frantically to get to them. I was able to sense if a dog was unwell or unhappy and understand the structure of the team, who was boss, who were his friends and enemies and which dogs liked to run together. I realised that they had been working animals for their entire adult lives and knew more about Antarctic survival than I ever would.

Some of the old timers had travelled tens of thousands of miles. I discovered that it was much more effectual to sink my teeth into an ear than hand out a harsh thumping; a good bite from me seemed to be a serious embarrassment to a dog. I learned to trust them implicitly when travelling on thin ice or among crevasses. I have cried in frustration trying to train my team to sit quietly and I've rolled among them in pure happiness and comradeship.

On my first sledge trip on Blakelock Island my dogs had a particularly bad fight; Devon had been aggressively challenging Gringo for the top dog position in the pack. Gringo was an old-timer and winner of a thousand battles – he was having none of it. In the ensuing battle Devon was left with his eyeball hanging out and it seemed likely that he would have to be shot. We emptied out the tent and used it as an operating theatre, tied up his muzzle and legs, and gave him a shot of morphine strong enough to kill most men.

He showed absolutely no sign of drowsiness and continued to struggle violently. Phil Wainwright and Thwaits sat on him trying to hold him steady while I shoved the eye back in the socket and stitched the eyelids back into place. It was a horrifying procedure with the dog thrashing about viciously and the constant fear of sticking the needle into his eye.

When we finally finished he gave us the customary licking and took his place outside with the rest of the dogs as if nothing had happened. The eye healed up nicely giving him a slightly Chinese look. This incident ended my first attempt to stop smoking!

Antarctica was a great lesson in self-sufficiency. If the radio broke down or your camera jammed you fixed it or did without. Sledges, tents and harnesses required constant repair and there was a stream of minor injuries to both men and dogs. Fortunately the common cold or flu was non-existent and in general we were surprisingly healthy.

11 | That's One Small Step for Man

Sastrugi, the wind ridges on the snow surface caused by constant drifting snows, are almost invisible from the air. John Aires, the pilot of our small Pilatus Porter aircraft made a bumpy landing on the polar plateau. On board was his aircraft fitter, John Walsh, and Martin Bramwell, a meteorologist who had come along for the ride. Watching anxiously as the small aircraft bounced to a standstill with one of its skis twisted around to the side were two sledgers, Charles Smith, a geologist, and Rod Ledingham, whom John had come to collect.

This should have been Charlie's last flight as he had finished his two years on the ice and was about to catch the boat home. Rod, now beginning his second year, was expecting to become base commander on Adelaide Island.

They spent an hour straightening out the wonky skid and tied it up as firmly as they could with a climbing rope. The pilot didn't like it but it was the best that could be done, and they loaded the two men and their dogs into the hold. The powerful little plane almost made it into the air when the offending skid hit a large sastrugi and slewed sideways. Instantly both skis collapsed and the plane belly-flopped into the plateau, throwing dogs, men and equipment into a writhing heap in the hold of the wrecked aircraft. Apart from pride and a few bruises, nobody was hurt. There were no aircraft able to come to their aid and after sorting themselves out they loaded as much equipment as they could on to their two dog teams and reluctantly set off down the Otter Glacier to Fossil Bluff field station, which they reached two days later.

Surprisingly, in 1968 the Bluff was a single hut, not much bigger than a garden shed. It stands on a rocky point on Alexander Island at the side of George VI Sound, a twenty-mile-wide, ice-filled channel separating it from the mountains of the Antarctic Peninsula. The rock strata behind the base is full of fossils and there are coalfields visible on parts of the island – at some time in the distant past this place must have been tropical.

By now the ships were heading north and there was no possibility of rescuing the stranded aircraft party before the winter set in. The four men were faced with the unhappy situation of an extra winter stranded alone until spring when the sea ice formed sufficiently for us at Stonington to sledge the hundred miles or so across Marguerite Bay and bring them out. They were an odd assortment of Fids, two met men, a geologist, and a pilot and his fitter.

The tiny base was well stocked with basic sledging rations and dog food but it must have been a dismal place to be stuck during the long period with no sun. Worse still, the diesel generator wasn't working so they had no electricity. When the crash happened I was out on a sledging trip and one evening listened to a radio conversation with their main base on Adelaide Island and heard a serious but hilarious discussion between Rod Ledingham and Barry Whitaker, Adelaide's diesel mechanic, as he attempted to instruct Rod in how to fix the generator. Rod had the machine stripped down and was tinkering about under Barry's instruction. Nothing seemed to be working until Barry had an idea.

'Swing the starting handle now,' Barry said elatedly.

'Okay, done it.'

'Now swing it in reverse.'

'Okay.'

'Does the spigot slide back from the carburettor?'

'Yes, yes, it's coming right out,' Rod's voice rose in excitement.

There was a long thoughtful pause. 'Well, I'd give up if I were you, it's fucked,' said Barry cheerfully from his warm radio shack on Adelaide base.

They spent a miserable winter at the Bluff with no power and not a lot of creature comforts. It was the same period of poor weather that we were suffering on the Heim Glacier. We were all concerned about them and as soon as the sun returned a party of four, Ali Macarthur, Ian Flavell

Smith, Shawn Norman and Lew Willy, set out to relieve them. Their hundred-or-so-mile journey from Stonington crossed the open sea ice of Marguerite Bay.

Normally by spring the sea ice was safe and about five feet thick, but for safety's sake they skipped from island to island across the bay, which is roughly the size of Scotland. They made rapid progress to Terra Firma Island and then made a long crossing to the Puffball Islets close to the ice front of King George VI Sound. Here they were caught in a strong katabatic wind blowing from the polar plateau.

The following day, to their horror, they were on moving sea ice. During the afternoon Lew broke through thin ice and joined the Antarctic Swimming Club. With open sea ahead of them and huge uncrossable cracks and leads behind, it was a very dangerous situation.

Flavell Smith's calm but anxious radio signal came as an awful shock to us at Stonington.

'Hi, I've just taken a fix on our position and we seem to be on the move and can't get off these flows to the Puffball Islands.'

To our knowledge, nobody drifting off on open sea ice had ever survived, there had been a fatal accident two years earlier when two dog teams had been lost while crossing from Pourquoi Pas Island to Horseshoe Base and the drivers had never been seen again. At Stonington we sprang into emergency mode.

Within the hour, Thwaits, Ken Doyle and I loaded our sledges as lightly as we dared, including an Avon inflatable rubber boat and outboard motor, and set off as fast as we could go. It was rotten weather, windy with snow showers and poor visibility. We made fast time on the first day round the exposed Red Rock Ridge and camped among the ruins of the old disused Argentinean base at the Debenham Islands.

The following day was horrible and we were very pushy. I never again sledged in worse conditions but my eyes were opened to what was possible. We pushed on to Terra Firma Island crossing a number of large open cracks in the ice.

The dogs were marvellous and seemed to respond to our constant urging and gave the impression of delight in the rush. We had a lot of trouble pitching the tent that night in the wind. All around us we could see long, dark shadows across the clouds – 'water sky', a clear indication of open leads in the sea ice – and out to the west the underside of the cloud was dark, open water below. We were exhausted but unable to sleep, fearful and anxiously listening and feeling for the slightest movement in the sea ice.

In the northern hemisphere sea ice is relatively stable. Antarctica is very different; the circulating storms cause the ice to break away with alarming frequency and little or no warning. Dog teams rarely ventured far from the coast and here we were pushing out twenty-five miles or so with cracks all over the place and open sea visible on the horizon. Ken and Thwaits made no mention of their concern but like me they lay in the tent wondering and worrying what tomorrow would bring.

The next day we started the long, open sea crossing to the Puffballs. We set off early and the weather began to improve – the cloud cleared and the temperature dropped, and we were still crossing small open leads, but the surface of the water was steaming and fresh ice was forming. I saw a number of mirages, lovely blue water stretching out in the distance and some strange distortions caused by the cold; mountains stacked on top of each other like Christmas trees and the dog team ahead twisting up into the air with Thwaits skiing alongside, looking twenty feet tall.

The leads were still open but, thank God, we managed to cross without using the boat and reached the Puffballs and joined up with Flavell Smith and co. at almost the same time that they reached the islands.

Here we were met by a colony of emperor penguins who turned out in a curious line to meet us – we had a desperate time keeping the dogs away from them. These giant and gentle birds had no fear of land animals and would walk inquisitively and unwittingly into the teeth of a team of excited huskies.

It's hard to describe our relief as the sea ice began to firm up. The last three days had been an extreme version of, quite literally, 'walking on thin ice'. The nights spent on the edge of the open polar ocean had been absolutely nerve wracking. Neither Derrick Postlethwaite nor Ken Doyle had made any mention of their anxiety, but all of us, including the four men we had come out to meet, were showing signs of fatigue and lack of sleep. We could still see open water ahead and water sky on the clouds and it was no great decision to give up the attempt to get to Fossil Bluff. The lads would have to wait for a few more weeks before we could relieve them; reluctantly we turned back to Stonington.

The castaways spent another three weeks at Fossil Bluff before the sea ice finally formed solid and the whole squad of us from Stonington turned up on their doorstep. By then the stranded men had accepted their fate that they were to be with us for another year. They had held out well in a miserable situation but were very glad of new company and were repatriated to Adelaide Island as soon as the new aircraft arrived. As far as I know, they got some extra pay from BAS; they deserved it.

My first full summer at Stonington was spent with Thwaits and Shawn Norman surveying the peninsula. It was interesting work and Shawn, like me, was an enthusiastic mountaineer and we managed a number of exhilarating days climbing on the coastal mountains.

One very scary episode springs to mind when we were camped on the beach in a very dangerous place called Windy Valley. As the name implies this particular spot is prone to a katabatic wind that regularly spewed down from the polar plateau.

Ten miles out from the coast at Terra Firma Island, Mike Fielding, another surveyor, was camped on the open sea ice with Jack Donaldson, and we were working together triangulating the island's position. One night there was a terrific blow. We had no way of measuring the colossal force but with winds well over 100 miles per hour, Shawn and I struggled out of the tent and tied the peak down with climbing rope and did everything we could think of to protect it. By morning the wind had stripped the glacier and the sea ice clean of all its snow, right down to bare blue ice. Our tent was left standing exposed on a heap of snow and we were terribly concerned for Mike's party camped out at Terra Firma Island.

Shawn and I climbed a hill behind the beach and looked out to sea where we could see that there were cracks all over the place and open water beyond the island, but we could just see that Mike's tent was still okay. We radioed and suggested that they get their skates on and come over and join us on the mainland. The wind had dropped but there was a lot of open water about.

Mike and Thwaits, the two surveyors, insisted that we continue the triangulations of the island before they came back. As guides the decision was really up to Shawn and me, but both of us were relatively new boys and didn't like to overrule old hands. One of the few very heated arguments I can remember took place with the surveyors adamant that they complete the work and Shawn and I angrily insisting that they come back.

We finally left the decision to Jack Donaldson, the assistant out at Terra Firma Island. Jack was able to climb up on to the island with a better view out to the open sea ice and he took the risk to stay for a few hours and complete the work, much against our better judgment. They finished in double quick time and sledged safely over to join us, but Shawn and I were furious. It had been a dangerous decision and I vowed never to be overruled again – the graves on Stonington Island were a grim reminder of Fids who had taken just such chances.

Twenty years later at a reunion dinner in the Lake District, when we were all a little merry, I walked into the gents' toilet to hear the sound of raised voices and there was Shawn and Thwaits once again arguing as to what we should or should not have done. Shawn was right of course, but at least we were still alive to have the argument.

That summer we surveyed among the fjords and headed back to base in time for the ship's annual call in March, the Antarctic autumn. In came old friends on the ship's crew and new Fids replacing the home goers, piles of mail and a whole year's supply of newspapers and magazines.

I remember tasting the first fresh hen's egg that I'd had in a year – we were well used to penguin and seabird eggs which were okay but tasted fishy and watery. By comparison a hen egg is superb. The taste was so good that I kept eating them till I was bloated; it's amazing how much we take eggs for granted.

All too soon the *John Biscoe* was ready to leave Stonington and three geologists, Flavell Smith, Mike Burns and Peter Rowe, with me to supposedly look after them, were taken on board with my Vikings and Flavell Smith's Komats dog teams and dropped off at the disused base on Horseshoe Island which we reopened for that winter.

The ship left the four us waving goodbye from the beach among a pile of boxes. Ali MacArthur, our base commander, Chris Madders, the radio operator, and Thwaits were all leaving for home and we had become the old hands. It was a strange, lonely moment watching the ship moving slowly out of sight among the icebergs. In a few weeks they would be back among their families, the humdrum of normal life, trees and grass and fresh fruit and perhaps the scent of a girl. I suffered one of those pangs of desperate loneliness that all of us must have felt at times. It was a rare feeling; usually we were too occupied to worry about home, so on these occasions I found it best to sit with my dogs.

The old base was in a bad way but we soon had the generator running and a roaring fire in the main hut and settled in for a cosy winter. The scientists were doing a detailed gravity and magnetic survey of the island and I followed along with the theodolite, mapping the position of their work. It was a relaxing time with just the four of us, a time to dream and make plans.

We listened to the news on the World Service – the cold war was at its height and young American soldiers were coming home in body bags from Vietnam. Closer to home, Bernadette Devlin was tearing up pavements in Northern Ireland. This, the start of 'the troubles', seemed unbelievable to us; such things couldn't happen on the streets of Britain.

It all seemed a long way away – our little world was one of ice, storms and stars, of dogs and cold, of warm fires and good books. With the return of the sun we set out to meet Ian Curphey and Rod Pashley who were sledging from Adelaide Base to meet us for the summer journeys.

Curph had returned to Britain as an engineer on the *Shackleton* and managed to get a job as a dog driver with the Antarctic Survey and here he was back again, as large as life. We sledged across Bigourdan fjord on thin ice as we passed Pinero Island and met the two men on a lonely beach at Rothera Point. They had driven their dogs across Adelaide Island in deep wallowing snow and were glad to join up with us. It was a lonely spot; there was nothing there but a few seal and penguins.[1]

An incredible event began to unfold as we set up our tent on the Jones Ice Shelf on our journey back to Horseshoe Island. The surveyor, Mike Fielding, along with Mick Pawley and Brian Sheldon, was camping on the far side of the shelf and called us up on the radio.

'Can you come over to our camp tonight?' Mike asked. 'There's something I want you to listen to.'

It had been a long, cold day and we had some difficulties getting on to the Jones Ice Shelf as there were some big crevasses to cross. It was getting dark but once on the shelf it was relatively safe on its flat surface and it was the most perfect night, not a cloud in the sky and a full moon lighting the ice shelf and surrounding mountains.

We set off on the last six miles of our journey, casting long moon-shadows on the perfect crisp and flat snow of the shelf, with the Milky Way, a gleaming mass of stars, leading our way overhead. With a mile or so to go we could see Mike's tent lights and the two teams of dogs with him began to howl. Our four teams burst into a gallop and we had an exhilarating race into their camp where the men rushed out to help us picket the dogs. Mick Pawley began calling urgently from the tent.

---

1. This is now the site of Britain's largest Antarctic base, with a jetty capable of mooring research ships and a tarmac airstrip running out into the sea, laboratories, aircraft hangers and a small town of buildings. Visiting it in 2002, I found it unrecognisable to the lonely place where our two parties had met thirty years earlier.

'Quick, come in, listen to this, and leave the dogs!'

We all scrambled into the tent and sat around the radio where we were just in time to join millions of people the world over, crammed around television and radio sets as Neil Armstrong's crackling voice came over the air.

'Houston, Tranquillity Base here. The *Eagle* has landed.'

It's hard to describe the thrill of the moment as Neil's voice came scratchily through the static. Surely in the entire world there wasn't a place more remote and beautiful to listen to such an event. It was a terrific moment; there were nine of us crammed in the tent and parked outside were well over fifty dogs. The full moon was gleaming overhead and the dogs howled into the night with us joining in. Incredibly there existed a better map of the moon's surface than the part of the world where we lived.

Sometime later Neil stepped gingerly out on to the moon's surface.

'That's one small step for man, one giant leap for mankind.'

Like everyone else we waited for the next thirteen hours with our ears pinned to the radio, praying for Neil and Buzz Aldrin's safe take-off in *Eagle*, to join Michael Collins orbiting in the main capsule before the long journey home.

Ian Curphey's diary from that day is well worth quoting, and gives a wonderful picture of what polar travel was like:

July 20th 1969

Very cold today minus 30 C. Left Blaiklock at 1045 and travelled up Bigourdan Fjord to the western end of the Jones Ice shelf, beautiful scenery on the east side of Blaiklock, towering pinnacles of rock enhanced by the light that painted the summits pink. A low bank of cloud that drifted out of the great valley that the Heim Glacier has carved, making everything seem very still and eerie.

Access to the Jones is on the north end where a large mass of ice stands proud of the shelf. To the left was a ramp which was quite easy to get up. The surface [snow] was very good but the cold was unpleasant, especially for Rod and I who were going too well and had to ride a lot [on the sledge to slow it down]. We encountered many crevasse and Rod turned over [his sledge] on one bridge. I went back to help him and did a bloody stupid thing by walking back without skis. Sykes, rightly so, went spare. I deserved a bollocking for behaving so bloody daft in such a desperate place. About 100yds further on I went through one [crevasse] and only my sledge loop stopped me. Not a very nice feeling. At the eastern end of the Jones we camped where we met the survey party of Sheldon, Fielding and Pauley. Went into their tent for a brew [nine of us all told] and listened to the Yanks land on the moon! What next? Fids on the moon, lunar sledging? A good day but very cold for travelling.

Curph's quite a bit bigger than me so it can't have been much of a bollocking. This was his first sledge journey and he and Rod Pashley had taken over dog teams at Adelaide Base with nobody to teach them the ropes. They had done a marvellous job of self-training and had only just joined us in the fjords. He seems less impressed with the moon landing than I was.

Sometime later I discovered that we were not the only polar travellers listening to Neil and Buzz landing on the moon. Almost directly opposite, on the other side of the planet, Wally Herbert with three companions was floe hopping, over breaking up pack ice, the final miles to Spitsbergen, after a 3,600-mile traverse of the North Pole. They had started from Point Barrow in Alaska on 21 February 1968 and reached the pole on 6 April 1969. They reached Spitsbergen fifteen months later on what must be one of the greatest of all sledge journeys. He became, undisputedly, the first man to walk to the North Pole. Unfortunately their triumphant return coincided with the Moon landing and hardly got a mention – it was to be many years before his great feat was recognised. He was knighted thirty years later in the year 2000.

So began my second year in Antarctica. I travelled much of the time with Ali Skinner, a young geologist from Portmahomack in northern Scotland. We sledged south to Fossil Bluff and then up on to the polar plateau where we visited the almost-buried wreck of the Porter aircraft. We continued south to the Eternity Range of mountains and then back over from the Larsen Ice Shelf on the east side of the peninsula, a journey of over a thousand miles, to arrive back at Stonington just as the *John Biscoe* was about to arrive.

My last day of sledging was in from the polar plateau and down the terrifyingly steep 'soda-bread' slope on to the North-East Glacier. Jack Donaldson and I had come across the plateau on a compass bearing and camped on the plateau edge. In the morning we just couldn't believe it was possible to get down and thought we were in the wrong place. We could make out Neny Island and Stonington in the distance, and after searching around realised that this must be it. The slope was about 3,000 feet of very steep snow with big crevasses on either side. If a sledge had somersaulted here or run off course it would have been lethal.

We lashed climbing rope and dog chains around the sledge runners and turned most of our dogs free; they would have to fend for themselves. With only three dogs pulling we launched over the edge, feet jammed down on the big spike brake between the runners, and went screaming off down the slope. There was no way of stopping once we were underway and I was prepared to jump for it if things went wrong. By halfway down the sledge had overtaken the poor dogs and they were being dragged along in their harnesses. We whizzed over a couple of crevasses and ended up wallowing in deep snow at the bottom of the slope, all in one piece. Jack came flying down a few moments later and we both fell about laughing with relief.

The final ten miles down the North-East Glacier was the best sledge dash I ever made. It was summer and the midnight sun was shining low over the sea ice with the mountains and icebergs in brilliant orange relief. We had reversed our day and were travelling at night-time when it was cooler. In the low sunshine the final run down the gently sloping glacier into Stonington Island was magnificent. The little island was shining in the snow with dog teams parked around on the sea ice and the base black against the mountainous backdrop. We arrived at 3 a.m. to find that everybody was fast asleep on normal time. I had been away for almost five months and it was wonderful to wander around the island at such a peaceful time.

The *John Biscoe* arrived a day or so later and we began the hard work of moving cargo from the ship and loading the scientists' samples on board. The dreaded moment arrived and I found myself having to reluctantly hand over my dogs to Henry Blakely, the cheerful Irishman who I had met on Deception Island almost two years earlier and who had come down from Adelaide Island to replace me. I took him for a run up the glacier and knew immediately that he would be okay; the dogs took to him right away.

'Look after them Henry, this is the best bloody dog team in the world.'

It was terrible, far worse than leaving people behind; these dogs had been my family and friends for the last two years. I realised what John Noble must have felt when he handed his dogs over to me.

That afternoon a small group of us stood at the rail of the *John Biscoe* – Ken Doyle, Flavell Smith, Ian Curphey and I – watching the group of Fids waving from the beach. The tiny island was dwarfed between the mountain of Neny Island and the huge North-East Glacier and slipped out of view as we sailed out of the fjord.

12 | Nevisport

Arriving home in the summer of 1970, I had a short spell on the dole. I wrote 'explorer' on the form for the kind of work I was looking for and strangely didn't get any takers. Leeds dole office was a miserable place and there was nothing cheerful about the little queue of us waiting for our weekly handout. It was a far cry from the peaceful isolation of Antarctica, a mad world. America was losing its war in Vietnam and the first shipyard riots were taking place in Gdansk, Poland. Inflation was about fifteen per cent and having been away for a while I just couldn't believe how expensive life had become. I got very angry about prices in my local supermarket and the poor checkout girl must have thought me totally insane.

At the first opportunity I went off for a few days' climbing on my own in North Wales. I walked up to Dinas Cromlech and was sitting at the foot of *Flying Buttress* when I saw my first climbers. In an almost four-year absence a dramatic change had taken place. Gone were the tatty trousers or moleskin breeks with red socks and scruffy pullovers. These guys were dressed in Lycra tights, sit harnesses, coloured crash helmets with an incredible array of nuts and ironmongery hanging round their waists. Had they been overdressed idiots I wouldn't have minded, but they set off up *Cenotaph Corner* like a couple of whippets and I realised that the world had moved on. There I stood in my old tattered kit feeling like Woody Allen emerging as the 'Sleeper'.

When I arrived home there was a letter waiting from Peter Downs who had become the warden at Locheil Centre, offering me a senior position in my old job as an instructor. It seemed a backward step but I was desperate and accepted it immediately.

I loaded my old minivan, which had sat hibernating in Mum's garage for the last four years, and headed north.

I thought Fort William had sadly changed for the worse. The new pulp and paper mill had opened at Annat Point on the narrows between Loch Linnhe and Loch Eil and was pumping out filth into the atmosphere and both lochs. A stinking chemical cloud hung over the town and cheap and ugly new housing was springing rapidly up the hillside.

Fort William has some of the highest annual rainfall of any town in Europe and in a bad year can have well over a hundred inches. Yet some enterprising architect was building hundreds of flat-roofed council houses, only suitable for a warm and dry climate, right up the steep sides of the mountain behind the town. In a misguided attempt to improve the view he had reversed the design so that the bedrooms were downstairs. This put the heating systems in the loft making the bedrooms freezing cold and damp, and the flat roofs pooled and dripped like colanders on to the miserable occupants. These revolting houses were crammed together on the steep hillside while all around the wild, untouched Highland country below Ben Nevis could easily have been transformed into a beautiful new town.

In the time I had been away there had been a series of climbing fatalities. My friends Ian Clough and Tom Patey had both been killed in separate accidents in May that year; Ian descending after the successful ascent of the south face of Annapurna when a serac, an ice-pillar, collapsed on him, and Tom in an abseiling accident at Whiten Head on the north coast of Scotland. We had been involved in so many rescues together and both Ian and Tom were such larger-than-life characters it seemed impossible that anything could happen to them. I remember Ian was so full of life, living for free in the morgue at Kinloss and then becoming a part of the community in Glencoe, and Tom singing all night to his accordion, climbing all day and then back to the singing without allowing time for sleep.

I called in to see Ian's wife Nicky at her cottage, Dingly Dell, in Lancaster, on my way north and found her in a very distressed state. More was to come. Ike Jones, one of the Lochaber rescue team members had died in a fall on Buachaille Etive Mor and an avalanche accident on Ben Nevis had wiped out five other friends. I spent my first few days in the Fort calling on their bereaved relatives. I had seen too many fatal accidents but this was the first time that close friends had been involved and the sheer number and amount of distress was horrifying.

The Locheil Centre had changed dramatically in the years that I had been away. Somehow the sailing had taken on a higher priority than the hillwalking, the four-day expedition had vanished from the course and there seemed to be too many instructors. For the first time in my life there didn't seem enough work to do and I was bored.

Ian Sutherland (Suds), my old climbing partner from the Dolomites, was instructing at Applecross, a remote outdoor centre to the north of Kyle, and we got together for a day's climbing in Ardgour. We walked in the long way from the Corran Ferry and were plodding up Coire an Lubhair to climb the Great Ridge of Garbh Bheinn. Both of us disgruntled with instructing and grousing about our lot.

'There's a small shop for sale in Fort William High Street, Suds, what do you think about opening a climbers' shop?' I asked impulsively.

Scotsmen are never people to make instant decisions. 'That sounds a bit serious Spike,' he muttered.

'We could guide during the week and open at weekends when the climbers are around,' I reasoned enthusiastically.

'Och, what the hell, it's worth a go,' he said.

We found ourselves grinning and shaking hands. Neither of us had great expectations of anything but a small business to keep ourselves climbing, nor could have guessed that this was the start of a friendship and joint venture that would last for the next forty years.

Suds' uncle had died leaving him a share in his house worth about £2,000 and I had the remains of my Antarctic savings of about the same. It seemed quite a large sum of money in 1970. We pooled the lot and within a few weeks we were in business.

We called it Nevisport and were never to regret the name. At the time there were very few shops selling mountaineering equipment in Britain:

George Fisher in Keswick and Frank Davies in Ambleside, Robert Lawrie in London, Arfons in North Wales, Ellis Brigham in Manchester and Graham Tiso in Edinburgh. There was Blacks and a mishmash of sports shops selling camping equipment but the outdoor revolution that exploded over the next two decades was yet to start. Most of our friends thought that we were going to lose our shirts as they rightly assumed that climbers would have bought their kit long before they arrived in Fort William.

We opened four days before Christmas in 1970. The shop, an old dairy, was tiny, with two floors each about 20 feet square. It sat above the pier and railway station alongside the Wee Free (Presbyterian) Church and the Highland exhibition shop, which cleverly charged sixpence to anyone entering the premises to watch an old lady pretend to spin wool in the traditional manner.

Upstairs became the boot room where I slept on an airbed and cooked my meals on a Primus stove. My husky lived on the flat roof above. Suds took a job stoking the furnace in the aluminium works earning the amazing sum of £40 a week, which was a princely wage in those days. This kept me in food! Neither of us had the foggiest idea how to run a business but we were encouraged by Fred Riley, the manager of the Linen Bank.

Fred was the old-style bank manager who took our savings and helped us sort out how to run the business. He was the first of a whole series of excellent bankers that helped us expand our business in the seventies. We had complete trust in the local managers in those days and thought of our relationship with the bank as a partnership, a situation that is unthinkable nowadays.

While I ran the shop Suds slogged it out in the furnace room in the Fort William aluminium smelter. It was hard graft but made enough money to keep us both alive during the first two or three months as we started the business. He tells the tale in his own words.

I worked in the aluminium smelter three times in the sixties, long before the factory modernised. I'd served my time as an apprentice shoemaker with the D&E Shoe Company in Fort William. There wasn't much work to be had and it was pretty poor pay so I took a job in the furnace room to make some cash.

The first time I went in it felt like entering hell itself. It resembled something out of a Dickens novel. Inside was a massive area about the size of a football pitch. There were lines of a hundred or so huge steel furnaces called pots, each about forty feet long. These were filled with pitch, bauxite and molten metal and were spewing out smoke and steam. The lights in the roof barely penetrated the smoky haze and it was impossible to see from one end of the factory to the other. There were about forty of us working in there. It was hard, brutal work and I remember it as heat, smoke and camaraderie in that order.

My first job was with the reconstruction squad. When one of the pots began to leak it was closed down, emptied and cooled with water and there was lots of steam and ammonia given off. Once the pot was lifted clear, the firebrick base had to be dug out and replaced in the pit below. This had become encased in a mesh of molten aluminium and had to be smashed out with a jackhammer. I was only nineteen when I started and could hardly lift the hammer. In the early days some of the older men would come down and help me start to break out the blocks.

A bogey full of molten aluminium spilled into one of these pits and a bricklayer called Cameron was incinerated instantly; you had to be very careful.

Another job I had was to clamber up on top of the furnaces to adjust the clamps holding the stubs. These were rods going down through the molten pitch that held the anode in position. The heat was intense and there were sparks flying and our clothes were full of small burn holes. You could boil your tea-can on top of the furnace.

We all looked after each other and socialised together. One or two of the men over-indulged and we would cover up for them while they slept it off. Someone would take a van around Inverlochy village

before the 6 a.m. shift and drag absconders from their beds. I can
remember hiding old Archie McPhee behind a sheet of plywood
at the back of the furnaces while the foreman was looking for him.

Quite a few of the mountain rescue team worked in there and
Arthur Hill, the team leader, was one of the foremen. In those days
there were not so many call-outs, something like thirty a year.

The police would call round and drop us off at the Long John
distillery and we would wallow across the Everglades and then follow
the Puggy Line (the narrow gauge railway) up to the start of the
Ben path. The road up to the dam was yet to be built. On the way
down we would put the stretcher on the Dead Man's Bogey, a small
pump trolley, and everybody scrambled aboard and we screamed
down the lines at break-neck speed hoping that the gate into the
aluminium works was open. It was very exciting.

The British Aluminium Company was very understanding
and we were allowed to go on rescues at a moment's notice and they
always paid our wages in full. In many ways they looked after the
workforce very well. None the less, the furnace room was an excep-
tionally unhealthy place to work in. It's very noticeable that many of
the long-term workers have had untimely deaths due to respiratory
problems and few have enjoyed a long retirement.

I left to work at the new pulp mill when it opened at the head of
Loch Eil but by then was very involved in mountaineering and got a
job as an instructor at Applecross Outdoor Centre. I returned to the
furnace room for a short stint while we set up Nevisport. At that time
in 1970 I was earning £40 a week which seemed like a king's ransom.

While Suds sweated in the aluminium works I was deliriously happy;
for the first time in my life I had a place of my own. I had gone from
boarding school to the YMCA and the RAF and then outdoor centres
and Antarctica, always living in communal accommodation; at last I had
a place for myself.

Outside my window were two old phone boxes where a couple of ladies ran a thriving business of the night. I lay in my sleeping bag howling with laughter at their antics attracting customers. When business was slack they would drop in for a cup of tea and fill me in with all the local gossip. Both have become respectable married women in the town and we have remained the best of friends.

Kate Ward, the wife of one of the rescue team, became our first shop assistant, manager and bookkeeper, at first for no pay and thereafter for what we could manage. Her son, Ian, was in a pram in the corner and I swear that the first word he uttered was 'crampon'.

We spread the boots out on the shelves mixed in with empty boxes to make it look as if we had a good range and bought one line in full sizes and another in halves. Our stock was very limited, there wasn't a lot available and we had no idea where to get it. We were still using old money but almost immediately were involved with the change to decimalisation. There was a great hike up of prices at the changeover and many of the local Highland businesses refused to accept the new money and continued to use old shillings and pence for several years.

Almost immediately we were faced with the telephone and mail strike in the spring of 1971, which happened while we were still trying to open accounts with our suppliers. What little stock we had was depleted almost to nothing and we had no means of contacting them. In desperation we commandeered Suds' brother Harry and his van and headed south in search of something to sell.

Our first call was in Newcastle where an oddly named company called Berghaus was reputed to be wholesaling climbing boots.

This we discovered was in the attic of the LD Mountain Centre in Dean Street and was run by two young guys, climbers just like us, Peter Lockey and Gordon Davison. They were somewhat taken aback at these two unknowns from the Highlands and probably disappointed at our request to purchase one dozen pairs of Scarpa walking boots. They sent us off to have a drink while they had a discussion and when we returned made a proposition that was to be the making of Nevisport.

Instead of the dozen or so boots, they loaded us to the gunnels, sale or return, no limit and a great deal of trust. This was to be the start of a friendship and company relationship that has endured throughout the whole of my time in business.

From there we drove over to the Peak District to Troll and Parba Products who reputedly made harnesses and chocks and who acted in exactly the same way. Troll was started by Tony Howard, Alan Waterhouse and Paul Seddon, who were members of the Rimmon Mountaineering Club. I knew Paul, who had been involved on the big rescue on the North-East Buttress of Ben Nevis, and all of a sudden the mountaineering grapevine was paying dividends. Once again we were welcomed with open arms.

Our next call was Deiniolen in Snowdonia where Denny Moorhouse was just starting up a technical mountaineering works called Clog in an old, disused watermill. We knew Denny already from our Dolomites exploits; he had been soloing extreme rock walls at the time that Dinger and I were cutting our teeth on the Tre Cime in the early sixties. Once again we were loaded with stock and headed over to Manchester where MOAC, Ellis Brigham's wholesale company, was just starting up. Bill Birch, another climber, opened doors for us and we fully loaded the van with a great heap of stock on credit.

Manchester was a tough place in those days and we watched a bunch of locals rip the windscreen wipers off the van. Like cowards we stood by and let them do it: they looked tougher than us.

Thinking back, it astonishes me how small the industry was and how friendly we all became. The international trade show, called SPOGA, in Cologne, was my first foreign buying trip. Outside the trade halls was a large clover-leaf motorway junction and we of the British outdoor trade kipped under its bridges, unable to afford the extortionate hotel prices. We tottered into the show with crumpled suits, hungover and with our toothbrushes in our pockets; it was a miracle that any of the continental companies accepted our orders.

Denny Moorhouse and his partner Shirley toted the first Clog climbing gear round the show, illicitly selling out of a polythene bag. The trade fare was huge by the standard of the day and we had never seen such a fabulous array of climbing equipment. Not only that but many of the climbing stars were there in real life: Reinhold Messner, Riccardo Cassin, Yvon Chouinard all selling their wares. There were fantastic French Galibier Super RD boots, Toni Eggers, Salewa crampons with tungsten points and rows of ice axes and hammers to set any climber's mouth dribbling.

Halls filled with tents, rucksacks and sleeping bags, André Jamet, Millet and Pierre Allain. We returned to Scotland brimming with ideas and realising that it was possible to bring home products that were new and exciting.

I think what really lit up the climbing scene in the early seventies was the advent of Ken Wilson's bi-monthly *Mountain* magazine. 'Wilson's weekly' was launched in 1969 and almost immediately became the bible of information and standards to the world of mountaineers. Ken's aggressive charge against the advent of bolts and his defence of climbing ethics along with a host of articles about mountaineering all over the world became an absolute must.

The photographs were fabulous and there was bucket loads of information about where to climb and what was happening on the world scene. *Mountain* is still spoken of in hallowed tones and set a standard that modern climbing magazines have found hard to follow.

Ken was very pro-Scottish winter climbing which at the time was developing at breakneck speed. We were selling his rag like hot cakes and I realised that our small advertisements in the magazine gave Nevisport a higher profile than we had expected. Climbers started to arrive in Fort William with the knowledge that our little shop existed.

Typical of the time, shops in Fort William were closed on Sundays. This was a great problem for us; the shop was very quiet during the week and hectic at weekends when the climbers were around. It seemed daft to be shut on one of the only days we had customers so we decided to take a risk and open on Sundays. All went well on the first day and trade was brisk and uneventful until the morning service at the Wee Free Church ended. An angry crowd of the congregation formed outside the shop and a deputation of church elders marched in and demanded that we close immediately; we were defiling the Sabbath.

'Go away,' Suds said, or words to that effect.

The protestors remained outside while the elders, bristling with righteous indignation, marched over to the police station and made a formal complaint. A few minutes later PC Angus McDonald, one of the members of the mountain rescue team, ambled in.

'You're breaking the law boys, you'll have to close,' he said, looking rather embarrassed.

'No way Angus, you'll just have to arrest us. Have a coffee,' Suds said.

Angus took his time and went back to the police station and we awaited the inevitable closedown but nothing happened. Seemingly there were no byelaws in Scotland to stop us, but on the next three Sundays we had a bunch of angry protestors at our door.

That week we were approached by Hugh McKenzie of Highland Homespun and Kenny (KK) Cameron, both highly respected businessmen in the town.

'How are you doing on Sundays?' they asked.

'Not bad, it's our busiest day,' I said a little apprehensively.

Both these men had been kind and helpful to us when we started up. They listened sympathetically to what we had to say and left us deep in thought. The following weekend both their shops opened and by the end of that summer most of the retailers in Fort William were open and flourishing. It seems churlish to crow over the church and established way of life but I think our small victory made a huge improvement to the tourist industry in the Highlands.

Suds became deputy leader of Lochaber Mountain Rescue Team when we started the business but when Arthur Hill retired he took over as leader and was to remain so for the next ten years.

The civilian teams were slowly replacing the RAF as we gained equipment and experience. We were averaging about sixty call-outs a year and in those early days had little backup from helicopters so rescues were generally quite long affairs. We either shut up shop or took it in turns to go on call. Both of us were climbing at every spare moment and we were using the call-outs as a way to keep fit.

On 12 February 1974, two young climbers, Barry Thomas from Bramhall in Cheshire and his friend John Beatty from Stockport, started up *Observatory Ridge*, a classic winter climb on Ben Nevis. Conditions were superb, cold with a deep cover of snow. They made reasonable progress up the initial system of gullies and ledges but somehow they missed the crest of the ridge and took a bad line, which led them leftwards and off route into the fierce and steeper region of *Zero Gully*. By now the weather was deteriorating, it was snowing lightly and misty.

John told me his story some time later.

> *My belay was poor but strangely acceptable, as the climbing was relatively easy. I used a coffin-shaped aluminium nut called an original Moac wedged into a slot at waist height, jammed precariously between the rock and a thick, clear icicle. I stood comfortably on a tiny ledge of snow gazing out at the rope snaking away into a wall of mist.*
>
> *When accidents happen it is usually without warning. For us, just a muffled hissing sound, then soft thumping. The rope tremored momentarily and tightened to a titanic heave, so powerful and sudden that instantaneous reaction is all that one has. The rope, attached to me with a friction knot called an Italian hitch, tightened and locked under tension. My mind spun into action, horrified at the realisation of the small weak belay. First thought, 'no weight on belay', second thought, 'add friction to the hitch'. I pushed my fingers*

*into the knot in order to save load bearing on the poor belay. These
were instant reactions because in a second Barry was now fifty feet
below me swinging freely in space over the gully wall of Zero.*

*Barry then made a rising, unprotected traverse and man-
telshelved on to a steep, snow-banked ledge and there he stuck,
unable to reverse down and with no easy way forward. This was
a terrifying situation with 400 feet of Zero Gully almost vertically
below him and over 1,000 feet to the top.*

His shouts for help were heard by a party of climbers on North-East
Buttress but it took them some hours to complete the climb and raise the
alarm. This was long before the days of mobile phones and the stranded
climber and his partner, fifty feet below, had a long, cold wait ahead of
them. The rescue team was not alerted until nightfall.

We set off up the Ben path by torchlight; every time I slog up that bloody
path I swear it will be the last. It's easy enough; just a long, upward trudge
that goes on forever, the darkness seeming to stretch the distance. Along
with our climbing equipment we were lugging some 500-foot spools of
pre-stretched Terylene rope on pack-frames; they were heavy and awkward to carry.

It was snowing and blowing and still dark when we reached the summit
but a grey light of dawn was breaking in the east as we apprehensively
approached the cornice at the top of *Zero Gully*. There was a slot where
climbers had emerged through the cornice and we peered over and shouted but could see or hear nothing. We knew that another party would be
trying to climb up to them from below but time was of the essence.

'Somebody's got to go down,' Suds said, looking at me.

It was cold and unpleasant standing exposed in the wind and a bit of
action seemed more appealing. 'It should be easy enough,' I told myself.
'The top half of Zero is a straightforward snow slope.' The difficulty
would be the lower 500 feet when they would have to knot on another
rope and pass it through the belay point.

Huddled on the edge of the cornice we dug into the snow to get some shelter and rigged a safe anchor point. Suds went over first, dropping awkwardly over the overhanging rim. I tied the rope firmly on to my Whillans harness and nervously dropped through the slot behind him, trying not to think about the enormous drop. Immediately we were out of the wind and it was a much more pleasant place to be than the summit, where the poor guys were paying out the rope. Suds was 100 feet below and we began the long, slow descent.

The ropes faded upwards into the cloud like two slender umbilical cords and I tried not to think how thin they looked. For once I had excellent radio contact and was able to chat to Andy Nichol who was controlling the lower on the summit.

After 500 feet of lowering there was a long pause and I could hear Andy and the boys cursing as they organised the frozen knot and passed it through the belay to attach a second spool of rope. Unlike modern climbing rope the hawser-laid Terylene was stiff and difficult to handle and everything was freezing up on them.

After a while the lower continued and we began to descend into the steeper part of the gully and almost immediately could see the two stranded climbers who were waving frantically at us. The lead guy was in a very exposed position and must have had a very frightening night.

'Down really slowly, Andy. Suds is going for the leader and I'll get the man on the belay ledge,' I called into my radio.

Suds got to the lead climber and began sorting out his ropes. I lowered on past and reached the man on the ledge and clipped into his belay.

'Hi, how are you?' I asked.

'Cold and stiff but very glad to see you. I'm John,' he shivered.

The rope above me began to slacken and I realised that Andy Nichol was still lowering. 'Hold it Andy,' I called into the radio. The rope, still reasonably taught, came to a stop.

'Right John, I'm clipping you in to this rope with me and we'll be down in no time. We just lean back and relax and the boys will lower us off.'

Suds was already descending with Barry Thomas. I unclipped the belay, leaving their ropes and tackle behind as booty for the next climbers up *Zero Gully*.

'Okay, here we go,' I said to John, as we leaned back into space.

The next instance we dropped vertically, both of us yelling in shock and I thought the rope had come away at the summit. Suddenly it came tight and then we began to spring upwards and then up and down, the two of us bouncing like a giant yo-yo. It was a terrifying few seconds before we settled and managed to swing back into a stable position.

What had happened was that Andy had continued to lower when I reached the ledge and the stretch in the 1,000 feet of rope had released. With the weight of an extra man we had dropped like a stone for almost thirty feet. Andy told me later that they hadn't felt anything on the summit and wondered what all the shouting was about.

Once we got ourselves settled things went smoothly and we lowered on down into *Observatory Gully* where we met up with the team heading up from below. John and Barry were able to walk down to the CIC hut unscathed and very much relieved. Considering their ordeal they were in very good shape.

The men on the summit had done a fantastic job. They had controlled the ropes for several hours in the most miserable conditions while Suds and I had been active and out of the wind. This was the first of a number of lowers from the summit plateau of Ben Nevis. Modern equipment is more advanced these days but the principles are much the same.

A few years later the guide Mick Tighe and I were lowered down *Hadrian's Wall* to an injured climber hanging where his rope had snagged. Just as we were about to reach him a helicopter flew in and the winch man was lowered down and snatched him to safety, much to our disgust. We felt robbed but had a grandstand view of the proceedings.

Crampon front-pointing was starting to happen. Johnny Cunningham had returned from Antarctica and developed a technique of climbing ice with droop-picked axes. It seems so obvious now but up until then our tools had straight picks and we hacked steps and handholds into the ice. To my mind the last great step-cutting event was Dave Bathgate's marvellous six-and-a-half hour ascent of *The Curtain* on Ben Nevis in 1965, a real tour de force. Within a year or so drooped picks and lobster-claw crampons came into use and we began to learn to front-point. It seemed so obvious once you got the idea. Suddenly the great classic gullies were open to us mere mortals!

Willy Anderson and I tried our first front-pointing on the ice pitch just left of the start to *Glover's Chimney*. I remember balancing quickly up for about twenty-five feet and thinking, 'This is great,' and then looking down at the two tiny front-points of my crampons holding me on to the ice.

'Bloody hell, Willy, what do I do now?'

'Cut a step you fool!'

'Right!' I hacked a large step and handhold and hung on for dear life. This was going to take some getting used to.

A few days later, Big Ian Nicholson, one of the Creagh Dhu club, ambled into Nevisport just in time for lunch having soloed *Zero* and *Point Five* gullies in two hours; it seemed unbelievable. Progress was amazing and Scottish climbers were the toast of the mountaineering world. Hamish MacInnes invented the Terrordactyl axe which became the ice tool of the decade and we climbed with swollen knuckles until we put padding into our Dachstein mitts!

In 1973 Nevisport began to expand and we moved to larger premises into what had once been the first garage in Fort William. An ancient petrol pump was fitted to the wall and the tanks and pits were still in the floor which sloped to allow oil to drain away. It was a great site though, right in the middle of the High Street and we did it up in a rough and ready way. The clothing and equipment was colourful and didn't need fancy display.

Business was great, the wet Highland summers ideal for selling water-proofs that we were having made to our own designs. A great little extra was selling anti-midge creams by the bucketful. By the end of that year we opened shops in Glasgow and Aviemore.

13 | Callop

I had rented a ruined farm, called Callop, at Glenfinnan for the princely sum of £1 a year … if asked for. It was a wonderful isolated place half a mile from the single track road to Mallaig. The rutted track up the field in front of the house followed the River Callop in the most idyllic situation surrounded by beautiful mountains, the nearest neighbour over a mile away. The house itself was in a bad state of repair and only partially roofed but one half was weather tight and there were a number of very service-able outbuildings.

It became the regular doss for climbers as one of the outbuildings had an old black lead stove and I put in bunks and some comfortable chairs. It also had the advantage of being not far from the best pub in Scotland, the Glenfinnan House Hotel, which ignored the ludicrous licensing laws of the time by remaining open night and day. Charlie MacFarlane-Barrow, the owner, ran a marvellous business. He was a raconteur, fiddler, piper and singer of extraordinary songs. The hotel was the centre of village life, hung with ancient pictures of Highland battles, antlers and musical instruments. Charlie piped his guests to dinner dressed always in his tweed jacket and ancient kilt and played the fiddle till the early hours of the morning.

'What time do you close?' A perplexed tourist asked when the bar was in full flight in the early hours of the morning.

'Och, about October,' Charlie said, lifting his fiddle to his chin.

Burt Lancaster, the actor, was a regular visitor and I once saw him at the bar, deep in conversation with Jimmy the tramp. Burt in a smart tweed country jacket, the very image of the star he was, and Jimmy in an old raincoat down to his ankles without a care in the world. If I'd only had a camera! Jimmy was one of the great characters of Glenfinnan and one of the last of the tramps who roamed the roads after the Second World War. He was a regular at the pub where he knew there was always a free drink on the bar for him. He played a mean penny whistle and loved to join in the singing and there were innumerable local stories about his antics. He stopped in at Callop regularly for a bite to eat.

Dougie Cameron at Corrie Beg croft told me of the occasion Jimmy was in for a meal and watching the television with deep interest. It was a decadent bedroom scene with a lady on the bed and a man standing over her with a glass in his hand.

'What do you think of that, Jimmy?' Dougie asked.

Jimmy screwed his eyes attentively at the screen. 'I think its Bells,' he said, referring to the popular whisky brand he dreamed was in the glass.

Jimmy was one of my many visitors during my time at Glenfinnan. Callop was a very isolated farm a couple of miles from the village. Herds of deer roamed the corries behind Callop and it was the perfect place for a spot of poaching. Needless to say we were never short of meat. The River Callop teamed with fish and the hills were alive with game. How we managed the social life and still managed to build the business and keep climbing I will never understand.

I was itching for an adventure so in 1973 Bruce Barclay, Ronnie Richards, Mike C. and I went on a climbing trip to Kenya. Jomo Kenyatta was still president and although stable there was still some unrest and anti-white feeling about, but we were very kindly welcomed in Nairobi by the Mountain Club of Kenya. At the time the unclimbed Diamond Couloir on Mount Kenya was one of the great targets for mountaineers and with the newly discovered front-pointing techniques our little Scottish contingent felt we had a good chance.

We started from Naro Moru Lodge where by coincidence I met Minto Nuttall, whom I had met previously at my disastrous interview at Admiralty for the South Georgia expedition. Minto had fared no better than me and was now running his own safari business in Kenya and was able to give us a lot of sound advice on the approach to the mountain.

The local mountaineers were very anxious that we would snatch the prize from under their noses. They need not have worried; after a long slog up the Tilaki Valley we spent a couple of cold nights in Top Hut and plodded up Point Lenana to get used to the height. It was my first experience of altitude and I literally crawled to the summit feeling desperately ill. I have found that I'm slow to acclimatise but improve after a day or two. On this occasion I disgraced myself, was violently sick and had to be helped off the mountain by Bruce and Ronnie.

Having recovered we set off up the Diamond in great style. The climbing was similar to *Point Five Gully* on Ben Nevis and we thought we had it in the bag. Unfortunately we were too slow and the sun hit the Diamond Glacier high on the upper reaches of the mountain before we reached the top of the gully. Almost immediately snow avalanches began to pour down the glacier and there was nothing for it than to beat a hasty and very frightening retreat. As we got clear the whole gully became a massive funnel of avalanching debris.

As a consolation we crossed over to the sunny side of the mountain and climbed the Fermin Tower route and spent a cold bivouac just below the summit at about 17,000 feet. After shivering through the night I watched the sun explode out of the horizon. It was a sight I'll never forget. We were looking down the Gorgeous Valley, a hundred-mile-deep rift of lakes, woodlands and gorges running out to the grassy planes of Africa. I promised myself that one day I would walk up this marvellous valley and climb Mount Kenya again. I hope there's time!

A few years later I discovered to my embarrassment that Mike C. had written to the Mountain Club of Kenya claiming that we had climbed the Diamond Couloir, at the same time claiming the first solo ascents of impossibly hard routes in North Wales. Why he should do this is a real mystery as he was a fine rock climber. I have never seen him since but heard that he had a nervous breakdown soon after we got home. I don't think the Kenyan mountaineers took the claim seriously but our name must be mud in the club hut in Nairobi.

Back in Scotland a young Scottish mountaineer, Gordon Smith, got a job in Nevisport and stayed in the bothy at Callop. He was making a name for himself as a hotshot climber. Gordon's hitch-hiking exploits were as legendary as his climbing; he managed to hitch back from Chamonix with two huge rucksacks of climbing equipment and his leg in plaster, without a penny to his name. He sneaked on to the ferry at Calais among a bus party and fed off the leftovers in the café, arriving home to Callop as cheerful as ever.

That summer Suds and I had climbed *Route II* on Carn Dearg Buttress, Ben Nevis, and scouted it out with a view to a winter ascent. The following February (1974) Gordon and I walked up to the CIC hut on one of those never to be forgotten days that happen in Scotland once every five years or so. Ben Nevis was almost buried in snow and Carn Dearg Buttress was plastered. Even the steep slabs of *Bullroar* were coated in ice. It was bitterly cold without a cloud in the sky. If we were ever going to venture on to the buttress this was the day.

Gordon led off at the lowest point of the cliff up a steep corner which is the summer start of *The Shadow*. The Terrordactyls were great on this kind of ground and we were soon perched on a steep slab below a series of overlaps. I managed to traverse right and worked into a slabby groove. At one we point tried to traverse into the middle of the face but found the climbing very thin. This place, I think, is now the superb line of *French Connection*, climbed seventeen years later by visiting Frenchmen Damilano and Lewale in 1995.

A couple of pitches further up found us level with the top of *The Curtain* and the summer's recce really paid off as I was able to find the unlikely traverse line of *Route II* to The Meadow. In summer this is a wet mossy area at the start of the main traverse; now it was a cascade of glorious

142

green ice and I managed to place two really good screws, the first decent belay so far.

Shouts of encouragement came from below from Alan Kimber, a local guide, and his client, asking how we were getting on and taking photographs which he kindly gave us later. We were getting very anxious about daylight as it had taken longer to climb the lower half of the buttress than we had anticipated.

Gordon joined me on my frozen perch on The Meadow. He's very short-sighted, and wore bottle-thick spectacles, which gave him an owl-like appearance and some advantage over me as he could only see half a rope length ahead and seemed totally unaware of the atrocious drop below. Nonetheless, neither of us liked the look of the traverse. He set off nervously, leaving the safety of the ice and began clearing snow off the slab in the most precarious situation as he moved out rightwards across the heart of the buttress.

'There's a peg here, Spike. Someone's been here before us,' he said in consternation.

We just couldn't believe it. We were over halfway up the buttress and until now there had been no sign of climbers and we could not imagine how they had got there, but sure enough there were clear tracks of somebody having crossed the traverse before us. It was too steep a place to lose concentration but very baffling and somewhat disappointing.

The climbing was very serious here; powder snow on steep glazed slabs with not much for the crampon points or the Terrordactyls to hook into. Gordon moved very slowly and I prayed for him to get a runner of some kind, but nothing doing. After a hundred feet or so of very airy sidestepping he finally reached a spot below the little scoop of *Centurion*. I was certain that there was a belay here from my summer reconnoitre and kept bellowing him encouragement as he scraped about. He finally got a nut into a small depression.

'It's all there is. Don't come off for goodness sake!'

I didn't intend to. The thought of leaving my safe perch was unnerving,

Gordon had clipped the peg of our unknown predecessors and then the rope ran out at right-angles across the face in a long unprotected loop. I teetered across the slab in a gibbering state which grew worse when I reached him and saw the useless nut he was pretending to use as a belay. Fortunately the worst was over and I continued on better holds and finally reached the hollow where *Sassenach* and *The Bat* converge.

It should have got easier from here but a steep rock pitch on the crest of the buttress proved harder than expected. We were racing against the falling darkness. Gordon led off round a huge overhanging block and vanished from sight and I stood stamping my feet and willing him to get a move on. There was a lot of scraping, scratching and muttering and then the rope started to move and at last the angle eased off. Gordon topped out and I followed by torchlight on to the crest of the ridge. We descended *Ledge Route*, following the steps of our unknown predecessors.

Back at the CIC hut we learned that Mick Geddes and Alan Rouse had reached the traverse pitch of *Route II* three days earlier by taking a tension traverse from *Route I* on to the ice bulge of The Meadow. This must have been a very scary thing to do and explained how the tracks appeared as if by magic.

It had been a fantastic day's climbing in perfect surroundings and we knew that it was a breakthrough as the first winter ascent of one of the Ben's major rock climbs. Terrordactyls are relics now, hanging on barroom walls, but they were the first tool that made this kind of climbing possible. Sadly, poor winters have meant that Carn Dearg Buttress is rarely in winter condition and this classic climb has had few winter ascents.

The call-outs were coming thick and fast and it's impossible to chronicle them all, but a catastrophe that I can't stop thinking about began one afternoon in Five Finger Gully on Ben Nevis on 14 February 1974. This long and uninteresting gully is one of the black spots for accidents. It lies on the not-so-steep flank of the Ben alongside the Red Burn, which is the ordinary footpath up and down the mountain. Less than a five-degree navigational error from the summit leads spot-on into the top of this gully which dips steeply down, looking initially very much like the normal footpath.

Almost all of us in the rescue team (including me) have mistakenly started down this treacherous slope at one time or another. There have been more mishaps here than in any other place on Ben Nevis, and many disputes among the climbing fraternity about whether or not to put up some kind of route marker to reduce the accidents.

That afternoon a young couple on their honeymoon, John Bowes, a London architect, and his new French wife, Gabrielle, climbed the Ben. With their friends, Alf and Carol Hughes, they reached the summit in fine, but deteriorating, weather. On the way down the cloud thickened and they made the classic error and began to descend Five Finger Gully. The snow slope steepens rapidly and somewhere in the upper reaches Gabrielle slipped and while attempting to stop her the entire party slid out of control and bounced and rolled for about a thousand feet into the open snow basin about halfway down the gully. This is a relatively safe place but below them the gully narrows into a deep gorge with a series of steep waterfalls.

John Bowes seemed to be in the worst condition and was unable to walk. Gabrielle had taken a bad knock on the head but got to her feet and was able to scramble over and join him. Alf and Carol Hughes were unhurt and climbed down to make sure John and Gabrielle were safe and then without delay set off to raise the alarm.

Luckily, Willie Anderson, George Grassam and I were sorting out equipment in the police station when the alarm call came. It seemed pretty straightforward and the three of us set off almost immediately, first asking for RAF helicopter support if it were possible, and leaving a message for the rest of the team to bring up stretchers and equipment as soon as everybody was available.

It was still daylight but snowing lightly as we scrambled up the lower slopes of the gully. Once in the gorge it became very nasty ground and we clambered up a lethal combination of rock- and snow-covered grassy ledges alongside the big waterfalls and finally reached the snow basin where almost immediately we found Gabrielle and John.

John had a broken leg and it was obvious that we would need a stretcher to move him, but he was cheerful enough though very concerned about his wife; Gabrielle was now in a much worse condition. After the fall she had been on her feet and fairly mobile, but she had a bad gash on her head and was showing signs of concussion. Both of them were very cold.

We had come up quickly without a great deal of equipment but had warm sleeping bags, poly bivvy sacks and hot drinks and we rigged a shelter and gave them all our spare clothing. Willie urgently called on the radio for a helicopter while George and I organised things. It was now snowing heavily, in a sea of cloud, and we knew that the chance of a helicopter was very remote. RAF Kinloss Mountain Rescue was on the way.

The rest of our rescue team was coming up the gully in dribs and drabs. It was one of those nights when the police had difficulty finding people. Most of the lads were on holiday and none of the usual experienced climbers were available. Sometime around midnight they reached the narrow gorge of the gully where the big waterfall spouts vertically over the chasm. The steep sides were now plastered in fresh snow and in the darkness the pitch looked appalling.

'There's no way we can get up in these conditions,' Andy Nichols' voice crackled over the radio. 'We'll have to wait until daylight.'

It was a dreadful predicament: I had climbed into the bivvy bag with Gabrielle, who was shaking uncontrollably and delirious, and was hugging her in an attempt to get her warm. Willie was looking after John who was in a lot of pain and constantly asking after his wife.

George set off alone down the gully to see if he could get a rope to the men below the waterfall. Willie was pleading over the radio for them to come up. A helicopter had arrived in Fort William from RAF Kinloss but was grounded on the car park. They were keeping the engines running and we knew they would come at the slightest clearance, but in these conditions there was no chance.

Sometime later George arrived back plastered in snow. 'It's hopeless, you can't see a bloody thing,' he said despondently. 'There's no way they'll get up in this. I managed to get within shouting distance of the boys but this snow is blinding. It's a waste of time!'

We were all very cold, Willie and I in the bivvy bags at least had some shelter, and George was stamping about in the open trying to keep warm. It was an endless night, shivering with cold and feeling utterly inadequate and defeated. Gabrielle died quietly while I was holding her. I didn't say anything but noticed that John had stopped asking how she was and must have realised how hopeless our situation was.

At first light the RAF arrived. As usual they came as soon as it was humanly possible, risking all and flying in through narrow gaps in the cloud. Within minutes we were winched up and flown down to the waiting ambulance in the West End car park.

I was terribly sorry for John who would have to face the world without his new wife. Time and again I have wondered if we could have done better. What if we'd left a fixed rope up the side of the waterfall? Should we have left the casualties and tried to get a rope down to the rest of the team? Perhaps we could have rigged up some kind of lower ourselves. What if, what if?

It's hard in retrospect to know what was the right thing to do. At the time we were hoping against hope that the helicopter would get to us, but that's always a second line of defence in mountain rescue situations. I was terribly upset by the whole episode and felt personally responsible that we failed to get Gabrielle to hospital. Mostly in mountain rescue situations we remain detached from the personalities involved. There is plenty to do without worrying about the effects on the family and friends and once the call-out is over we slip off quietly and leave that to the hospital and police. In this case I had felt very close to Gabrielle and John and that whole terrible night still haunts me.

Five Finger Gully is a very dangerous place. Some years later I was involved in my own private rescue there. On New Year's Eve 1986 both the Lochaber and Glencoe rescue teams were involved in a difficult call-out on Beinn a Bheithir, the lovely mountain above the Ballachulish Bridge. For some reason I arrived late; all the teams were already on the mountain and I was just starting up when a call came over my radio asking if anybody was available to guide a helicopter into Five Finger. I offered my services and jumped aboard an RAF Sea King. As it was New Year the crew were a stand-in unit, inexperienced in mountain flying, and the pilot, quite rightly, was taking things very slowly and carefully.

We flew into the gully, the powerful searchlights of the chopper lighting up the big, snow-filled basin almost like daylight and it was easy to see two figures lying in the snow almost in the same place that I had spent that terrible night with the newlywed couple. One of them was waving frantically.

I was hitched on to the winch and the helicopter eased in towards the slope. At the winchman's signal I swung out and had a terrible shock. We were still well out from the face and I was hanging about 500 feet above the mountainside. I dangled there very frightened as the chopper eased me slowly into the basin. It finally dropped me on a steep wind-slab snow slope about 200 yards from the casualties and I began kicking steps across the slope, scared of setting off an avalanche.

Much to my surprise the winchman came down and followed me. He was dressed in aircrew overalls, and wearing a pair of soft-soled aircrew boots, and he had no ice axe or crampons. He unclipped from the winch and started slipping and sliding across this very dangerous snow towards me. I managed to get over to him and asked him, in no uncertain terms, to get back to the helicopter. He was quick on the uptake and was winched up almost immediately. I then managed to climb across the slope and reach the casualties.

The man sitting in the snow was Andy Fanshawe. I knew him slightly: a competent, young mountaineer on the staff of the British Mountaineering Council. His friend was dead. Andy had a broken leg but was very

TOP Riccardo Cassin in Roybridge with Suds and me. What he really wanted was a shot at a stag! BOTTOM Eiger. John Barry and Dave Nichols at the Swallow's Nest bivvy.

TOP Suds lugging up snow fencing in early tests on the Snow Goose on Aonach Mor.
BOTTOM The Briton portable ski-tow on Aonach Mor, during our helicopter day, 1986.

TOP LEFT Nevis Range car park during the construction of the ski area.   TOP RIGHT The mountain transformed into something that resembled a ski field.   BOTTOM LEFT Alphons Mattis, the Austrian site manager, running the Gondola cables.   BOTTOM RIGHT Willie Anderson digging tower foundations in the snow-covered frozen ground.

TOP Our Kässbohrer winch-cat heads into the back corrie at Nevis Range.   BOTTOM The Queen meets me and Ian Jones at the opening of Nevis Range.   OPPOSITE PAGE The Lotus Flower Tower. The climb takes a central line up to the tiny snow ledge then follows the line between sun and shadow.

LEFT Lotus Flower Tower upper wall from the snowy ledge.
RIGHT Smiler Cuthbertson trailblazing through waist-deep snow below the tower.

TOP The administration offices in Central Square, Kemerovo.   BOTTOM The gulag in Tashtagol.

TOP Valeri Maltser and the Sheregesh ski lift above Tashtagol. All was not as it appeared. BOTTOM LEFT A fallen lift tower on the Sheregesh ski slopes. BOTTOM RIGHT Bridge over the Mras-Su River, built by convicts from the gulag. OPPOSITE PAGE, TOP LEFT Almost impenetrable jungle protects the hidden valleys of Cochamo in Chile. OPPOSITE PAGE, TOP RIGHT Dave Clem managed to land in a tiny clearing, his blades missing the trees by inches. OPPOSITE PAGE, BOTTOM The summit of Pico Eilidh just before the storm.

OPPOSITE PAGE, TOP Jungle bashing in Cochamo, the bamboo-filled rainforest was almost impenetrable.
OPPOSITE PAGE, BOTTOM Huge polished slabs of granite overlooking Lago Ness.   ABOVE The huge 5,000-foot
wall of El Condor (El Monstruo). This is possibly the world's tallest unbroken granite wall. The volcano Tronador
and Cerro Trinidad in the background.

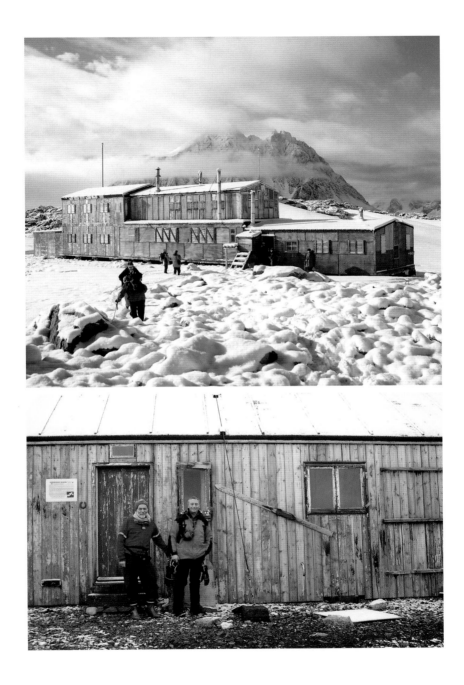

OPPOSITE PAGE, TOP LEFT Tony Howard in Wadi Rum. A living guidebook. OPPOSITE PAGE, TOP RIGHT Dave Pierce on the Tignes dam just before our arrest. OPPOSITE PAGE, BOTTOM Wadi Rum. Great glaciers of sand running between perfect rock walls. THIS PAGE, TOP Stonington Island base, Antarctica, derelict and boarded up. BOTTOM Ian Curphey and I outside our old base on Horseshoe Island in 2002, forty years after our time at the base with the Survey.

TOP The horses in Wind River Range, Wyoming, seemed to know what they were doing.
BOTTOM Eilidh avoiding mosquitos in Wind River Range. OPPOSITE PAGE, RIGHT Pingora Peak,
Wind River Range. Pitch after pitch of superb rock.

Our horses arrived spot on time to take us home.

composed and under control. The two men had done a hard climb on the North Face and then made the same error that we all make at the top of Five Finger Gully.

I now discovered that the RAF helicopter's radio was on a different frequency to my police radio set. The chopper was circling with its lights blazing but I had no way of talking to it. Luckily I managed to contact Fort William police station who telephoned RAF Pitreavie Castle in Perthshire who radioed the pilot and relayed my message. This radio problem with the military took years to resolve and was always a frustration.

I strapped Andy's broken leg to his good one and splinted them with his ice axe.

'How do you feel about being winched up like this,' I asked.

'I'm fine,' he said, gritting his teeth. 'Let's do it.'

The helicopter winched up his dead friend first. A macabre task that must have been very distressing for Andy, but he remained composed throughout. The winchman came down to help him on to the cable and up he went. Within minutes he was in the Belford Hospital and the whole rescue couldn't have taken more than an hour from start to finish.

I called in to the hospital the following day. Andy was very despondent as the dead man was his best friend, John Taylor. Nevertheless, within four months he was climbing again. He continued with an expedition to Melungtse with Chris Bonington and climbed its west peak with Alan Hinkes, and the following year led a trip to Makalu while in-between making lightning raids on the big Alpine walls of the Eiger and Croz Spur. He died after a fall on Lochnagar's Eagle Ridge in 1992.

Regular visitors to Callop were Don Whillans, the Villain as he was known, and his friend and self-imposed minder, Barry Kershaw. Barry, or Dobber Kershaw as he was known, was great fun but a desperado and terribly dangerous to be with when alcohol was involved. He was a steeplejack by trade and earned a living dropping factory chimneys.

His standard dress in all weathers was an open shirt to the waist with a shark's tooth pendant dangling on his hairy chest. We had the tendency of driving rather fast in those days and Barry had the frightening habit of suddenly covering the driver's eyes on a particularly bendy bit of road, with terrifying results. We never actually smashed the car but ditched on a number of occasions.

Don had missed out on a trip to Everest and was getting a fair bit of sympathy from the press. The Triumph motorcycle company had designed a new Bonneville bike for off-road use and asked him to ride it up Ben Nevis as a publicity stunt. The bike was far too big for the job and Don's feet could hardly reach the ground but he sat astride the bike while a small group of us pushed and heaved the monster up the Ben path.

Don sat comfortably on the bike, shouting encouragement like a Roman charioteer. It was a desperately hot day. We pushed and heaved the entire 4,000 feet. The bike was far too heavy and not designed for this kind of terrain and was of little use in powering us on. When we finally staggered to the summit a cameraman produced a bottle of Champagne which Don proceeded to swig in its entirety while the rest of us looked thirstily on in consternation. I could have murdered him.

I had married in the early days at Callop. It had been a difficult place for a girl to live and we had got along badly and the marriage had broken up quite quickly – I was devastated. That Christmas I went home to my mother's house in Leeds to lick my wounds.

Mum was very understanding and didn't ask too many questions and I planned to take her out for a meal on Christmas Day. On Christmas Eve there was a knock on the door and there stood Don and Barry. The Villain was holding a huge, five-gallon bottle of wine that he had acquired from a company that had sponsored him.

'We heard that things weren't too good, Spike, so we've come to take you out!' Don said. 'I'm not going to open this bottle unless we finish it.'

There followed one of the most outrageous nights I can remember. We started out at their favourite pub, The Shoulder of Mutton on the moors above Hebden Bridge, and a group of us finished up at Barry's home in Halifax where he kept a blacksmith's anvil in the living room. His party piece was to lift the anvil above his head; it must have weighed about three-hundredweight. I had a go but was unable to move the thing, but Don hefted it up with apparent ease. Barry, determined not to be outdone, managed to get it up to shoulder height and then dropped it. There was a tremendous crash and it went right through the floor and down into the cellar.

We all peered down the hole in alarm but Barry seemed more concerned at how to retrieve the anvil than the appalling mess he had made of his home. At some time in the early hours of Christmas Day they bundled me in to a taxi and I made it home to bed and slept through the entire day. My mother never got her Christmas dinner that year.

14 | A Mandarin Murder

The usual watering hole of the Lochaber Mountain Rescue Team was the Nevis Bank Hotel at the entrance to Glen Nevis. I was having a quiet pint one evening when I overheard a local businessman talking to his friends. Ronnie MacLeod was a shrewd old crofter who was jokingly famed in Fort William for having trouble making ends meet, the 'ends' being the properties in the High Street, most of which he owned.

'Someone's going to get that site at the east end of the High Street and then we'll all be buggered, it's the best spot in town,' he said.

I couldn't think where he meant but the following day I wandered along to the east end of the High Street and there it was. A piece of waste ground that had once been the site of the 'hanging tree' and was only used when the fair came to town for the dodgems and waltzers and suchlike. Unused and spot in line with the centre of the street, I realised that this could be a marvellous position for a shop as the focal point of the town.

The land belonged to British Rail and had once been an old railway siding until the station had been moved to its new site. The town council had a legal agreement that it could not be sold privately. Finding out who to negotiate with in a massive railway bureaucracy that didn't even know it owned the land was a nightmare. How we survived the next two years negotiating with BR and the council, raising the money to buy the land and build the shop, I find barely credible. We hocked everything we had; our friend Alex Smith, who ultimately became our financial adviser and confidante, helped put together a team to purchase the land with a quantity surveyor and architect for the design work. We put our old shop on the market and committed ourselves to fate.

David Meek, an architect based in Oban, had a real creative flair – the octagonal shape he designed was radical for a Highland town and we had trouble convincing the planners. As well as catering for the climbers we incorporated a restaurant and gift shop. The latter was worrying as we did not wish to spoil our technical image but interestingly it was never a problem. Many of the climbers were on holiday leaving long-suffering wives at home. It was a good place to purchase gifts to purge their guilt. It also allowed me to pursue my interest in books and maps and we began to build up a reference library of climbing guides.

Among our early customers was Walter Poucher, the well-known mountain photographer and guidebook writer. Walter, by then an old man, was a one-off. As well as his writing he was the chief perfumer at Yardley's. Highly eccentric, he still wore the breeches and red socks of the sixties along with plenty of lipstick and rouge and gold lame gloves. One of his moments of glory was being the other guest on the Russell Harty TV chat show in 1981 when Grace Jones jumped on Harty's back when he tried to ignore her. Janet Street-Porter described Walter as 'a fully paid-up member of the British Academy of Potty People'.

Nonetheless, he was a master of the Leica camera and would be in the mountains at 4 a.m. to get the perfect light for his photographs, his guidebooks always sold out straight away. He did a number of book signings for us and I spent happy hours listening to his outrageous stories.

By the time we moved into our new premises Britain's fortunes had changed. It was the so called 'Year of Discontent' – the government was at war with the unions and there were strikes everywhere, many businesses were on a three-day working week and there were almost daily power cuts. The new shop was over twice the size of the old one but our income hardly increased and we were struggling to pay off the loans.

Fort William was in an abysmal state; the pulp mill closed with a loss of almost 2,000 jobs and the British Aluminium factory was bailed out by the government, modernised and ultimately sold to the Canadian minerals corporation Alcan. The modernisation reduced the workforce from 1,750 to about 350. In a small town of only 11,000 people, almost 3,000 were out of work, shops closed and the High Street looked derelict. We were no exception; throughout the whole of Britain companies began folding one after the next.

Many of the workers in the pulp mill had moved from the cities to start a new life in the Highlands. For a while Fort William had the highest suicide rate of any town in Europe, there was no point in leaving as there appeared to be no work anywhere. Something had to be done.

In a desperate bid for ideas a meeting was held in the Mercury Hotel under the auspices of the town council and its energetic and enthusiastic chief executive, David Blair. All local businesses were invited – garage owners, lawyers, forestry, shops, estate personnel, and so on.

Nevisport had just started to sell ski equipment. Neither Suds or I were very experienced skiers, we much preferred mountaineering but felt we ought to understand what we were selling and had recently carried our skis up Aonach Mor, one of the Ben Nevis range of mountains, and had been amazed at the size of its snowfields.

On impulse I got to my feet still bursting with enthusiasm about our local snowfields and suggested that we could build a ski resort on Aonach Mor, enthusing that the Forestry Commission could build a road up to the snowline and perhaps we could attract Reo Stakis or one of the big hotel companies to invest in the project. Reo Stakis was a high-flying Greek hotel owner and entrepreneur in Glasgow and seemed an ideal candidate at the time. Much to my surprise there was a general murmur of assent and the suggestion was put on to a list of possibilities. I had no idea that the proposal to build the ski resort would become a burning obsession that would put me at odds with many of my friends in the climbing world and the controversial project would begin a ten-year battle with the government. At that time a committee was formed with the intention of looking into the various options and trying to take the idea forward.

We managed to get out of the financial problems by selling our Aviemore shop. We had spent months converting an old croft at the end of the High Street into a nice little climbing shop and it was a terrible wrench letting it go but the recession was awful and there was nothing else we could do.

An unforeseen problem occurred at our Glasgow store. It was a bitterly cold winter and the shop closed at New Year for its annual Hogmanay bash. Apart from liquor stores and pubs the city has a long history of closing down and entering into a two or three-day drinking spree. This year was no exception and Ian Smith, the manager, Biggles as he is known, locked up as usual and went home to join the revelry.

Our shop in Sauchiehall Street was on the edge of Chinatown. On the three floors above us was the Mandarin Chinese restaurant with whom we shared the back stairwell. The proprietor was Mr Wong, a classic Chinese gentleman, bald with a topknot. We knew that his restaurant was really a front for an illegal gambling den; the top two floors were filled with mah-jong and roulette tables and suchlike. There was always a strange smoky smell about the place that we took to be opium or dope. The Glasgow police kept a wary eye on them but we never had any trouble and turned a blind eye to the goings on in our back stairwell and upper floors.

As Glasgow closed down for Hogmanay we were called to an accident on Creag Meagaidh. A climber had taken a nasty fall from 1959 *Face Route* and was hanging on his rope with back injuries. Both the Fort William and Cairngorm teams were called out. Bill March, one of the instructors from Glenmore Lodge, and I clambered out along Tom Patey's famous *Crab Crawl*. It was relatively easy climbing kicking steps leftwards along the steep snow traverse, but with near-vertical walls above and below us it was a very airy and frightening situation. Suds and Molly Porter (the Cairngorm team leader) kept the mountain in almost permanent daylight by firing off parachute flairs one after the other and the whole of Coire Ardair lit up in a strange half-light that extenuated the steepness. It would have been very exciting except for the urgency of the situation. When we reached the injured man he was in a very bad way. It was a horrible place but we managed to rig a safe belay and were able to very carefully lower him down to the team below.

It was a long and difficult night and the stretcher carry down to the road at the side of Loch Laggan seemed to take forever. We got back to Suds' home in Roybridge at about 9 a.m. and were just sitting down to a cup of tea when the phone rang. It was Biggles, our manager in Glasgow.

'There's a problem here. The Chinese restaurant above our shop turned its heating off over the holiday and all their pipes have burst. We're flooded out, the ceiling has fallen in and there's one hell of a mess!'

There was going to be no rest for us. Leaving Suds to hold the fort I set off immediately on treacherous roads following snowploughs across Rannoch Moor and reached Glasgow as it was getting dark. When I finally got to the shop I had a terrible shock. There was no electricity and Biggles had lit up some paraffin lamps. The boys were in the process of tearing up the waterlogged carpets; our stock was lying under heaps of soaking wet plasterboard and water was still pouring down from the ceiling. The basement was totally flooded. It was like a scene from a ghastly movie.

I'd been on the go for almost thirty-six hours and my brain just couldn't take it in. I had no idea what to do so I went back out into Sauchiehall Street, bought a bottle of whisky and a large box of cigars and went back in.

'Not much more you can do here, Biggles, let's have a party.' I said, uncorking the bottle.

It was a surprisingly cheerful evening. Everybody was absolutely filthy, soaking wet and covered with plaster. The staff had done an amazing job trying to rescue some of our stock and had been on the go since the early hours. We sat round in the squalor of our devastated shop and laughed hysterically at the chaos. There wasn't much else we could do until the water drained out of the ceiling and we could get a pump going in the basement.

Surprisingly we managed to open again within the week. The place was in a dreadful state but we held a water damaged sale. Glaswegians are always up for a bargain and we managed to clear the damaged stock but it was some months before things returned to normal. I spent many months arguing with the insurance company and although they finally paid up it was very little in compensation for our losses.

This wasn't quite the end of the story. Some months later we managed to purchase the whole building in Sauchiehall Street and planned to expand into the upper floors. Mr Wong kept the Mandarin restaurant running right up to the last gasp, in fact right up to his very last gasp. The morning we were to take over the upper floors we discovered that the restaurant, although closed, was still set up and ready to open. All the tables were set and the kitchen was still fully stocked and the bar full of drink. We were not sure what to do, shop fitters were ready to start modifying the building. I managed to contact Mr Wong's accountants who assured me that he had left the premises. It turned out that most of the fittings were rented. We set about sorting out the mess when about mid-afternoon two police officers arrived in the shop and demanded to see me.

'Do you know Mr Wong?' they asked.

'Yes,' I said and worriedly explained what had happened and what we were doing with the contents of his restaurant.

'Would you mind coming with us?' they asked, and I was taken across Sauchiehall Street to a taped-off area on Garnet Hill about fifty yards away.

There was Mr Wong; he was tied to the railings at the road side. Both the arteries in his groin had been opened and he had been emptied out on to the pavement. His topknot had been removed so that his soul couldn't go to heaven, indicative of a Chinese Triad murder. From then on we always treated our Chinese neighbours with the utmost respect, and as far as I know the culprits have never been found.

Our troubles were far from over. For the last few years the Lochaber rescue boys had spent the Whitsuntide bank holiday climbing on the sea cliffs at Mealister Point on the Isle of Lewis, at a time when the weather was usually glorious. The guide, Mick Tighe, was the main instigator and there were few people who knew the secret crags in the Outer Hebrides as well as Mick. We camped on the beautiful white Uig sands where there were miles of superb, unclimbed sea cliffs, a climber's dream with the possibility of new routes of all standards.

The star of the show was Jock Finnen, the Nevisport joiner, a mighty man who had served his time in the Glasgow shipyards. He was the old style of weekender, a singer of songs, poacher and beer-swigging teller of amazing stories. Mick and Jock were perfect foils for each other, the former a superb rock climber and the latter very strong and determined not to be outdone.

On this last trip we had a large contingent of Nevisport staff, the usual suspects from Fort William, GL from our Glasgow shop along with our manager from Altrincham, Jim Moran, a well-known gritstone ace and Dave (Cubby) Cuthbertson who was at the time the finest rock climber in Scotland. Dozens of new routes sprang up the cliffs, which have now become a classic rock climbing area.

The euphoria of this great week's climbing was soon to turn very sour; Suds and I returned to a series of events that shook the company. We had noticed that our Glasgow shop had been losing stock at a much higher level than normal. Shoplifting was rife in the city but it was hard to believe that the amount we were losing was not an inside job. This was before the days of computerised tills and we were uncertain which department was the culprit.

With the help of the Glasgow police we set up a watch from a room in Trerons, a large department store across the road. The managers, Biggles Smith and Robert Ferrell, took the day off, leaving the shop unattended, and joined the police on watch in Trerons. It wasn't long before GL and two other staff members left the shop. GL vanished into the crowd but the other two were apprehended; both were carrying rucksacks full of climbing gear. GL was lifted on his return and the police found a railway luggage locker key in his pocket and on searching it discovered a veritable hoard of our climbing equipment.

The police kept the boys apart for questioning and the full story began to emerge. By that evening we discovered that both the Glasgow and Fort William shops were involved. In a Fort William flat we discovered a stack of mountaineering boots and altogether recovered about £6,000 worth of goods. We also found that our mail order department had been sending large quantities of goods to a climber in Leeds University known as the Brat, the inside joke being that Nevisport paid the postage. Some of the people involved had been with us on the fabulous climbing trip to the Isle of Lewis the previous week – it was terribly upsetting. It's bad enough being robbed, but when it's by folks you consider your friends it can be doubly disappointing. GL, the youngest person involved, turned out to be the ringleader and was put on probation. I hope he learned his lesson.

All in all we survived the loss but it was a hard lesson and we tightened up our systems. It's a funny thing that robbing climbing shops seems to be fair game to many young climbers, not just at home but also on the continent. Snell's wonderfully friendly shop in Chamonix, where we were able to get up to date information about new climbs, was a prime target as were the local supermarkets. It's a sad reflection on our sport that although many young mountaineers are world class our status is tarnished by a reputation for thieving.

Not long afterwards I was involved in a very bizarre call-out. One of the mountains in the Creag Meagaidh group on the west side of Loch Laggan is Beinn a' Chaorainn, a fairly innocuous Munro with one nice scrambly ridge and a large, flat summit plateau that curves around two steep corries.

For some reason it is an accident black spot; huge cornices build out over the corrie edges and a simple navigational error can be fatal. On this occasion a father and his son were out in poor visibility and strayed too close to the edge and the father dropped through the snow leaving a neat hole in the cornice. The son frantically shouted down the hole but heard nothing but the wind and finally set off as fast as he could to raise the alarm.

His father had fallen about 300 feet down a steep slope and landed unhurt in a drift of deep powder snow. With little difficulty he could have easily scrambled down into the corrie but he was disoriented and decided to stay where he was. An hour or so later another lone hillwalker, following the same set of tracks, did exactly the same thing. The man sitting below thought he was being avalanched as the second man dropped in beside him. Some time later another party passed and this time a dog fell through the cornice and joined the party sitting in the snowdrift below – and there they all sat, awaiting rescue.

An hour or two later a party of us walking up into the corrie were perplexed to hear shouts and barking and found the group sitting like three wise monkeys in a pile of snow in the bottom of the corrie. This humorous and happy outcome was not always the case.

A year later in almost the same place a similar accident occurred. A man and his son walking round the same corrie stepped too close to the edge and the father fell through the cornice. In the ensuing search there was no sign of him. For almost a week we hunted a vast area in the hope that he had wandered away from the mountain but to no avail. We probed the snow slope where he fell but found nothing and the search was finally called off. When the melt came in the spring we looked again and there was still no sign of the man but it had been a heavy snow winter and that summer the corrie still held an almost permanent snowfield.

Coincidentally, at the same time the newspapers were full of the Fred West murders and the police searching in his garden used the newly invented ground-penetrating radar for the first time to search for bodies. Hamish MacInnes, never one to miss a trick, contacted the university with the radar and persuaded one of the scientists to bring up his equipment and help us search for the missing climber. We trudged up Beinn a' Chaorainn lugging a sledge rigged up with a large box of tricks, some car batteries and an oscilloscope and spent several hours sceptically hauling the sledge across the snow with Hamish enthusiastically shouting encouragement.

Staring at anomalies on his screen the scientist signalled us to a spot almost directly below where the man was thought to have fallen and sure enough about six feet down we dug out the body. As far as I know this was the first time this kind equipment was used in a mountain situation and at least some good came out of the Fred West murders and the family were able to retrieve their loved one.

That summer, Nick Banks, his wife Lindsey, my girlfriend Carol and I had a very successful Alpine trip. We went first to the Bregaglia, on the Swiss-Italian border, and managed a number of climbs in the area culminating with a wintery ascent of Riccardo Cassin's marvellous route on the North Face of the Piz Badile.

Realising that we were on good form we decided that there was never going to be a better chance to have a go at the North Face of the Eiger. We drove to Grindelwald, took the funicular railway to Alpiglen station, and pitched our tents below the mountain's colossal North Face. The following day we climbed the west flank of the Eiger to get a good look at things and check out the descent route. The face was enormous and although it was August, that year it was in a very wintery condition which suited our climbing technique.

The following afternoon Nick and I left the women camping on the grassy alp below the wall and walked up to the foot of the face. We were unsure where to start and messed around for a while before getting on to the obvious route where there was loads of tat and old pitons. From here we made rapid progress up the Shattered Pillar and Difficult Crack and then traversed below the startlingly steep wall of the Rote Flüh and reached the famous Hinterstoisser tension traverse.

It's normal here to leave a back rope in case of a retreat, but we had none to spare so crossed anyway, pulled down our rope and got committed. A short pitch later we reached the Swallow's Nest bivouac site where sat two familiar characters, John Barry and Dave Nichols. The usual shallow cave and ledge were covered in ice and did not exist. John and Dave had already taken the only reasonable ledge so we made the customary abusive greeting and moved out on to the First Icefield, cut a large bucket ledge and settled down for the night.

It's impossible for anyone who has read Heinrich Harrer's book *The White Spider* not to be awestruck by the myth of the Eiger. What Harrer didn't say, however, was how stunningly beautiful the climb is. While we were at that bivouac the mountain was encased in a gleaming winter coat and there were none of the famous rocks whistling down the icefields. Here was a silent vertical world of rock and ice and I sat spellbound in a huge glittering amphitheatre hanging out over the Bernese Oberland munching a slab of smoked German bacon and feeling very content.

Somewhere not far below us must be the Gallery window where the Jungfraubahn cog railway tunnel has a viewing point and is a possible escape route from the face. We were climbing using twin 200-foot, hawser-laid nylon ropes and felt confident that we had enough rope to reach this should we be forced to retreat.

During the night it rained and at one point a rush of water poured down the First Icefield soaking us and our bivouac bags. John and Dave fared somewhat better on their perch at the Swallow's Nest; they breakfasted and vanished upwards leaving us wringing out our wet sleeping bags. We finally made our way up the First Icefield and then the Ice Hose, which proved to be like good Scottish ice, on to the huge 1,800-foot Second Icefield. Our Terrordactyls were excellent for this kind of climbing but our wet sleeping gear was heavy and I found myself dreading the thought of another one or two nights out.

We had hoped to finish the climb in a single day from the Swallow's Nest but this was not going to happen. We could see the steep rocks of the Ramp were covered in ice and we were moving very slowly. We were almost two thirds of the way up the face but the hard part was yet to come and we had almost reached the point of no return. It was debatable that it would be quicker to complete the climb, a retreat would be huge, by far the longest I had ever made.

We stopped and made a brew and discussed the situation. It's always a hard decision to retreat but forward was unknown territory and we reluctantly decided to turn back. Almost immediately as we started to descend a helicopter flew in close and signalled to see if we were okay – somebody had been watching over us. We waved cheerily back indicating that we didn't require assistance and set off on the enormous descent. Making rapid progress down the Second Icefield we abseiled the Ice Hose and reached our bivouac site at the Swallow's Nest in good time. There was plenty of ice on the Hinterstoisser Traverse and I managed to move back across and hook my Terrordactyl into some very ancient tat on the far side and risking all, swung across to safety.

From here it was a long but relatively easy descent to the foot of the face. We joined the women in the tents at dusk, surprising ourselves that we didn't have to spend another night out. Any sensible mountaineers would have called it a day but we were tired and thirsty and decided to walk down to Alpiglen station for a meal. It was about a thousand feet below us and a short walk along the railway line below the avalanche barriers. They had stopped serving food when we reached the station but readily sold us a couple of bottles of wine, which we devoured with relish. That was when our troubles really began.

We tottered out of the station bar into the night, none of us having thought to take a torch. In total darkness we felt our way back along the railway line but we had not the slightest idea how to find our way up the alp to our tents. The women were furious, but tiredness and alcohol had finally taken its toll and Nick and I could only stagger about stupidly. After various sorties up the alp we finally lurched back to the railway line and huddled together for the night under one of the avalanche barriers. Sometime in the early hours of the morning the moon rose and we shivered our way up the hillside to the tents and at last collapsed into our sleeping bags, it had been a very long day. It might have been safer to remain on the Eiger; the haranguing we got from Lindsey and Carol when we belatedly surfaced the following morning was far more dangerous.

So ended my attempt at the Eiger. John Barry and Dave Nichols had two more bivouacs and had great difficulty breaking out of the Exit Cracks but completed the climb safely. I feel we made the right decision in retreating but it was a bitter disappointment. Nick Banks successfully climbed the face the following year.

15 | The Snow Goose

I had this dream to transform a very beautiful mountain into a ski area but was acutely aware that I may be spoiling the very thing that I loved. Scottish climbers had an indifferent attitude to skiers and many of them thought that ski development was invading the wild country. This may well be true but I felt that this was hardly an isolated mountain and that recreation for people was as important as conservation. There were only four ski areas in Scotland. By comparison, Austria has 700 areas in a much smaller region than the Highlands and I would argue that it is hardly spoiled.

By 1980 Fort William was in decline. The recession had devastated the High Street which was scattered with empty shops, the Town Hall burned down – uninsured and was never replaced, and the cinema closed because it was a safety hazard. The A9 road up the east coast of Scotland to Inverness was upgraded while our trunk road to the west, the A82, was in an abysmal state of repair; part of it fell into Loch Lomond and for the last thirty-five years it has remained single track there with passing places and traffic lights. (As a publicity stunt a thirtieth birthday party was held at these traffic lights where the road collapsed and we held up drivers who were treated to a piece of birthday cake.)

Meanwhile, the towns in the east had prospered: Inverness became a booming city, enjoying the fastest growth in Europe while eating up the resources of the rest of the Highlands and leaving towns like Oban, Fort William and some of the islands to rot. In a country whose highest earning industry is tourism this has to be the result of a series of bad government decisions.

The committee formed to look into the possibility of building a ski area was flagging. People drifted away and our occasional meetings turned into an annual event. We bemoaned our lot and wondered why 'they', the mythical powers that be, didn't do something about it.

On an impulse I rang Sir Bob Cowan, Chairman of the Highlands and Islands Development Board (HIDB), and asked if I could have a word with him and he kindly invited me to his home in the village of Farr in the beautiful Strathnairn Valley just south of Inverness. He was a charming man with his heart firmly entrenched in the Highlands.

'How much would we need to raise ourselves if we were to start a small ski area?' I asked after first explaining my plan for a forestry road up the mountain with a cafe and two ski tows to start things off.

'You find me a million pounds and we'll talk turkey,' he told me kindly.

I drove south from Farr feeling glum and defeated – where the hell would I be able to find that kind of money? That evening I despondently talked it over with Ian Milton. Ian owned a group of Highland hotels and was a Fort William man, born and bred, and knew almost everybody in the Highland business world.

'How much could Nevisport raise?' he asked me.

'I think we could scrape up about £300,000,' I stammered, exaggerating, and wondering where on earth it would come from.

'Okay, I'll match that and we're halfway there,' he said. 'I'll go round the town and see who else might come in.'

Ian was as good as his word and with a bit of arm twisting a number of local businesses came on board. Alistair MacLeod, a local financier, and Tommy Wynne, the butcher, and many others. It was a wonderful feeling to find that so many townspeople were behind us. Within the week I was driving back to the HIDB in Inverness with a million pounds in promises and ready to call their bluff.

It was a disappointing meeting; far from being welcomed with open arms, two young economists gave me a very dismissive grilling and it seemed clear that the HIDB had already discussed the project and given it an emphatic thumbs down. I returned to the Fort as glum as ever. I think now, had I known the difficulties that we were going to face over the next ten years,

I would have packed the scheme in there and then and got on with life.

Almost all the residents of Fort William and the local district council were in favour of the idea, as was the ski fraternity. Scottish skiers were suffering from long queues on the ski lifts and it was felt that another area was desperately needed. We were not alone though, there were plans afoot from three other would-be developers: Ben Wyvis, just north of Inverness; Dalwhinnie Corries above the Drumochter Pass; and the existing main ski area at Cairngorm that was trying to extend into Lurcher's Gully.

The government, HIDB, Nature Conservancy and Highland Council were all resolutely against our project. The Highland Roads Department vigorously opposed us. They were protecting a limited budget and rightly guessed that a new road would have to be constructed and realised that my idea that the Forestry Commission could build the road would almost certainly be rejected.

Strangely enough the other ski companies were generally on our side. Scottish skiing was in its ascendancy; the winters of the late seventies and early eighties were excellent with plenty of snow and long periods of cold fine weather. It was before the days of cheap flights and few people could afford the luxury of a foreign ski holiday. The big problem was overcrowding; at Cairngorm and Glenshee it was possible to spend a whole day standing in lift queues and only managing three or four runs.

It wasn't all doom and gloom, Suds and I were still climbing most of the time and occasionally skiing at Glencoe where the uplift system was very primitive. It had a single-seat chairlift up to the plateau and then a long walk up to the three upper lifts. Nonetheless it was a lovely place to ski with a great variety of runs. They had no piste-bashers and the runs had to be beaten down by the skiers, but it had a distinct Scottish flavour and was a great place to learn.

We still had to get on with Nevisport, which continued to expand. An amusing incident happened at that time when Riccardo Cassin, the great

Italian mountaineer, did a lecture tour. We had become the UK agents for Cassin climbing equipment and organised the Scottish venues. Riccardo spoke no English and lectured with a translator. At the time he was in his late seventies.

During the war he had been the leader of the partisans in the Italian Dolomites and apart from mountaineering, his other great passion was hunting.

'I much preferred shooting Germans to deer,' he joked.

At the end of his tour the translator left and Riccardo stayed at Suds' home in Roybridge for the weekend where he spent much of the time chasing my mother around the kitchen table. Language became a serious difficulty!

We organised a clay-pigeon shoot for him. He was a great shot but he kept holding his hands up to his ears and wiggling his fingers and I suddenly realised that he was signalling antlers and what he really wanted was a shot at a stag.

In Scotland, stalking was out of season and, anyway, it's done on private hunting estates, but undeterred we organised a day with 'Shotgun', a local poacher, who took Riccardo out on the hills above Glen Roy. It was miles up the mountainside before Shotgun got him within range of a big stag. Riccardo was a good shot and got it okay but we then had a long haul into the night dragging the carcass back to Roybridge. The old man's knees were bothering him terribly by the time we got him home. The next day we put him on to the plane back to his home in Lecco, Italy, a happy man with a large haunch of venison hidden in his luggage.

Suds had the antlers mounted with Riccardo's name and the place and date of the shoot and we presented this to him that autumn on the Cassin stand at the international trade fair in Munich. The Italian press went wild and we were photographed with the old poacher holding the antlers triumphantly in the air. The pictures were headlines in the Italian newspapers with Suds and I looking rather sheepish in the background and hoping they were never seen in Scotland.

One of the greatest mountaineers of the twentieth century, Riccardo continued to climb well into old age. In 1987 on the fiftieth anniversary of his famous ascent of the North Face of the Piz Badile, he repeated the climb. For some reason the Italian newspapers did not believe he had done it so a week later he did it again. He was seventy-eight! He died in 2009 having celebrated his one-hundredth birthday.

The ski project moved along very slowly but by the mid-eighties our plans had advanced considerably. Michel Mercier, the very determined sales-man for Poma ski lifts, had taken me out to France and introduced me to a number of experts – Suds and I were getting a better idea of how to lay out a ski area. A more accurate set of drawings showing the possible line of ski lifts was taking shape and our architect friend, David Meek, started the designs of the cafe.

We took on the engineering firm Halcrow as consultants, at the outra-geous cost of £400,000, to look into the viability of the project. It seemed a ludicrous waste of money to prove the figures that we had already worked out, especially as most of the consultants knew nothing of the ski in-dustry; the HIDB were covering their backs. Such is government; in the eighties consultancy was absolutely the business to be in.

Alcan, the Canadian mineral corporation, owned the mountain, and 300 square miles of surrounding country which is the water catchment to power the hydro turbine for their aluminium works. The manage-ment of the factory put every possible difficulty in our way to prevent the scheme; their chief engineer, Jim Roebottom, was nervous that we might cause erosion above the intakes for their hydro scheme. Our assurance that we would be skiing on snow above the ground surface and we would not infringe on the main water collecting areas did little to placate him.

The beautiful unused narrow-gauge railway line running to Loch Treig passed through the area we wished to rent and the local council were keen to invest in opening it up to the public. In what I believe to be a piece of mindless vandalism the company ripped up the lines and destroyed the bridges making any future tourist development out of the question.

In another attempt to stop the project, Scottish National Heritage (SNH) designated the mountain a Site of Special Scientific Interest (SSSI) and claimed that it was the habitat of golden plover and that there was an interesting and rare moss on the summit. It was certainly interesting as it was the same stuff that was messing up my lawn. We lost a year and several thousand pounds having a bird survey done to prove that there were no golden plover and found that SNH already knew this. Their argument was that it was the kind of country in which the bird might nest. This argument didn't do them much good as even the Highland Council realised that this was ridiculous.

As the objections grew in ferocity I became more and more determined; I didn't mind people having fair-minded opposing views, but some of the venomous attacks on the ski industry were outrageous.

It is impossible to detail all our ups and downs during the nine years it took to convince the powers that be, and for us to find the ten or twelve million pounds that it took to make the Snow Goose fly, but there are one or two highlights that are worth the telling.

Throughout most of this period the Conservatives were in power at Westminster and in principle were neither for nor against the project. Scotland is anything but Tory and as they had no MPs to act for the Highlands, the work was undertaken by members of the House of Lords.

Lord Glenarthur, a helicopter pilot from Aberdeen, became Minister of State for the Highlands. On the face of it he seemed a likely candidate to approach for help. David Blair, Fort William's chief executive, managed to twist the arm of a few high-ranking Highland councillors, including Duncan McPherson, the head of the council, to take a delegation to parliament and lay a petition before the minister. All kind of difficulties were put in our way and after several setbacks we were told that the only possible date was 2.30 p.m. on Christmas Eve.

How David convinced the councillors that we would get them home in time for the bells in Inverness that night I'll never know, but we flew to London in the morning and made our way to the jumble of offices that is the inner sanctuary of the Houses of Parliament. There we sat in an uncomfortable waiting room like a bunch of naughty schoolboys awaiting our doom.

The hours passed and the possibility of a flight home for Christmas faded. The noble Lord was nowhere to be found. Finally, having missed our flight, and as we were about to leave in search of a hotel for the night, we were ushered into an office where Glenarthur was sitting, clearly full of Christmas spirit. Dispassionately he turned down our petition and we were ushered out of the office before anyone could get a word in edgeways. A delegation of Highland hicks was certainly not going to spoil his Christmas.

As we walked out of parliament into a drizzly London night I fought back tears of frustration. Five years of work and several hundred thousand pounds had gone up in smoke, my dream was in tatters and I felt utterly defeated.

It's at times like this that one realises the resilience of the Scots. David Blair, Ian Milton and I spent Christmas Eve with an angry bunch of outraged Highland councillors in the Gatwick Hilton. The councillors were spitting blood; their pride had been deeply offended. What seemed to me to be the end of the road was the start of Tantalus's rock rolling over the top of the mountain. We had a surprisingly cheerful night at the bar in the Hilton and to my amazement not one of the councillors showed any signs of giving up, in fact the very opposite.

Duncan McPherson, the head of the council, put a hand on my shoulder. 'Don't you worry laddie, we'll see what can be done.'

He was as good as his word; from this point on the Highland Council were in full support. Somehow we got everybody home the following day and it didn't seem such a bad Christmas after all.

Up until then our plan had been to persuade the council to build a road to the foot of the ski area, similar to that in the Cairngorms. We would then raise the money to build the ski centre. Keith McFarlane, the head of the Highland Roads Department, was adamantly against this and suggested a cable-car up the lower slopes and the Highland Council offered to pay a million pounds towards this should the project go ahead.

We realised that a cable car would cost millions and our group furiously rejected this suggestion feeling that we were being manipulated into something that we could never afford. Afterwards, I had an uneasy feeling that this was not a bad idea and a million pounds, our first offer of public money, was not to be sniffed at. I knew of a second-hand gondola that was to be removed from a garden festival site at Stoke-on-Trent and it occurred to me that a cable car would be an attraction in its own right and could be used in summer to take tourists up to enjoy the scenery.

When I voiced this opinion it caused the only serious rift among our small committee in the entire nine years of putting the ski development together. I felt like Judas, particularly to the local councillors and business people who had been fighting on our behalf to build a road. It is always risky to make a U-turn, but I stuck to my guns and after a lot of arguing managed to convince them that this was the right way forward and we conceded to the will of the Highland Roads Department. Another barrier to our progress had fallen.

Doctor George Matheson, the head of the Scottish Development Agency (SDA), flew up to Fort William in a helicopter and asked me to show him the ski area. At the time Scottish industry was going through a period of expansion and the agency wielded enormous power and influence. He gave me a tough grilling, particularly about the way that the HIDB were going slow on the project and the troubles we were having with their economists.

We flew up the mountain and landed at the planned site of the restaurant. It was a gorgeous summer's day, there was still plenty of snow lying in the Snow Goose corrie and it was possible to see the islands of Skye, Rum and Eigg and the pulp mill smoking at Corpach at the head of Loch Eil. George Matheson gave nothing away but I gathered that he was a skier himself and had the feeling that he was reasonably impressed by the time he flew back to Glasgow.

Following his visit the agency took a much deeper interest. They were able to do much of the work in-house instead of the never-ending number of consultants the HIDB were using. Help arrived from the agency with two men, Alan Dale, a high-powered executive with a 'can-do' attitude, and Duncan Harvey, an experienced project manager. A team was developing that began to push the venture forward.

While all this was going on Ian Milton had met a merchant banker called Ian Jones. Ian had a reputation of being a maverick and his company, Quayle Munro, was willing to take sensible risks. The sums of money we were beginning to have to raise were growing horrifically and he realised that nobody would lend us the amount we needed without some form of security and this we didn't have. Ian Jones was himself an enthusiastic skier and understood that there was a great need for another ski area. Instead of a single loan he used his influence around the Scottish banks and put together a consortium of investors all of whom individually did not have to take an enormous risk.

I had never considered myself to be much of a financier so it was a relief to have somebody on board who understood how to put this together and as we progressed Ian became chairman of our fledgling company. In the years that followed he and I did not always see eye to eye but without his expertise I doubt that we would have been able to put the financial package together.

Until then, most of our dealings were with Poma, the French ski-lift company, but in 1987 I was approached by Briton Engineering, a ski-tow manufacturer based in Huddersfield. The managing director, Brian Thomas, was agent for Doppelmayr, the Austrian lift maker. Brian took Ian Jones and me out to their factory in Wolfurt, on Lake Constance.

The Austrian cable cars and ski lifts were much less stylish than the French but seemed to us to be more robust and able to withstand the kind of winds and weather that we have in Scotland. Austria has 700 ski areas and skiing is its biggest national industry. I was able to set up a competition between Doppelmayr and Poma which helped make the competing companies sharpen their pencils.

The Austrians were difficult to deal with and had yet to join the European Union and we had endless problems trying to find a way to avoid huge amounts of VAT being paid. William Simons, our lawyer, and I went out to Wolfurt prior to Christmas to try and sort out the problem. I was probably the wrong person for the job as I hadn't a clue about tax. I fell out with the Austrians and was at the same time getting a lot of earache from Quayle Munro in Edinburgh. William ultimately lost patience and flew home leaving me still arguing with the Austrians.

Everything closed down for the Christmas holiday and Doppelmayr left me high and dry with nowhere to stay, so I took a few days skiing in Muhlbach, a charming village in the Tirol where I had some good Austrian friends who had a small guesthouse. I was distraught but they convinced me that this was probably normal business strategy and not to worry. The fireworks and consumption of alcohol in Austria is almost equal to ours in the Highlands and I staggered back to Wolfurt after the holiday to a beaming, friendly reception of accountants who had finally solved the VAT problem – I returned to Scotland triumphant and very relieved.

In the spring of 1987 we organised a day's helicopter skiing on Aonach Mor and took a number of Brian Thomas's portable ski-tows on to the ski slopes. Approximately 200 Scots had a great day's skiing and I managed to fly a party of press and local councillors to the summit.

One senior politician, Councillor Malcolm Mackay, stepped statesmanlike out of the helicopter and walked smiling up the slope almost losing his head in the whirling blades. Luckily the pilot, Dave Clem, spotted him, increased power and lifted the aircraft just in time to give him a neat parting and, for us watching, the fright of our lives. For me it was a blissfully exciting day that seemed to be the moment that the ski company truly sprang into existence.

There was never a moment that we got the go ahead. To build in 1989 we had to order the gondola in the spring of the previous year. Alan Dale and I took the decision to purchase from Doppelmayr and awarded the building contract to Morrison Construction.

It was decided that Morrison would construct the gondola and associated buildings up to 2,000 feet and I would form the Nevis Range company and take on the erection of the ski lifts and buildings above the gondola top station. I decided to employ mainly climbers and experienced hill people who were used to being up in the mountains. Doppelmayr recommended a New Zealander called Warren Newlands to oversee the ski-lift assembly and in the autumn of 1988 I left Suds running Nevisport and moved into a portakabin office in what was planned to be the Nevis Range car park.

Business and climbing have much in common, there come these moments of total commitment, you either go for it and accept the consequences or fail and forever dream of what might have been. This was one such moment. Somehow the stone had rolled to the top of the hill and now only needed a light touch to trundle over the other side and we were committed.

16 | Nevis Range

Duncan McPherson cut the first sod on 1 April 1989. We had eight months to build the entire ski complex and at all costs it had to be open by Christmas that year whatever the weather, a daunting prospect. Morrison started immediately digging out the peat, which was three metres deep in the car park. It had been a long, cold winter and the Goose corrie was still deep in snow.

On the mountain I held back the start for six weeks hoping for a thaw but finally could wait no longer and set about digging down through the snow to excavate the foundations for the ski lifts. It was slow and frustrating work as each night the holes refilled with snow and I was already a month and a half behind.

What had to be achieved in the next eight months was overwhelming. In the valley Morrison were digging out the car park and laying the foundations for the gondola bottom station with its cafe, ski hire and offices. Then there were power lines, a dam, water mains, and the control cables.

The car park is only 300 feet above sea level, which makes the bottom of ours the world's lowest ski area. The top gondola station is at 2,100 feet, where a road, a four-seat chairlift and five ski-lifts with a second dam had to be built with all their ancillary water and power lines and transformers.

Unexpectedly, Alcan demanded that we build a large settling tank to protect the water intake for its hydro scheme. I argued that this was unnecessary as we would be skiing on snow above the surface and anyway, the skiing was well away from its water intake. We had already taken out several million pounds of insurance in its favour and were paying compensation for any loss of water during the construction. It was humiliating and seemed unnecessary but I got short shift from it and it had to be done.

In fairness to the aluminium company, which has recently become Rio Tinto Alcan, in the twenty-odd years since the building of the ski area a new and more energetic and positive management has become more understanding and receptive to our development. Our other landlord, the Forestry Commission, have opened the forest to the public and allowed vast swathes of it to be used in a joint venture with us to develop mountain bike trails. Time is a great healer!

Almost immediately we discovered that our quantity surveyors had made a mistake in their calculations and we were a million pounds under funded and as yet not a brick had been laid. Something had to go and we took the decision to reduce the top station restaurant to a less radical design. In hindsight this was probably a mistake as the original building would have been a true statement and an attraction in its own right, we could have saved the same sum by building one less ski-lift. (This would have reduced the capacity of skiers but in retrospect we would have coped.)

At the time none of us had predicted the rapid change in climate that would seriously affect Scottish skiing in the next ten years. Shortage of money, bad weather and a race against the clock were my constant companions during those eight months. I was lucky that it was a mostly fine summer, and this far north in Scotland it never really gets dark. The sun sets at 11 p.m. and rises again at three in the morning. I realised that we could catch up by working through the night and the mountain squad worked twelve-hour shifts round the clock. It was incredibly exciting watching the ski centre develop.

Warren Newlands was a hard taskmaster setting out the foundations for the lines of the ski-lifts. He had brought a Maori friend with him, Wayne Limyock (Yocky), who headed the squad working up on the mountain, and Wayne Watkins, who had been the manager of the Queenstown gondola in New Zealand and who eventually became our chief engineer. There was a great air of camaraderie and without the total dedication and friendship from everybody I don't think I would have survived the summer.

Morrison proved to be a good choice of contractor and after a few early spats our two teams worked together sharing a helicopter. All told we spent over a million pounds on airlifts and developed enormous respect for the pilots who flew thousands of tons of concrete and equipment with astonishing accuracy. Our mountain squad spent a lot of time in thick cloud where it was often impossible to fly, while lower down Morrison's gondola team forged ahead in better weather.

Duncan Harvey was a brilliant go-between for us and the other contractors and fought a battle alongside me trying to keep the finances under control. While all this was going on I was trying to set up the ski company that would ultimately take over the site. Beryl Austin's daughter, Marian, was sorting out the ski-school, and Tony Cardwell set up the ski patrol and worked as a liaison between ourselves and the environmental agencies as we began to dig very big holes into the mountain. Marian quickly became indispensable and eventually became a director. Running the offices were Caroline Lucas and Jan Marshall without whom I would never have kept my sanity.

In August I had a note from Doppelmayr to tell me that a low-loader truck, which weighed over sixty tons, was on its way from Austria with the cables for the gondola. The huge truck with a police escort was trundling up the M6 and as I had already sorted out its route with the highway authority all seemed well. The last mile of road to Aonach Mor was an old forestry track with a tiny humpback bridge over the railway line. We had improved the surface and put in passing places but it was hardly adequate for the amount of traffic that we were hoping to attract.

The day before the low-loader arrived I noticed men in yellow jackets and hard hats inspecting the old humpback bridge on the forestry road.

'Any problem?' I asked.

'No, we're from British Rail, it's just the annual check on the bridge,' the foreman replied.

I glanced up and noticed to my horror a sign saying 'Maximum Load 10 Tons'. I'd passed it almost daily for the past year!

The sixty-ton low-loader had already passed Edinburgh. I fretted all day wondering what to do, there was no other way to go and the load would be here the following morning. I took the coward's way out, did nothing and didn't go into work the next day. At lunchtime I drove apprehensively up to Nevis Range expecting the worst. The huge truck was sitting there with a crane lifting off the spools of very heavy cable.

'Any problems?' I asked the Austrian driver.

'Nein problem,' he said making no mention of the bridge. My heart missed a beat and restarted.

By October, Warren had all the foundations in place, the gondola was up and running and the top station was taking shape. The mountain looked no different, we had returfed all the broken ground and were ready for the big lift. Dave Clem's fleet of small Squirrel helicopters could only lift a maximum load of one ton. His pilots were used to working with a mirror below the fuselage and could place girders on to bolts with great accuracy, but the job now was to place the ski towers into position on their foundations. The seventy towers were laid out in rows in the car-park and each weighed almost exactly three tons.

We hired a Super Puma helicopter from Aberdeen with an uplift capacity limit of just three tons. The pilots were more used to flying men to and from oil rigs rather than the exacting task of lowering heavy towers accurately on to holding bolts. At £10,000 an hour we had a big problem and the last thing we needed was damaged foundations. A two day standoff between me and the helicopter company was solved with the arrival of their chief pilot who was terrific and flew all seventy towers into position in a single day and by that evening the mountain transformed into something that resembled a ski field.

My poacher friend, Shotgun, headed a small team who built almost twenty miles of snow fencing. By the time they were finished snow was falling almost daily. In Scotland it arrives horizontally with high wind and without these fences we knew it would be impossible to keep the snow on the ski-runs. It was a race against the clock and winter arrived early. The boys on the mountain were still attempting to set up the ski-lifts, pulling heavy new cables and attaching chairs and T-bars.

The temperature in December dropped to minus sixteen degrees. We foolishly opened the stopcocks on the dam for the first time and the water blocked instantly in the empty, frozen pipes. We planned a big opening party on the 19th in time for the Christmas holiday and I spent the final forty-eight hours with Wayne Watkins, shivering below the dam with a blow torch trying to free the blockage.

Nevis Range opened spot on its planned date with great success and the first skiers hit the slopes. None of our staff had ever worked ski lifts or driven Kässbohrer, the three big snow-grooming machines I had purchased. I was once again relying on New Zealanders, this time a driver called Zoom Zimmerman who set about training our boys to push snow on to the ski runs.

We were a strange little company to be running a ski resort – almost nobody could ski. Marian Austin had set up the ski school and the few instructors that she had were frantically teaching our lift operators how to get around the mountain. For all that I was deliriously happy; the summer had gone in a flash with far less problems than I had anticipated.

Most of the contractors and Austrian engineers had departed and we were at last on our own. I was utterly exhausted but relieved that we were up and running and beginning to relax and dream of an easy time. I should have known better – our long run of luck was about to run out.

On Christmas Eve 1989 a party took place in the restaurant at the top of the gondola – we had been open for less than a week. It was snowing and windy but well within the safety parameters that the cable car was able to operate. The Forestry Commission had hired us for their annual bash and a crowd of local people had booked for a Christmas party. It was a lovely way to spend Christmas with a light snow falling and the lights of Corpach shining over Loch Eil 2,000 feet below. Around midnight the first of the revellers began to descend and head for home.

Suddenly and without warning there was a jolt and a mighty crash and the whole system shuddered to an emergency stop. The startled operator watched as one of the empty cabins entering the top station crashed off the line and fell out of the front of the building into the night. The horrified man hit all the alarms; he knew that there were a number of cabins with people on board swinging in darkness out on the cable and that one of these held two 80-year-old ladies.

I was leaving Beryl Austin's house when the phone rang. My first reaction was that it was a joke but within minutes I was driving frantically to Nevis Range. I arrived at the car park to a blaze of arc lights as a TV crew had arrived before me; somebody in the top restaurant had phoned the media as soon as the accident had happened. It was a terrible situation, Wayne, our chief engineer, had already set off walking up the mountain to try and figure out what had happened and what to do next.

I ducked past the line of press and joined the anxious gondola operator in the bottom station.

'I've tried to phone Doppelmayr in Austria but there's no reply,' he said. 'A party has gone down the line with a loudhailer to tell the people to sit tight and not worry.'

'Don't worry?' I thought in consternation. It must be a very lonely and frightening experience for the dozen or so people swinging up there in darkness. Our only means of communication with them was a loudhailer from the mountainside and what on earth were we to tell them? The chances of getting hold of Doppelmayr at one o'clock in the morning on Christmas day were very slim indeed.

We had practised all kinds of rescue methods in case of just such a happening but I was loath to start lowering people out of swinging cabins on to a snowy mountainside in the middle of the night and decided to leave them where they were until we figured out what had happened. I also phoned the top station and told them to keep the bar open and drinks were on the house. At least somebody up there could have a cheerful time.

Wayne phoned down from the top that he could find no fault with the gondola and told me he had moved the fallen cabin out of sight of any press photographers. Our local pressman, Ian Abernethy, somehow slipped in and joined me and seemed fairly sympathetic. There wasn't much to say and I was more concerned at getting the passengers down safely than the unwelcome publicity; we would almost certainly be head-lines in the morning. At the time Ian was cheerful and encouraging and I was glad of his company.

The engineers checked and rechecked but still found no fault and I took the decision to restart the motor and run the gondola very slowly and bring the people off the mountain. Everything seemed to be working perfectly. The first cabin down contained the two old ladies, who were immediately pounced on by the news crews. I had been dreading this but their reaction was astounding.

'Oh, it was wonderful, the most exciting thing that ever happened to me!' said one lady as she posed by the cabin for a photograph. Both refused to say a bad word about their experience and much the same happened as the other passengers were lowered safely down the line. For this I am eternally grateful. By daylight all of our customers were down the mountain, and some of the ones from the gondola restaurant were in a very inebriated state.

We would, and should, have made headline news but world events came to the rescue. That Christmas morning Romania was in the throes of a popular uprising and the dictator Nicolae Ceausescu and his wife Elena were arrested, tried and shot. This was world-shattering news and our little epic was off the front pages. It can't have been very pleasant for the Ceausescus, but they sure got me out of a hole.

We finally contacted Doppelmayr who immediately flew a team of engineers out to assist us. The defect in the gondola proved to be an in-correct setting of the guide as the cabins entered the top station.

An empty cabin swinging in the wind had entered the station and missed its guide completely. The manufacturers assured me that it couldn't have happened to an occupied cabin but this did little to calm my nerves. The final outcome was that we were able to demand a massive upgrade on the system and this has made it possible for the machine to operate safely in much higher winds than we originally expected.

It had been the most exciting year of my life and I wouldn't have missed it for the world. The gondola incident fizzled out almost immediately but I'll never forget the awful night with people stranded out in the dark on the cable and I'll always be grateful to Ceausescu.

I was physically exhausted, had lost weight and was desperately in need of a break. I took a six-week sabbatical holiday and flew to New Zealand. I arrived tired and jetlagged in Auckland after a short stop in Hong Kong and drove to Whakapapa ski area where I met Zoom's father who immediately insisted on taking me on a ski tour to the summit of Mount Ruapehu, the highest volcano on North Island, which was having a minor eruption at the time. It was a fantastic sight looking down into the boiling crater as we made our way around the rim and then an exhilarating slide back down to Whakapapa where I was staying with the ski area manager, Scotty Barry.

'There's a telex from Ian Sutherland, Spike. He wants you to phone him urgently. He sounds anxious.' Scotty said.

I phoned Suds immediately.

'There's no snow and the Royal Bank are trying to pull the plug on us. I think you ought to get back here as quick as you can.'

Lack of snow is something all ski areas have to face and this seemed ridiculous. We had a fighting fund for just such an event and it was right at the beginning of the ski season. What on earth was the matter with them?

I missed the flight back via Hong Kong by minutes and the next flight took me back via Hawaii and San Francisco. I had been in New Zealand for less than forty-eight hours. Suds met me at the airport in Glasgow and I tottered off the plane having flown round the world in less than a week.

We drove immediately to a board meeting in Pitlochry where I saw

Ian Jones at his very best. The Royal Bank had tried to take the funds we had put aside for lack of snow. At least we had a powerful and confident banker on our board. Ian point blank refused to deal with the Royal and had our cash moved to another bank at the same time threatening legal wrath should the bank attempt to take our money.

Without snow a ski company has absolutely no means of income. One can only watch the weather forecast and pray. It was my first taste of the precariousness of the ski industry; we rely entirely on a product that falls from the sky. At the time the board meeting was taking place snow was already falling and within a day or two we were back in business.

The gondola was formally opened later that summer by the Queen. The local Laird, Donald Cameron of Lochiel, did us a great service in organising the royal family who sailed up Loch Linnhe in the Royal Yacht Britannia. The whole town turned out to welcome them and the subsequent good will and publicity far outweighed the problems we had at Christmas.

The warm Gulf Stream current runs down the west coast of Scotland and although we are at roughly the same latitude as Hudson Bay in Canada our climate is relatively mild. For the previous ten years the winters had been cold with long periods of good weather and skiing had developed at a rapid rate. From 1990 onwards things were to change dramatically.

The term 'global warming' was hardly mentioned at the time. Our opinion of change was that it would be a gradual phenomenon and would have little effect on the ski industry. In reality we were about to get much more extreme conditions. Very cold snaps of weather followed by warm, heavy rain. The big winter storms dropping vast quantities of snow seemed to be eluding us. Winters started later and finished earlier with warm, wet and windy weather mixed with the snowfall.

Cheap flights were making it possible for skiers to visit the Alps and United States. Until now our market had been as far south as Birmingham and ski-buses regularly ran from Manchester and Newcastle. The advent of low-cost foreign package holidays cut deeply into our market. The heyday of the Scottish ski industry was in decline.

Fortunately for us Nevis Range had the gondola which gave us a year-round tourist business and although skiing was to remain at our core we set about changing to an all-year-round tourist destination. My plan to stay as managing director for three years and then return to Nevisport never happened. My office looked directly out on to Aonach Mor and the shoulder of Ben Nevis with the cable car running directly up the mountain in front of me, one of the world's finest views – who could ask for more? Suds took over the running of Nevisport and I settled in for the long haul. I was to remain at the Range for the next twelve years.

During the construction of the Nevis Range ski area it had been almost impossible to go out on rescues, but now as things settled down I was able to resume my position in the team although I was never able to be as active as I had been in earlier days. Half the workforce belonged to the rescue team and the number of incidents seemed to be increasing. During rescues we often found ourselves very short staffed. On the plus side, the RAF were very accommodating, Coastal Command had re-equipped the air-sea rescue squadron and replaced the smaller Wessex with the Sea King helicopter. This was initially unpopular as the Sea King is a much bigger and less manoeuvrable aircraft but it has the ability to fly in poor visibility and much higher winds. They're also equipped with night-vision and heat-seeking equipment. We very much appreciated the skill and professionalism of the aircrew, who we got to know well.

Flying on rescues was great practice for the pilots, particularly in peace time when air-sea rescue was the only fully operational wing of the service. Every now and then some idiot in the press would complain about the high costs of helicopters on the public purse, while the reality is that the precision flying in real life and death situations has far greater value than any ordinary training exercise. The crews flew in all weather, in very dangerous situations and saved many lives. The political argument continues and there are moves afoot to privatise the rescue helicopters. I believe this to be a mistake; the costs will escalate and privately owned aircraft will be far less willing to fly in the kinds of conditions that the RAF pilots accept, and they have none of the night-vision aids or technical gadgetry. The RAF will still have to practise, so why not kill two birds with one stone?

The statistics on the number of call-outs remain remarkably similar year on year. Lochaber team has approximately sixty rescues a year (not counting the twisted ankles and false alarms on the tourist paths) and there are about eight fatal accidents on Ben Nevis. Mostly things are much quicker now because of the helicopters, but many of the calls are in poor visibility when they are unable to fly.

The advent of mobile phones has been a mixed blessing, climbers began calling for help at the first sign of difficulties. In the past we would have no option but to retreat or spend a cold night's bivouac, now help is available at the end of a phone. It can be very frustrating to be called out from a pleasant evening meal to some idiot on the Ben Nevis footpath suffering from cramp.

One event on the Ben stands out as the worst call-out I was involved in. Two young climbers having reached the summit had missed the easy descent route to the Carn Mor Dearg Arête and headed down the steepening slopes of Coire Eoghainn on the south side of the mountain. When they failed to return, a full-scale search began and on the following day a searching helicopter spotted an ice axe in the snow above the steep slopes of the corrie. Fearing the worst we began to search the face.

We found the body of one of the men quite quickly, but although it seemed obvious that the second man would be close by there was no sign of him. It was late spring and much of the snow had melted leaving deep patches in some of the gullies. One of these gullies had a waterfall that ran down slabs and gushed behind one of these deep beds of old snow; one of the search and rescue dogs was giving this a lot of attention. It seemed probable that the man may have been swept down the waterfall and slid into the crevasse between the snow and the rock. Noel Williams poked his head as far into the hole as he could and thought he could see some cloth-like material deep inside.

The old snow in the gully was ten feet deep and very solid and it became clear that our attempts to dig through were futile.

'If he did slip down the back of the snow it might be possible for somebody to crawl down to him,' I said rather foolishly. There was a long silence and I realised that everybody was looking at me.

John Hinde, who was now demobbed from the RAF and working as an instructor at Outward Bound Loch Eil, rigged up a deadman snow belay and I put on all my waterproofs, tied in to the rope and nervously slid into the crevasse with my back against the rock in the waterfall and my face jammed against the snow as I began to wriggle apprehensively downwards.

About twenty feet below I found the body. He was jammed firmly between the snow and rock, some of his clothes had been washed away and he was somewhat bloated having been soaked constantly by the waterfall. It was a horrible situation wriggling about in near darkness in pouring water and trying to remain calm. I managed to get below him and untied the rope from myself and fastened it round his waist. Up on top they tried to pull him up but although they could move him it was almost impossible to move the body in the confined space.

Noel Williams squirmed down and joined me, both of us were getting claustrophobic and freezing cold in the pouring water but we began to manoeuvre the body slowly up the crevasse. The team above had rigged a pulley system and were hauling away when the deadman belay came out and the body slid back down the crevasse on to us. I have never been in a worse predicament, both Noel and I were struggling to avoid panic and not get jammed in this ghastly place.

John Hinde was shouting apologies and encouragement as he rerigged the pulley system. As tension finally came on the rope we managed to reorientate and began worming ourselves and our macabre cargo upwards and a few minutes later emerged, frozen, wet and retching, into the sunshine. Fresh air has never tasted so good and neither Noel nor I ever want to repeat such an experience again.

In 1993 Alison Hargreaves and her husband Jim Ballard and their children Tom and Kate were living in Fort William. Jim had run a small climbing shop in Matlock, Derbyshire, and we had been friends since meeting in the Dolomites in the early sixties. Alison had her own small manufacturing company called Faces which made some specialised climbing gear that we sold in our shops. She amazed me one afternoon in the Peak District by solo climbing up and down two classic hard routes, The Rasp and The File at Higgar Tor, running up the vertical gritstone with natural ease.

A diminutive and lovely woman, her skill as a mountaineer was phenomenal. She had tremendous technical ability combined with unstoppable energy and a grim determination to succeed. She now set about the improbable task of climbing the six classic north faces of the Alps, alone and unaided in a single season. These are the Eiger, Matterhorn, Grandes Jorasses, Dru, Cima Grande and Piz Badile.

Suds and I were out in the Alps that summer and joined up with the family to help with the project and we walked up to the Piz Badile with Alison. The beautiful Alpine meadows of the Bondo valley had changed little since I had last been here. The great shovel of rock of the Piz Badile towering alongside its near twin, Piz Cengalo, and the cirque of lovely granite peaks shining in the morning sunshine are a climber's paradise. I was surprised to find that the glacier that Nick Banks and I had walked up when we climbed the face twenty years earlier no longer existed.

Alison started up the lower slabs, a tiny figure almost running up the rock, while Suds and I set off up the easier North Ridge of the Badile with the intention of meeting her on the summit. Two and a half hours later when we were only halfway up the climb, Alison appeared, soloing down from the summit having already completed the North Face. Nick and I had taken a full day to climb the route with a forced bivouac on our descent.

Alison completed all six solos that summer, a magnificent achievement, the only climber of any gender to do such a thing. That ought to have been the culmination of her ambition but she then set about the improbable task of climbing the world's three highest mountains, Everest, K2 and Kangchenjunga, unaided and without oxygen in a single season. Nevis Range was one of her sponsors and in her year of preparation she and Jim spent a great deal of their time teaching their children Kate and Tom to ski. They were by far our most regular visitors, turning out almost daily whatever the weather for the entire winter.

On 13 May 1995 she reached the summit of Everest without the aid of Sherpas or oxygen. She returned briefly to Fort William to see the family and left in June for K2. That August I was leaving for a climbing holiday in Spain when word reached us that she was missing. I can remember thinking 'she's far too competent, she'll be ok' and catching my flight trying not to worry. The following day the news was confirmed: she had reached the summit of K2 unaided and in fine weather and reported over the radio that she could see a number of thunderstorms over Tibet. Somewhere on the descent one of these terrible storms struck the mountain and in one of the worst Himalayan tragedies all seven climbers that summitted that day perished.

It was a terrible shock for all of us in Fort William, and devastating for Jim and the children. There was a lot of ballyhoo in the press questioning the ethics of a mother engaging in such a dangerous sport.

Alison had countered this in an interview saying, 'I thought about taking my husband and children to base camp, but feel that it's rather "inhospitable" there. Besides, none of my male climbing partners had taken their young families along for the climb.'

The following year Jim organised a trekking expedition to K2 Base Camp and took the two young children to see where their mother had died and I suspect to find closure. Again there was a lot of controversy; death in the mountains is always a tragedy and all of us have different ways of dealing with it. For me Alison will always be that tiny figure running gracefully up the gigantic slabs of the Piz Badile.

17 | Lotus Flower Tower

In 1994, Steve Long, Dave 'Smiler' Cuthbertson, Suds and I planned a trip to climb the Lotus Flower Tower, a spectacular isolated rock climb in the Logan range of mountains in the Canadian Yukon. First climbed by Tom Frost, Sandy Bill and Jim McCarthy, this stunning tower, standing in what is called the Cirque of the Unclimbables, is recognised as one of the fifty classic climbs of North America and has been called 'one of the most aesthetically beautiful rock faces in the world'.

I had married the previous year and to my surprise Helen announced that we were having a baby and the due date was in July, right in the middle of our planned expedition. I was desperate to go and selfishly promised my wife that I would be home in time for the birth. I managed to persuade the team to go a month sooner knowing full well that this would be very early for an ascent of the tower and that there would almost certainly be snow on the ground.

We flew to Watson Lake, a truck stop on the Alaska Highway, where we employed a bush pilot, Warren Lefebvre, to fly us the hundred miles into Glacier Lake from where it was a long, steep slog up into the cirque. As we flew into the mountains I was horrified to see that the whole range was still plastered in snow and there was no sign of the spring thaw. The tiny Beaver floatplane flew right into the Cirque of some of the most spectacular towers of rock I had ever seen. We had boxed up some of the heavy climbing gear in plastic barrels and as Warren flew low over the snow we threw some of these out on to the area where we intended to set up camp.

Warren landed us at Glacier Lake, where we left a radio and some equipment, and we set out on the long 5,000-foot slog up into the Cirque.

We had been told that there was little likelihood of problems with bears so were somewhat concerned as we spotted a grizzly and cub almost as soon as we set out. Worse still, as we approached the Cirque the snow was so deep that our best way was to follow a trail already broken by a very large bear which we expected to meet at every turn; the little tube of bear spray we carried seemed totally inappropriate. I was hobbling along suffering from what I thought to be a groin strain and not sure if I would be able to run for it. When we reached the campsite the snow was so deep that a whole day was wasted searching for the barrels of climbing equipment we had slung out of the plane.

Lotus Flower Tower looked spectacular, but what should have been a short walk through gentle alpine meadows took a full day trailblazing through waist-deep snow. Our improvised campsite under a large boulder was a miserable place, the weather was cold and snowing and we settled in for a long wait. It had been an arduous slog up into the Cirque and the two younger members of the team were pleasantly shocked when Suds produced a litre bottle of Scotch from the bottom of his pack and even more so when I pulled another out of mine – sometimes the extra weight can be very worthwhile! The freezing campsite under the boulder became a place of cheer.

The weather gradually improved and we established a cache of gear at the foot of the tower. There had been a rock fall at the first pitch, which was also pouring water, and Steve made a marvellous lead to get us established on the face. This was my first big-wall climb of this kind. Steve and Smiler did most of the leading while Suds and I, the two old men, worked away at heaving the haul bags.

There is a small, level grass ledge about a thousand feet up the face where we intended to bivouac. I had seen photographs of climbers lying out relaxed and sunbathing on this ledge. For us the weather was so cold that we had brought a small tent in our haul sacks. The ledge turned out to be a high-angled bank of snow and we set about trying to cut a shelf with inefficient summer rock climbing gear while skating about on the ice in our rock-shoes. We finally pitched the tent, angled at about forty-five degrees, leaning out over a very vertical drop and all four of us scrambled in still roped-up and attached to the wall in case it slid off. God knows what we would have done if this had happened, the thought of dangling upside down in our harnesses in the dark and tangled in a tent was too terrifying to contemplate.

After a long, miserable night it was decided that Smiler and Steve would make a fast push for the top while Suds and I set about sorting out the ledge and rigging up the abseils for our escape. It was the logical thing to do but disappointing for us. All the previous day I had been struggling with my sore groin but the climbing was fabulous and here on one of the world's most beautiful rock climbs I felt very much at home. We watched Steve and Smiler working their way up the twin cracks known as the ski-tracks on the vertical final arête of Lotus Flower Tower.

To the west we were looking out over the amazing ridge of Mount Proboscis, known as The Great Canadian Knife and site of one of the most isolated and audacious big-wall climbs in Canada. South we could see Glacier Lake and into the Tahini River basin, and east a thousand miles of rough outback with no roads or habitation as far as the Great Slave Lake and beyond. In the event of Warren being unable to collect us in the float-plane we had the vague idea of rafting down the river in the direction of Hells Gate, but this would be a very extreme undertaking.

Steve and Smiler topped out on the tower and Suds and I set about dismantling the extraordinary campsite and organising the abseils. It was a great temptation to load the haul sacks and drop them off into space on to the glacier a thousand feet below. It would have been a clean drop but our experience of the previous search for our aircraft drop made us wary and we decided to abseil with the loads on our backs.

The boys reached us in late afternoon and we set about the long series of free swinging abseils down the wall, Steve discovered a sequence of bolts that a previous party had conveniently left and this made our descent considerably easier than we had expected. At this latitude the sun hardly sets and we had plenty of daylight. The rope jammed on one of the abseils and Smiler valiantly prusiked back up to free it. Late that night we finally reached the glacier and ploughed our way back down to our camp under the boulder.

Smiler and Steve were anxious to leave, with dreams of warm rock and sunshine in Yosemite Valley. Suds and I would have preferred to stick around in the Cirque but bowed down to the younger enthusiasts. None of us looked forward to a double trip down to base camp at Glacier Lake 5,000 feet below, so we ditched anything unnecessary in a crevasse, including all our food with the exception of a packet of porridge, just in case, and set off down the long scree slopes under the weight of enormous rucksacks.

When we reached Glacier Lake, to our consternation, the radio wouldn't work. Without contact it would be another week before Warren planned to fly over and check us out. It's amazing how hungry one gets when facing a week with three half-starved climbers and only a small packet of Scott's porridge oats!

It was at this point I realised what seriously useless woodsmen we were. We had no gun, but the trees were alive with squirrels and birds. We could see herds of caribou and in the distance the odd moose lurking about, the lake was alive with fish and beaver dams blocked the river. We set about trying everything we could think of to catch something. Snares were set; I had carried a short length of fishing line and hook in the top of my rucksack but without bait there was nothing doing.

By day two we were getting frantic. Not a single catch or trap and the mosquitoes were draining out what little blood we had left. I spent hours messing with the radio to no avail, not a squeak. Steve and Smiler padded up to the top of a hill with the radio in the hope of contact but although the set seemed okay nothing could be heard. I can see how one begins to contemplate cannibalism – Smiler would have been my choice!

On day three our luck changed. Suds swatted a large wood wasp and using this as bait managed to fish out a large Arctic char. Using its guts for bait we soon had a nice pile of fish, a blazing fire and a veritable feast. We were saved.

Late that evening the radio suddenly crackled into life and we made contact with another Yukon wilderness group canoeing down the Tahini River. They managed to radio our predicament to Warren who immediately flew out to pick us up. Apparently there had been a large solar flare which had affected radio communications.

I sat in the co-pilot's seat as the little Beaver floatplane skidded out over Glacier Lake and flew out into the midnight sun through the Cirque of the Unclimbables, passing the wall of Lotus Flower Tower, up over the great blade of Canada, Mount Proboscis, and out across the snow-covered Yukon highlands. As the boys slept in the back of the plane the most stunning range of mountains came into view.

'That's the Vampire Peaks,' Warren said. 'As far as I know they have never been visited.'

A whole range of granite spires towering into the sky from a wooded plateau surrounded by a myriad of lakes. Spellbound we circled this beautiful scene, their long shadows casting across the highlands and the low midnight sunshine gleaming on the smooth granite faces. I determined that one day I would come back to this lovely place.

Back at Warren's outpost we were unable to change our flight times and so relaxed for a few days canoeing down one of the local rivers. Suds and I then flew to Vancouver while Steve and Smiler headed to Yosemite in search of El Capitan and glory. Suds and I headed up to Squamish, where we climbed on the Chief, a fabulous rock mountain between Vancouver and Whistler.

I had been trying to phone home with no reply but finally managed to contact friends in Fort William who told me that my wife, Helen, had been taken into hospital. This was earlier than I had expected and I shot back to Vancouver and managed to catch the next plane back to Glasgow. I spent the long flight willing the plane to go faster and drove frantically north to Raigmore Hospital in Inverness where I arrived two hours late for the birth of my daughter. I was jet lagged and shell shocked and filled with remorse for missing the birth but at the same time gloriously happy to be holding Eilidh, our new baby in my arms.

18 | An Autumn in Siberia

Sitting in my office at the Nevis Range in the summer of 1994 I stared dreamily out of the window. Things were beginning to run smoothly and although the winters had not proved particularly cold since we opened Nevis Range was beginning to settle into a fairly organised operation. I looked out on to the Aonach Mor ski fields and the gondola with its steady flow of cabins heading up the mountain through the trees. In the background was the stunning north face of Ben Nevis with its gullies still filled with the remnants of the previous winter's snow.

Life had settled and after the high adventure of the previous few years I was bored. To make matters worse I was in a lot of pain in my left hip and the hard trip to the Lotus Flower Tower in the Yukon the previous year had finally worn out my joint and I was on the waiting list for a hip replacement. I was climbing okay but the walks up to the crags were brutal and I staggered along using ski poles and hobbled terribly when walking downhill.

One afternoon I had an interesting phone call from a company called Enterplan International.

'We're running a project in a place called Kemerovo in Siberia,' the man said. 'We're looking for an expert in ski development to take a look at a defunked ski area and see if it can be turned into a viable business. Can you recommend anybody who might be able to help us?'

'I'll go,' I said without hesitation, leaping at the opportunity without the slightest idea where Kemerovo was or whether my co-directors at Nevis Range would let me go or not. I hadn't the vaguest idea of what I was letting myself in for but I was certain that this was an opportunity not to be missed.

Five years earlier in 1989 the Berlin Wall had fallen and by 1991 the Iron Curtain had disintegrated with the resultant breakaway of many of the

USSR satellite states and the collapse of much of the Russian economy. Boris Yeltsin had replaced Mikhail Gorbachev as the president of the new Federative Socialist Republic. Britain was not sending aid to these countries but was prepared to give technical help through a project called the Know How Fund.

The man explained that a Siberian iron ore mine had closed leaving the small town of Tashtagol destitute. In better days the workers had built two ski lifts and somebody had the idea of trying to turn the place into a resort.

Within a short time, having negotiated a three-month leave of absence from my sceptical colleagues, I was on my way.

If you pull out an atlas and look at a large-scale map of Asia including the whole of the Soviet Union and China, and stab your finger right in the middle, chances are that you will be somewhere within a few hundred miles of Kemerovo. It's about 3,000 miles due east of Moscow, 700 miles west of Lake Baikal and 1,200 miles south of the almost permanently frozen Kara Sea. Tibet lies about 1,200 miles to the south and to the south-east lie Mongolia and the Gobi Desert. The nearest cities of any size are Novosibirsk on the Trans-Siberian railway line, about a hundred miles to the west, and Almaty in Kyrgyzstan, 800 miles to the south.

This is the very heart of Siberia, an area known as the Kuzbass, rolling, fir-tree-forested mountain country rich in iron ore and coal. Here are the towns and small cities built by Stalin to feed his war effort and provide the steel for his armaments. Hidden are the Gulags, the prison camps where millions of dissidents were removed and placed out of harm's way, and tucked in the forests are the silos with their nuclear warheads facing west.

I went through the usual bureaucratic delays in Moscow Airport feeling very nervous. I was carrying about £1,000 worth of roubles hidden in my money belt, in those days well above the going price for which the less reputable Soviet citizen would commit murder. I took a taxi for an hour's drive across the city to a small local airport on the south side. Alongside the runway were parked literally hundreds of military aircraft, presumably out of use and in various forms of decay.

I joined the inevitable queue trying to find where to get rid of my luggage; the passengers were wrapping their bags in brown paper, presumably as a precaution against theft, and I did the same feeling that mine stuck out like a sore thumb. Everybody was shouting and pushing forward, all the signs were in the Russian alphabet and as the only words that I knew were nyet and da and I hadn't a clue where I was going. By some miracle I finally made it out to my plane which turned out to be a huge ex-military transporter.

There followed a fight among the passengers to get a comfortable seat and to my amazement those of us who lost were issued a deckchair by an unfriendly and brutal-looking stewardess who looked like Tamara Press, the Russian Olympic shot-put and discus champion who failed her gender test. I was beginning to think that this adventure was turning out to be a really bad idea.

The giant aircraft somehow lumbered into the night sky and we were on our way on the long 3,000-mile flight to Kemerovo. Tamara handed out blankets and most of the passengers spread out on the floor to sleep. I watched one family light a paraffin stove and brew up – nobody took the slightest notice. I sat back in my deckchair and snoozed uncomfortably through the endless night.

Morning saw us flying over dark, uneven forest with the occasional river or lake, an endless rolling landscape of trees with no sign of roads or towns or human inhabitation.

Later that day the giant plane circled down over a tree-lined runway where I couldn't help but notice two craters part-filled with the remains of aircraft remarkably similar to ours. We hit the tarmac and bounced along with reverse thrust and brakes screaming, me hanging on to my deckchair, eyes shut. The plane finally came to a stop alongside one of the craters. Nobody had taken the trouble to remove the debris.

Kemerovo airport was a small, dusty building with no facilities and much to my relief my luggage turned up intact. As I walked out to find a taxi I couldn't help but notice two of the locals walking up the airport steps;

two girls dressed up to the nines, the miniskirt had hit Siberia with a vengeance. I'm not sure what I expected, but it was hardly this.

I was taken to the only hotel in town, a fine old building with a court-yard where men were polishing two very new black Mercedes cars with tinted windows; I would learn later that this was probably a mafia-owned business. An agreeable old lady showed me my room, which looked comfortable with a TV, shower and a nice bed.

'Da,' I said happily, accepting graciously as she smiled and left. Things in Siberia, I was to learn, are never quite as they seem. I sat down on the bed, which promptly collapsed, the shower was fine but there was no water and the TV didn't work – it couldn't, there was no wire connecting it to the wall.

That afternoon I walked to the city administration building in the main square where a huge statue of Lenin pointed accusingly at us. We had seen the destruction of many of these statues on television but clearly Lenin was still popular in this part of the world.

The situation in Kemerovo was difficult to grasp. The city was bankrupt and most of its industries had closed down. None of the administration staff had been paid for some months but everybody still turned up for work and seemed to be taking a fatalistic view of the future. A barter econ-omy appeared to be the way that most people existed, there wasn't much work to do and most of them sat at their desks wasting time.

The British delegation's Know How Fund consultant's office was here and they told me that the ski area at Tashtagol where I was to work was about a hundred miles away. I was introduced to my translator, a thin, sallow-faced girl called Tanya, half Russian and half Iranian from Almaty who I was later to discover was suffering from anorexia. She spoke only a little English but after some practice we managed to converse in a sort of pidgin English, Russian and hand signals. The manager explained with some embarrassment that none of the local interpreters volunteered for the job and she was the only taker. I was beginning to have a very uneasy feeling about this exploit.

One of the consultants, Ben Hargreaves, showed me around Kemerovo, a typical Stalin city with austere Soviet housing blocks along wide, rubble-strewn streets with tram lines. Abandoned vehicles of all kinds were scattered in the side streets. There was one large, department store that carried a surprisingly large range of Western luxury goods and an indoor market, supplying a small amount of fruit and vegetables, where most of the population queued for hours. The city was on a branch line of the Trans-Siberian Railway and apparently trains bringing in food and goods only arrived spasmodically as the Kemerovo administration were unable to pay the coal bill for the railway.

Ben took me to a large factory that manufactured electric cable, where he was acting as a consultant. The manager was at his wits' end, he had plenty of wire, in fact there was tons of the stuff, but he had been unable to outsource any plastic for insulation and work had ceased. He explained sadly that there was no money to pay his workers but they still turned up daily and hung around in hope. I didn't envy Ben his job!

That evening, Valeri Maltser, the manager of the ski area in Tashtagol, arrived. He was a similar age to me, a very determined-looking individual who grasped me in an iron handshake nearly breaking all my fingers, slapped me on the back and loaded Tanya and me into the back of his ageing military pickup. At breakneck speed we roared off down a dirt road in a cloud of dust into a land of rolling hills and endless trees.

We reached Tashtagol after several hours of hair-raising driving. I had visualised a small ski resort with well-ordered pistes cutting neatly down through the trees. Well, perhaps not, but in my wildest dreams I couldn't have imagined a more unusual place.

The first thing to come into view was the Gulag. Massive electric fences in a huge rectangle with watchtowers at each corner encircling a group of dreary wooden huts. Teams of very ill-looking men were marching out to work on logging operations in the forest.

'Who are these men?' I asked.

Valeri shrugged disinterestedly. 'Bad People,' he said.

During my stay I was never able to get anyone into conversation about the prison, which local people seemed to tolerate with embarrassment.

At one side of the Gulag stood a playground with a rusty, disused Ferris wheel from which local children must have been able to look straight over the prison camp fence. Beyond this was the massive structure of the iron ore mine, which must have employed several thousand men. Valeri assured me in broken English (slightly better than my translator) that although the mine was closed the men still showed up for work each morning. Later he showed me enormous workshops, which could easily have been put to use by the ski company but nobody seemed able to take the responsibility.

The small town of Tashtagol stood behind the mine. It was a single street of classic Communist high-rise buildings and was no bigger than a small village. There didn't seem to be any shops, which I suspect were instead run from people's flats, although I was never invited inside. I discovered later that, surprisingly, the town had a population of over 20,000.

Running into the mine was a railway line that linked to the Trans-Siberian Railway at Novosibirsk and this had a small side-line that ran into the trees where the ski company operated. As we bounced into the entrance yard I noticed a cage with a gloomy-looking brown bear pacing forwards and backwards.

'Our mascot,' Valeri smiled, pointing at the badge on his ski jacket which pictured a bear on skis.

The ski slope was quite impressive with tows running up cleared pistes through the trees. The lift was painted a bright blue and parked alongside was a bright red East German rat-track grooming machine. Tanya and I were given rooms in the ski lodge at the bottom, a nice meal in the cafe and shown round a spacious building with a comfortable sauna and spa. Things were beginning to look up.

That evening I took a walk up the ski tow and began to realise that, as usual, things were not entirely as they appeared. Whoever had painted the lift blue had done a hell of a job. He had not only painted the towers but all the sheaves (that is the wheels carrying the cable) and the cable itself for about a metre out as far as he could reach from the tower. The whole thing was totally gummed up with paint.

One of the towers had fallen over. Looking at the foundations I was shocked to see that there were no holding bolts set in the concrete but it had been fixed to the foundation by long and very rusty wood screws. The lift had still been running and the fallen tower pulled to one side. The main cable almost touched the ground and it must have been terribly difficult for skiers to manage.

Very few of the spring boxes on the drag were working and the uplift capacity of people must have been tiny. As for the red grooming machine, weeds were growing through its tracks and it had clearly been a long time since it moved.

Feeling lost, helpless and alone I wandered back to the ski centre and joined the poor old bear still walking sadly up and down his cage. It was hard to see how I could be of any use in this alien and strange place.

During the next few weeks I was to learn much about the resilience of the Siberian people. Their economy had totally collapsed; it seemed that the only functioning organisation was the local Mafia who seemed to control almost everything. In Britain every company I dealt with would have been declared bankrupt; there was no money to pay the workers who still turned up daily for work.

None of the companies that I spoke to would have dared to declare a profit for fear of being heavily taxed. Valeri told me that there had been a demonstration at the mine but it had been a peaceful affair and quite jolly. It's hard to imagine what would have happened at home under similar circumstances. On one occasion while I was there, a delivery of bricks turned up at the town's administration office; this was treated as currency and to everyone's delight was shared out among the staff and used for barter.

There was no hotel accommodation in Tashtagol, but a siding had been built from the railway line to the ski centre. During the winter sleeper trains from Novosibirsk parked at the ski centre. They were apparently packed with people and were advertised as health trips rather than ski holidays. In the frozen Siberian winter on a relatively uncomfortable Russian passenger train it can't have been that healthy or comfortable but skiing is a wonderful pastime wherever you are and I guess that in the kind of winters they have in Siberia most people will be able to ski.

(On my return home I did contact ScotRail to see if such a thing could be organised on the West Highland Line that runs past the foot of our ski resort at Nevis Range, but the idea fell on very stony ground.)

I soon realised that Valeri's plot in getting me to Tashtagol was to use me politically to help him raise the money to buy a new chairlift. This seemed a good idea to me and would greatly enhance the ski area but I found it difficult to understand why there seemed to be no attempt to repair the existing two drag lifts.

The skiing was split into two distinct areas: the main lift at Tashtagol and a second smaller area over the shoulder of the mountain in a lovely valley at a village called Sheregesh. Here were some small accommodation sheds and a ticket office and it seemed to me that if a new chairlift were cut up through the trees connecting the two areas it would transform the whole place into a gorgeous and varied ski development.

The whole concept of renovating almost anything seemed non-existent, everywhere I looked broken down trucks, cars and forestry equipment were scattered and abandoned. Doors hung off trams and buses where very little effort would have been needed to put them to right. Valeri seemed astonished when I told him that a number of the ski lifts at our resort in Scotland were second-hand, put into working order and running perfectly well. It seemed that in the Communist era, as the state owned the equipment nobody took any responsibility for it.

I agreed to help Valeri as much as I could to push the authorities for a new chairlift under the condition that he help me put a team together to get the existing lifts working. Within a few days I had an enthusiastic bunch of very knowledgeable helpers hard at it restoring the lifts.

To my surprise I seemed to have become a celebrity who was interviewed on television and visited a number of times by local politicians, and it became obvious from these visits why the ski lifts had been painted in bright colours. Valeri briefed me on who were the important players. These visits culminated in the arrival of a very high-ranking commissar who looked just like the late Mr Brezhnev and got the full red carpet treatment.

After the inevitable knuckle-breaking handshake, a long and very serious conversation ensued. Translated by Valeri and Tanya, I understood none of it and was highly suspicious of what they were saying on my behalf. Eventually the commissar gave an agreeable roaring laugh and invited me to join him in a sauna with some of his drinking friends. Rather foolishly I accepted.

This was a mistake; the heat of the sauna was dreadful.

'This is too hot for me!' I gasped.

The commissar slapped me happily on the shoulders and poured an enormous vodka. In an effort to fly the Scottish flag I attempted to match him drink for drink. The heat was insufferable and I staggered out of the furnace only to be grabbed by an attendant, beaten with birch twigs and then thrown into a freezing bath of cold water and then back into the sauna where the Russians sat happily quaffing their vodka by the bucket load, seemingly oblivious to the heat.

Totally comatose, I was finally rescued by Valeri who carried me back to my room where I slept the clock round. He told me later that he was very pleased with the outcome. Apparently I had told the commissar that should we get a new chairlift, that Sheregesh could easily become an international ski destination and would be an ideal area to train the Russian ski team.

At this time of year, early autumn, the Russians spent their weekends at their dacha, small summer residences, where they had a garden for vegetables and fruit. Everybody was working hard collecting for the winter and scouring the forest for fungi and edible plants. I was invited to a number of these weekend trips and loved the long walks in the forest with the families searching for food.

One morning Valeri invited Tanya and me to join him on a trading trip into the forest. To my surprise there were native people living here, the Shors – or Shortzs – tribes of people who looked very similar to Inuit, still living in their traditional way in the forest with their own languages and traditions. We crossed the Mras-su River on a very large substantial bridge built by convicts from the Gulag and arrived at a tiny and very broken down village in the forest where we traded cans of petrol for sacks of pine needles and mushrooms with these smiling Mongoloid people. Valeri told me that many of the hunters in this area claim to have seen a yeti and that a number of expeditions have been combing the region in the hope of photographing one.

That afternoon we borrowed a boat from the Shortzs and drifted down through the most beautiful gorges on the Mras-su River through an area known locally as Hollow Mountain. Deep limestone gorges with caves and enormous cliffs threading through beautiful pine forests. Valeri told me that some of the caves had been partially explored and were enormous. In the future this gorgeous unspoiled area could be a huge tourist attraction but the distances from any centre of population was vast.

A few miles downriver the outboard motor packed in and we had to beach the boat and were rescued by a group of Shortz fishermen who dragged us up river for a while and then left us to walk the remaining miles back to Valeri's pick-up. I was hobbling terribly with my arthritic hip and the walk back to the Shortzs' village was a painful affair.

The drive back to Tashtagol was uneventful until we passed through a village where to my astonishment I noticed a ski lift cutting up through the trees. In all my time in the Kuzbass I had been told that Tashtagol had the only ski area in Siberia. This clearly was not true; Valeri was very evasive when I questioned him and muttered that it was only a practice lift but this lift looked very substantial. It seemed highly likely that there were other lifts in the area built for recreational use and probably other small groups of enthusiasts trying to develop into ski companies.

My time in Tashtagol was thankfully coming to an end. It was a lonely place and my translator and I were still struggling to communicate. I had a plan that it might be possible for the Know How Fund to pay for a small group of the ski company engineers to visit Nevis Range for a couple of weeks and work with us. This fell on deaf ears and I got the distinct feeling that the consultancy companies were only interested in projects where they could make money. I had become great friends with Valeri and his staff but was glad to be leaving the difficulties of trying to make myself understood and the altercations with my translator who I was convinced passed on very little of what I was trying to say.

My journey home was relatively uneventful other than a difficult time at Moscow airport when my money belt was discovered in the border search. It was an expensive bribe that finally got me on to a Lufthansa flight to Munich and suddenly everything seemed comfortable and luxuriously Western.

Now, twenty years later, I see that Sheregesh has become the training resort for the Russian ski team. This was the site where we planned to put the chairlift that Valeri asked me to help him acquire. Hotels and restaurants have sprung up in Tashtagol and the town has become a resort – who would have believed it? I could find no sign of the Gulag which hopefully has been dismantled and its inmates set free. It is a must on the list for the powder hounds who have skied everywhere. The bitter-cold Siberian winter must give some of the best conditions for snowboarding and skiing through beautiful forests, but it's a long way to go for a free ride!

19 | Cochamo

It's funny how adventures start when you least expect. The poor winters in Scotland were a nightmare and there was little we could do but cross our fingers and toes and pray for snow. January 1998 was just like that, sitting in my office at Nevis Range, looking out at the rain and wondering if skiing was ever going to happen. All was saved by the arrival of a letter with a South American postmark from our pilot friend Dave Clem.

Dave had set up a helicopter company in Puerto Montt in Chile. This incredible country is more than 2,500 miles long and hugs the strip of land between the Andes range of mountains and the Pacific coast of South America. At its narrowest it is only about 40 miles wide. Santiago, the capital, lies about halfway down and Puerto Montt is about 600 miles further south.

The helicopters were working in fjords where some of the world's largest salmon farms were situated, flying smolts (baby salmon) from the hatcheries to the fish farms in the fjords. It was a lovely place on the narrow coastal strip behind which reared up well-nigh vertical mountainsides covered in thick rainforest with almost impenetrable bamboo and thorn groundcover. Above this were the snow-capped peaks of the Andes, interspersed with some very high and active volcanos.

Flying over this very remote area Dave had noticed an incredible area of gorged valleys and lakes hidden behind these almost impenetrable ramparts.

Dave's exciting letter enclosed a number of photographs and said that it looked very similar to Yosemite Valley in California and that some of the vertical valley walls must be over 4,000 feet high.

'I don't think anybody has ever been there. Up above are some beautiful glaciated mountains, the climbing ought to be marvellous and there's miles of it!' he wrote.

It was too good to miss so in January 1998, Suds and I took a long leave and planned a month's visit to Chile.

As usual, nothing went smoothly. Suds booked a cheap flight to Santiago for less than £200 only to discover that he had booked us to go to San Diego in the USA. Humble-pie and admission that we were just a couple of idiots sorted out the problem with British Airways and we finally arrived at Puerto Montt very jet lagged to discover that all our climbing equipment had been sent to San Diego in California. With a lot of help from Dave Clem we got our stuff back three days later.

Dave and his son Alastair were all set to join us on the trip but at the last moment Dave was urgently called off to another flying job. Bitterly disappointed he promised that he would still be able to fly the three of us into the valleys.

I had discovered that there had been an old Indian trail over a pass in the Andes from near the Argentinean ski resort of San Carlos de Bariloche to the small Chilean fishing village of Cochamo where there had once been a meat processing and canning plant. Butch Cassidy and the Sundance Kid had once owned a ranch on the Argentinean side of the mountains and had used the pass to take rustled cattle over the border to be slaughtered at the cannery. There's a well-documented account of a bank robbery they had committed at Rio Gallegos where apparently Sundance shot out the insulators on the phone poles while Butch robbed the bank.

During the time of the Spanish conquistadors the area around Puerto Montt had been settled by Jesuits and the Pope had decreed them heretic and attempted to have them murdered. They had escaped over the Cochamo pass and it is believed that their gold is hidden somewhere up there. We were keen to keep an eye open; a stash of loot would be a great bonus to our trip!

The weather was perfect – warm, blue sky with not a cloud to be seen. The great thing about being helicoptered into a climbing area is that you can carry a lot more food and equipment than normal. We went off to the market in Puerto Montt and bought a big ice box full of steak, a sack of onions and potatoes, a case of wine and a couple of bottles of whisky, all the home comforts; this was going to be a real holiday. We also bought a 500-foot reel of polypropylene to use as fixed rope.

The short flight into the mountains was extraordinary. A lot of Germans settled here after the war and as we flew over a secluded lake we saw an island with a large building and compound with the German eagle and a swastika flying. Dave circled round and waggled his tail but we saw no one. Probably just as well!

I gasped as the valleys came into view. This was Yosemite on a magnificent scale. Valley after valley with enormous side walls, lakes and glaciated snow-capped peaks. Over the top we could see into Argentina, arid and dry in contrast to the dense rainforest of Chile, and in the distance the high, smoking summit of the volcano Mount Tronador – 'The Thunderer' (11,453 feet).

The valley floors were a dense, virgin, temperate rainforest, one of only three such remaining in the world. The very rare Alerce trees were growing here in secret abundance, some well over a thousand years old. Climbers and vines and thick thorn and bamboo undergrowth that had never known human footsteps.

We never actually landed in the Cochamo valley where I knew that there had been a German adventurer who cleared an area of the scrub and a chalet had been built. It was far too tempting to get into the secreted and untrodden gorges hidden behind Cerro Trinidad, a granite dome mountain very similar to Half Dome in Yosemite.

Unknown at the time, others were looking with similar interest in the Cochamo valley. A trail to the foot of Cerro Trinidad had been hacked by Crispin Waddy and his girlfriend Nell Doust in a three-day tour du force using machetes. Disappointingly, they were forced back through lack of gear. Waddy's trail was followed by American climber Tim Dolan and Briton Simon Nadin who climbed a weakness to the left of the original line, which they named *Stirling Moss*. The valley had its first route.

Sometime later Waddy and Doust, with their friend Noel Craine, returned to complete their original project. As often happens in Cochamo their hike out became a bigger epic than the climb itself. Ahead of the others Craine heard a loud crack which he first thought was rockfall but soon realised that puffs of smoke were turning into a fully fledged forest fire. He ran back to warn Waddy and Doust and the three of them legged it up the slabs. They spent the next few days trapped there watching trees explode at the side of the ridge. They finally got down wading through thigh-deep ash which Waddy recounts was fortunately not too hot.

Compared to Craine and his friends our use of a helicopter must have seemed a bit of a cheat, but it was a fantastic way to get into the hidden valleys behind the mountain.

We circled the area. From Clem's photographs we had planned to climb a wall that we had named El Condor, but as we passed it in the helicopter I realised that we had completely underestimated its size. This was an undertaking on the scale of the Nose on El Capitan and over 3,000 feet high. It was totally isolated and any descent from its summit would be very complicated. There was a huge corner leading to a crack system running up the entire wall, which from what we could see was the highest wall in the valleys.

We had the excellent excuse that we didn't have enough gear for a long, multi-day climb. There was so much to explore that we wimped out, but planned to come back the following year better equipped and with a stronger team.

We flew into the next valley, which came to a blind end but there seemed to be a number of possibilities for climbing. The bottom was filled with scrubby trees and after a very careful hover Clem managed to land the helicopter in a tiny clearing, its blades missing the trees by inches. A quick unload and he was off leaving the three of us in as isolated a place as we had ever been, even though we were probably less than twenty miles from the nearest road. We set up camp alongside a small stream.

We were surrounded on three sides by 2,000-foot granite walls that looked great for climbing, but the scrub in the valley floor was almost impenetrable. We had machetes with us but these proved useless, they simply bounced off the bamboo and had no effect on the thorn. Our best way through was to wade along the streambeds until we got within range of our goal, put on waterproofs and padding and simply barge at the scrub and sometimes we would make a few feet of progress.

Another problem was a fly, the Calehueache, which we called the Quasimodo. These horrors were a kind of slow-flying giant bluebottle, which dived like Stukas and if they got you would bite off lumps. I had watched local children in Puerto Montt catch them, stick a barley straw into the thorax and then let them loose and watch the heavyweight stunt flying. I had no sympathy with the horrible critters.

Our first climb looked relatively easy, the walls around us were about 2,000 feet high. We followed a stream to the back of the canyon and set about climbing out. Expecting little more than an easy warm up we found that lower down the cracks were flared and filled with moss and vegetation with not much protection. Once we got higher the granite was rough and superb. Our every move was watched by circling condors and at one time a huge eagle soared overhead which I photographed and later identified as a Lone eagle. These beautiful birds are thought to be almost extinct. We topped out the wall and then plodded up a small mountain from where we had a splendid view over the Andes into Argentina, dry and sandy country compared with the Chilean rainforest.

So far the weather had been perfect. We climbed with minimal gear in shorts and T-shirts and fell into a false sense of security that it would always be like this. From the chopper we had seen a long diagonal fault running across the main face of a mountain, which I had called Pico Eilidh. Below the fault the wall was overhanging and above very steep and impregnable-looking, but the rake itself looked as if it might just avoid the overhangs. The whole thing was about 2,000 feet and came out on to a smaller subsidiary peak. Our plan was to put fixed ropes up the first five or six pitches and the following day make a push to complete the climb.

We struggled through the undergrowth to the foot of our climb. As expected we had two very gungy first pitches, the cracks filled with moss and lichen and then above remarkable clean rock where we fixed ropes for four or five pitches and then returned to our camp for a well-earned steak and a bottle of wine.

The following day we set out for the big push. With still perfect weather we took minimal gear but each carried a Gore-Tex bivvy bag and spare pullover just in case. This was Alastair Clem's first big wall climb. He and I had climbed together in Wadi Rum and he was very sound. We were confident that we could reach the summit in a single day and a night out on the way down would be no great hardship.

The climbing was marvellous, Pitch after pitch of steep overlapping slabs, mostly about Very Severe grade, but with poor protection in the flared cracks. We topped out in the late afternoon and lay in the sun for a few minutes on a perfect rocky summit with every possibility of being well down the abseils by nightfall. There was a great view from here where we could just make out the Pacific Ocean and to the south, the Andes chain with snowy peaks, and as far as the eye could see Chiloe Island.

Not far to the south the mountains are backed by a permanent ice plateau, which stretches down to the Towers of Paine where South America finally dips into the sea at Cape Horn. Where we were had been glaciated until very recently, clean polished slabs with not a sign of lichens, a clear sign of global warming. This was the kind of place I loved to be, totally isolated on a virgin mountain that nobody else had ever seen. Every climber's dream.

As we basked in the sunshine I noticed some rather odd, small puffy clouds forming in the south. This was the first cloud we had seen in Chile and I suggested it might be an idea to start roping down as quickly as we could. Too late!

We managed three or four rope lengths before the storm hit us. The speed it arrived at was horrifying. One minute I was abseiling in warm sunshine, the next we were in lashing wind with hailstones the size of golf balls hurtling at us. Within seconds our line of retreat became a huge flowing river of hail and impossible to descend.

Any other way down was overhanging and totally out of the question. We just had to get clear of the terrifying line that we were descending. I swung out over a small sloping ledge that lead across above the main overhanging wall and then petered out. Suds and Ali slid down and joined me. There was no shelter here but we were out of the line of the flowing hail.

The only thing to do was stay where we were and pray that it would stop. Our belay was the top of the abseil. We managed to scramble into our Gore-Tex bivvy bags and there we sat like three wise monkeys with very little insulated clothing. As night fell the hail turned first to heavy snow and later to lashing rain. The line of our climb became a huge cascading waterfall roaring past. Water was pouring down the rope that lead directly to my harness and began to fill my bivvy bag. I was half hanging in the bag with my feet in ankle-deep water and trying ineffectively to bail it out. My teeth rattled with cold but there was no point in asking Suds how he was getting on as I could actually hear his rattling beside me and I had no doubt that Alastair was in the same state, some experience for a teenager on his first big wall. At one point I unhitched from the rope in an attempt to stop the water pouring in and then realised that one false move and I would be sailing into space with my arms inside the bag. I hastily clipped back in and continued to bail.

Our tent down in the jungle was pitched alongside what had been a pleasant stream but now the valley was roaring as the burns began to explode into spate and I had the terrible vision of the loss of our campsite. We had no means of communicating with the outside world. The endless night continued, time and again I checked my watch determined that I wouldn't check it for another hour, as the hour passed I checked again only to find five minutes had elapsed.

The storm continued and it was still pouring when daylight finally came. The mountain had changed dramatically, the wall above the ramp we had climbed the previous day was now a series of waterfalls and snow had settled on the summit. At our level it was torrential and our descent route was a rushing watercourse. There was nothing to do but sit there and shiver and pray for it to stop. All three of us sat in silence in our own private misery.

About midday the downpour ceased almost as rapidly as it had started. A weak sun emerged and the water moderated. We emerged soaking and stiff from our bags and started exercising to warm ourselves. The line of our climb was still a rushing watercourse but it was now possible to swing back into it and we had no choice but to climb into the torrent and try to get down. It was difficult to find abseil points in the water and one of our ropes had to be sacrificed to arrange safe belays.

We now realised why the rock was so polished and the cracks were all flared – in wet weather our line was the main drainage on this side of the mountain. Drenched to the skin we splashed down the abseils but it was a great relief at last to be able to do something rather than sitting help-lessly. As we descended the weather improved and once we reached the fixed ropes it became a relatively easy retreat. We struggled back through the scrub and much to our relief the tent was still intact. Within minutes we were crawling blissfully into our sleeping bags.

That evening came the sound of engines and the squirrel helicopter inched down into the clearing. The storm had been violent in Puerto Montt and Dave had seen the fresh snow falling in the mountains. Knowing that we had been planning a big climb he decided to come over and see if we were okay. We quickly scrambled our stuff together, loaded the chopper and jumped aboard glad to escape. An hour later we were sitting in a comfortable bar in Puerto Varas recounting our exploits. Helicopters are wonderful!

Alastair had taken a job guiding a raft trip down one of the local rivers so the following day Dave flew Suds and I back into the valleys, this time to a more open site alongside a lake that we called Lago Ness. It was a beautiful place with a glacier-covered mountain at the head of the valley that we named El Grepon. Our camp was on a gorgeous beach quite close to the cliffs on the valley walls. As usual it took about an hour's bush-whacking to get through the couple of hundred yards to the climbing.

Our first attempt was up what looked an easy gully but we were stopped almost immediately by huge chockstones blocking the way. Suds drew the short straw and climbed a horribly steep moss-filled crack and belayed at the foot of a huge slab. I climbed on to this to discover that it was easier than it looked from below and we were able to take off the ropes and solo for several hundred feet until we reached a sharp summit ridge. We were now on a crest that separated our valley from a much deeper one to the east. What followed I consider to be the best ridge walk I have ever done.

We were walking on perfectly polished granite slabs that would have graced the front of any major bank, with absolutely vertical walls falling away on either side. Following this for a couple of miles over a number of minor summits we left cairns to indicate to any future climbers that we had been there. It must have felt like this in the golden age of mountaineering, when the first pioneers topped out on Alpine summits. At the high point we realised that we were on top of the huge wall we had named El Condor. The summit was ice-capped but the enormous face was clean, shining granite dropping away thousands of feet below us and I realised that this was one of the world's biggest walls. We lay in the sun trying to figure out how one could get down to the foot of the face. It was not going to be easy. Both sides of the mountain were broken ground and almost vertical jungle had spread up for over a thousand feet and there were extraordinary lochans trapped in pockets on the cliffs. Next year we would come with a strong team.

Continuing along the beautiful ridge we came to another of the extraordinary easy-angled slabs that lead down into our valley. We decided to risk dropping into the jungle and finding a stream to get back to our camp. The alternative being to retrace our ridge with the possibility of a night out. We dropped down the slab for about a thousand feet till it came to a huge, unescapable overhanging wall. With no choice we plodded back up the slab for a few hundred feet until we found a gully which we scrambled and abseiled down into the scrub.

This top end of the valley had a beautiful waterfall flowing over a tremendously overhanging wall. This was meltwater from the glacier of El Grepon. There was the excellent possibility of a very remarkable climb turning the overhangs of the waterfall on its right, it was short, steep and spectacular and we planned this as our next outing. We scrambled into the stream from the waterfall and splashed our way down the valley in a tunnel of bamboo and scrub and arrived at Lago Ness tired and jubilant after a most glorious day.

That night another of the weird Antarctic storms hit and once again the rock faces exploded into torrents. This time we were safe in a warm tent listening to the storm and very much relieved that we had not tried to retrace our steps along the ridge where we would with certainty have had to spend a night out.

Our attempt on the waterfall climb failed. We splashed our way back up the river but were so exhausted when we got there that we packed it in. Getting to other cliffs in the area through the jungle took so long that we didn't manage any other climbs. In our times in the lost valleys we had seen very little wild life. There are reported puma sightings and wild boar but I doubt they would enjoy fighting through the scrub any more than we did. Above the trees we saw some marmot-like animals, lots of condors and some giant hummingbirds.

The helicopter picked us up and the Clem family took us for a few days touring. We visited the town of Osorno, a few miles to the north with its active volcano behind. I was very interested that there was a ski area, which was abandoned when the mountain erupted. I was keen to see if the lifts could be reinstated but gave up the idea as the mountain was still smoking.

We flew home leaving the South American summer sunshine for a freezing northern hemisphere making plans for our next year's trip. Unfortunately PDG Helicopters packed in their Puerto Montt company later that year, the politics in Chile making it very difficult for a foreign company to operate.

We never did get back to the beautiful valleys. An attempt by the Chilean Government to build a road through the Cochamo valley to Argentina was started but thwarted by conservationists as was a project to build a hydro dam. The great risk is logging. I had seen a mountain of wood chip at the docks in Puerto Montt waiting for transport to Japan for conversion to sterling board. On the narrow coastal plain the gorgeous thousand-year-old Alerce trees no longer exist and the thought that loggers would go into the beautiful valleys is appalling. Climbing however has exploded in abundance.

The mountain that we had called El Condor was spotted by local climbers sometime later and is now called El Monstruo. As trails were cut through the jungle, access to the Cochamo valley routes became easier but it was not until eight years later, in 2006, that two famous Polish climbers, Jerzy 'Jurek' Stefanski and Boguslaw 'Bodziu' Kowalski, finally climbed the great wall. In a twenty-hour push they transported their equipment over the Barrancas Pass and must have padded along the perfect granite ridge that Suds and I had followed in 1998. They spent the night there and then, risking all, left their cooking equipment and sleeping bags and abseiled down the horrendous 5,000-foot south side of El Monstruo into a thousand feet of vertical forest to reach the valley at the foot of the face.

They started up the great corner on the right side of the face that we had spotted from Clem's helicopter. The corner turned into a series of cracks and chimneys and topped out on the summit snow ridge after two long days of climbing and a very cold and uncomfortable bivouac. Three hours later in darkness they traversed over to the main ridge to reach their campsite. They called the climb *La Gran Raja*, 'The Great Crack' (F7a, 1,300 metres, 4,265 feet, 22 pitches).

Having seen the horrendous descent from the summit of El Monstruo I have nothing but respect for the two climbers who took off down the complicated 5,000 feet of wall and vertical jungle without sleeping bags or bivvy gear. I cringe at the thought of what happened to us a mile or so up the valley when we were hit by the Antarctic storm. I'm sure that like us, Jerzy and Bodziu had some gear for just such an emergency but I wonder if they realised just how violent things could get in this very exposed place.

A second climb was added to the wall in 2013 by Nathan Conroy and his father and several others over a thirty-day period of trail blazing and various sorties on to the face starting from the lowest part of the wall: *La Presencia de mi Padre* (5.10+, 1,600 metres. 5,249 feet, 26 pitches).

So El Monstruo becomes at present the longest clean and unbroken granite rock climb in the world.

Looking at the internet recently I was amazed to see a video clip of a party of hillwalkers traversing the beautiful ridge above El Monstruo. How in such short time things have changed. In just one decade an unassailable wilderness has turned into a climber's paradise. I can only pray that some of the valleys hold on to their secrets.

20 | Wadi Rum

In 1999 Dave Clem invited Suds and I to join him on a climbing trip to Wadi Rum in Jordan. It was to be a family holiday; Dave and his wife Helen and son Alistair, Suds and wife Catherine, and me as the odd bod. We found ourselves flying into the Arab port of Aqaba at the north-east tip of the Red Sea. The heat and smells of this small town were in sharp contrast to the regimented skyscrapers and apartment blocks of the Israeli city of Eilat, threateningly visible less than five miles away across the gulf. Here the Bedouin and Arabs in their bleached white robes jostled among the stalls and street vendors in the bustling streets in a town that must have looked little different to how it did a century ago.

Among the crowd I spotted a familiar figure, Tony Howard, one of the founders of the Troll climbing equipment company and the Rimmon Mountaineering Club. Tony had been wandering the desert for years and was one of the original climbers to have discovered Wadi Rum as a major rock climbing area and had done much to popularise desert climbing. He and his partner Di Taylor had become friendly with King Hussein and were accepted and respected among the Bedouin having popularised the area and brought much-needed tourism to Jordan. Tony and Di invited us to join them at their camp in Wadi Rum and it was like having a living guidebook of the area to show us around.

The camp in Rum village was at the edge of a group of small houses with a herd of camels grazing on the few diminutive plants growing in the desert. Most of the Bedouin lived in tents but with the beginning of tourism a few had built rough block buildings that looked primitive but inside were beautifully lined with carpets and were cool and comfortable.

The majority of Rum Bedouin belong to the Howeitat tribe and their black tents had been in the Wadi for as long as anyone can remember.

The hospitality of the Howeitat is as legendary as their fighting ability which became internationally known after the First World War through the writings of T.E. Lawrence. In the Second World War they fought as soldiers in the Arab Legion against the Vichy French. Tony told us that when he first met them they had warned, 'If you are soft with us, we will squeeze you; if you are hard with us, we will break you; if you are straight we will be your friend.' To us they were courteous and welcomed us into their tents wherever we went.

Wadi Rum reminded me very much of parts of Antarctica, a great glacier of sand running between vertical 3,000-foot mountainsides into the shimmering desert and running out as far as the eye could see towards Saudi Arabia – extraordinarily similar to glaciers running down from the polar plateau. It was easy to imagine Lawrence of Arabia amassing his Bedouin army and riding across the desert to take Aqaba from the Turks. Tony introduced us to an old Bedouin sheikh who had ridden on the pummel of his father's camel with Lawrence to the siege of Aqaba.

We climbed early in the mornings in the shade and rested up in the afternoon heat. There were acres of red sandstone rising vertically out of the desert. On one occasion we climbed Sheikh Hamdan's route to the summit of Jebel Rum. This difficult climb was first ascended and used by the Bedouin to reach the summit plateau on hunting expeditions. Barefoot and with a rifle slung over their shoulder, these agile men put our climbing abilities to shame. They made long, unprotected leaps on to tiny holds across the most horrendous sheer drops, jumps that none of us would contemplate even with a rope.

At one point I scrambled nervously along a very unstable scree ledge crossing a vertical face to find the branch of a dead tree balanced against an overhanging wall. The only way up was to climb the branch to reach a small hold cut in the soft rock above the overhang. Tony assured me that he had watched a Bedouin hunter swarm up this barefoot with an AK47 rifle slung over his back. I managed the same thing myself only with great difficulty and masses of rope protection.

One morning we drove twelve miles out into the desert in one of the Bedouin trucks to climb on Jebel Burdah where there is a huge natural arch, one of the great sights of the area. Climbing with Alistair up one of Tony's more conventional routes I began to feel unwell. By the time I managed to abseil off the climb I was vomiting and suffering from diarrhoea. I vaguely remembered eating some sweetmeats from a street vendor the previous day.

We now discovered that two of the truck's tyres had punctures and although the driver had at least half a dozen spares, all of them were full of holes. We all climbed aboard and drove with flat tyres across the desert until the wheels collapsed then the driver shrugged and told us to get walking. There was nothing for it but to set off in raging heat back towards Wadi Rum. After a mile or so I began to feel very wobbly, at the same time Helen, who had eaten from the same trader, also began to suffer. In this heat neither of us could go any further and we huddled against a large boulder trying to get some shade. A very concerned Dave set off as fast as he dared to get help.

Luckily a few miles further on he came across a Bedouin truck bouncing through the desert with what appeared to be no driver. It turned out to be a cigarette smoking small boy who could not have been more than eleven years old. Wooden blocks were attached to the truck's pedals so his feet could reach them and he was just managing to peer over the control panel. With much bribery and promises he was persuaded to come to our rescue. To Dave's consternation he refilled the tank from a rusty petrol can with the lit cigarette stuck firmly in his mouth and they bounced at break-neck speed back over the desert to where Helen and I were lying. A few hours later I was back in my tent.

For the next couple of days I spent my time crawling to a filthy toilet that I shared with a giant cockroach, which circled constantly round my pot and seemed totally unable to cross the shadow of the door to make his escape. By day three I was hallucinating and very ill and Tony spoke to two Bedouin who offered to take Helen and me to a doctor who they were certain lived about twenty miles away.

We were dumped unceremoniously on the back of a truck and bounced our way across the desert only to find that the doctor had left the area some years previously. We were then driven on for another twenty miles or so and finally arrived at a small village where there was an Arab hospital. It was a rough and ready place with sick people sitting around in groups on the floor. Helen, who was not as ill as me and was a lot more attractive, was taken away and fussed over while I sat against a wall quietly awaiting my fate, unable to walk and having difficulty speaking.

Finally an Israeli doctor appeared who realised that I wasn't just Helen's chaperone and had me carted into a surgery where I was put on a saline drip and given antibiotics. As the fluid entered my body I felt my strength returning almost instantly. Within the hour Helen and I were back on our truck bouncing through the desert with a stack of packets of pills and instructions to eat lots of yogurt (which I did) and not drink alcohol (which I did for a short while). Both of us recovered rapidly in the next day or two and I am forever grateful to the Israeli doctor whom I never got to thank. That evening I returned to my toilet determined to set the cockroach free only to find that some other miserable occupant had unceremoniously trodden on him.

Before the holiday I had been negotiating the purchase of a north of England group of shops called Wilderness Ways. The deal had fallen through and I had left Robert Ferrell running Nevisport while we were away. He had managed to contact Suds and me as we left Glasgow airport, to say that the owners of Wilderness Ways had asked to speak to us again and we'd left leaving Robert to find out what they wanted.

There was a small Arab police station in Rum Village and with Tony's help he managed to persuade them to let me use their telex machine.

'They're willing to accept your original offer, Spike, what shall I do?' Robert's urgent message came through.

Suds and I looked at each other and grinned. 'Accept, Rab, it's a good deal,' I managed to send back. We had purchased eight shops while standing in an Arab police station in Wadi Rum. It was a grand finale to a great holiday.

21 | The End of the Century

I watched the fireworks exploding over the ruins of the old Fort William as the bells chimed in the new century; rockets and shimmering curtains lighting up Loch Linnhe and the surrounding mountains in a breathtaking display of bursting light while my daughter, sitting astride my shoulders, slept peacefully through the spectacle. The whole town had turned out and was lining the waterfront cheering in the new millennium.

I remembered as a boy thinking, 'I'll be fifty-seven in the year 2000'. At the time it seemed to be a great age but here I was still relatively fit and thoroughly enjoying life as the new century arrived. Looking back I realise how lucky I've been. My generation must be one of the few who have not had to fight for our country. Those of us born during the Second World War have lived through a period of high prosperity. The world does not seem a safer place but the small wars we have been involved in have not required a large population of young men to be called to arms.

I had left the day-to-day running of Nevisport with Suds, Rab Ferrell and two other directors and set about changing Nevis Range from a ski centre into a year-round visitor attraction. We built mountain bike tracks in the forest and a steep and exciting 2,000-foot downhill course using the gondola for access. Taking advice from some French enthusiasts, we built a terrifying track down the mountain, increasing the obstacles and zig-zagging hair-raisingly through the trees. It was steep, gnarly, looked very dangerous and I was sure that Continental health and safety laws were not as stringent as ours.

As construction commenced I began to panic that we might cause a fatal accident. Nevis Range staff held a sweepstake on how many broken bones we would have on the first race. Amazingly nobody won. By some miracle there wasn't a single injury. We had found a summer business.

Everything seemed to be running smoothly, we had been doing well and there seemed to be no reason why things should change, but it became obvious that my plan to spend three years at Nevis Range, put in a manager and go back to Nevisport was not going to work out. The ski company was struggling from horrible winters, lack of snow and competition from abroad with cheap flights to the Continent, America and Canada. The industry was in disarray; instead of growing, the Scottish ski resorts were losing customers at an alarming rate. We were unable to pay some of our loans and had to restructure borrowing from a jittery and unhelpful bank.

I had been on friendly terms with Nick Escourt's shop in Altrincham for many years and we had come to the decision to amalgamate the two companies. Dave Pierce, who had taken over the running of Escourt's after Nick's untimely death on Everest, was going to join us as technical director and this would inject some new ideas into the company.

Dave and I had often climbed together and had a mini adventure climbing a crack in the wall of the huge dam below the Tignes ski area in France. We were arrested as we topped out; the local police seemed to have been more aggrieved that it had been Brits and not French men who first climbed the dam wall. It was all very jolly and our short stay in the cells ended in a cheery party, which the local gendarmes attended.

They say that trouble comes in threes. Up until now Nevisport had been on a lucky run. It hadn't all been easy but our little company had grown smoothly over the years and there seemed to be no reason to think that we wouldn't continue to expand.

When the first bombshell struck there was no prior warning. Dave was due to join us over a weekend and we planned to sort out the paperwork merging the companies on the Monday. During the week he called me on the phone.

'My son's home from Australia, Spike, and wants to go climbing, can we put off the meeting for a couple of days?'

Of course there was no problem and that weekend they went to Gogarth on Anglesey. Dave abseiled down to a ledge above the sea that hundreds of climbers had scrambled along previously. A huge block broke away and he took a fatal fall into the sea. His son abseiled into the water and held him till a helicopter crew arrived, but they were unable to save him. The tragedy affected me terribly. Dave and his partner, Caroline, had become such close friends and we had great plans for the future. Somehow a spark went out and although we joined up with the Escourt business, without Dave it never had the intended effect.

The second bombshell came a few weeks later. I had been diagnosed with a weird throat disorder called Barrett's oesophagus. It had never been much of a problem but I had to have a yearly check-up. One afternoon, David Sedgwick, the surgeon at the Fort William hospital, asked me to drop in for a coffee. I was under the impression that it was mountain rescue business and was somewhat shocked as David spelled it out to me.

'Your oesophagus is turning cancerous, Spike, we need to act quickly, I'm sending you up to see a specialist.'

Still feeling perfectly well I was rushed to Inverness where a Professor Munro told me in no uncertain terms that my survival depended on the removal of my oesophagus, and pretty damn quick!

Life had been so good; I was as fit as I had ever been. I had a new woman in my life, Gay, and we were deeply in love. My daughter, Eilidh, was just six and being a dad was wonderful. That night Gay and I made the mistake of looking up oesophagectomy on the internet – it made terrifying reading. The operation involved opening up my diaphragm and moving my stomach into my chest cavity, making a new oesophagus out of half my stomach, removing the old oesophagus and attaching the new pipe to my throat. A very workmanlike plumbing job with a failure rate of about eighty per cent. Not exactly bedtime reading but there didn't seem to be an alternative.

I have never been religious and can't imagine myself in heaven or hell or sitting on a cloud. The thought of oblivion – nothing – seems to me not very frightening. What would be distressing would be the huge disappointment in not being there to see what happened; how my daughter or Gay would get on without me. The shock to my mother, already in her eighties, and what would happen to Nevisport and Nevis Range haunted me. In addition to that came the selfish stuff; the long list of climbs and expeditions to be done. God, I'd not even managed to retire!

It was a hectic few days. Marian Austin took over as MD at Nevis Range. She had started out running the ski school and rapidly became indispensable and had become a director. She knew the ski industry better than anyone I know. Previously she and her partner had set up a bicycle business in Fort William. Marian now set about getting us on to the mountain bike world cup series. Her fantastic effort has made Nevis Range more famous worldwide for its bike track than its skiing.

Within three or four days I was on my way to Raigmore Hospital in Inverness. Gay and I drove up the east side of Loch Ness and stopped off at my old climbing haunts at Loch Duntelchaig where we sat quietly with our feet in the water and watched the sun go down.

That evening I checked into the ward and was examined by a cheerful anaesthetist.

'Your operation's tomorrow afternoon, you can slip out for a while this evening if you wish. No food but have a dram if you like, just one,' he said.

I dressed, slipped out of the ward and took his advice.

Doug Scott was giving a talk about his Himalayan adventures in Inverness that night so Gay and I went along. I'm sure it was brilliant but the whole thing went over my head. I spoke to Doug afterwards and suspect he thought I was acting strangely. I had a large dram, hugged Gay and slipped back into the ward where I realised that nobody had even noticed my absence.

I slept fitfully and got up at 4 a.m. and watched the sun rise over Dava Moor from the ward window. We had done mountain rescue navigation exercises here when I was in the RAF. Was this to be my last sunrise? A few hours later I lay thankfully drugged after my pre-med and was rolled quietly into theatre where I was, as the Scots would say, well and truly 'gralloched'.

For the next few weeks it was touch and go in the intensive care unit where I was lovingly looked after but managed to catch MRSA, the ghastly anti-immune infection that was the scourge of the NHS hospitals at the time. I also became very dependent on morphine. It was hard not to notice the shock on friends' faces when they came to visit me.

'It's not looking too good, Spike,' my surgeon anxiously told me on one of his morning rounds.

'I know, I know,' I muttered, wallowing in self-pity and frustration.

Gay came every day. A homeopath, she quietly began to help me back to health. I stopped taking medication and started homeopathic remedies, which without doubt helped me give up my reliance on morphine. It's incredible what the human body can take. Astonishingly, I began to improve and put on weight. Although I now had a rather peculiar anatomy with a half stomach in my chest I began to be able to eat remarkably well.

A few weeks later I went home to the long, slow process of rehab. How Gay put up with me I'll never understand. I must have been very demanding and was at times frightened, but slowly she nursed me back to health. I had a second hip replacement and various setbacks, but within a year I began to feel more like my old self.

Suds turned up one morning and insisted that I get my boots on and we plodded slowly up to Ardverikie Wall on Binnein Shuas, one of the most beautiful climbs in Scotland. The sheer joy of being back in the mountains, even on a rope as tight as a piano wire, is almost impossible to explain to a non-climber. I hobbled along on my crutches, staggering down the mountain with Suds waiting till I caught up and then setting off just as I thought I was getting a rest. No change there, I was back!

I had remained a non-executive director at Nevis Range but decided to return to Nevisport. I needed a job but did not feel well enough to go back to my old post as MD. Everything had become computerised in the years I was away and I struggled to get my head round all the new systems. I became office bound and tried desperately to catch up on the new technology.

Climbing shops were opening in almost every town in the country and their style was changing. I had been away from the industry for almost ten years and although I had remained as chairman of Nevisport, we weren't the kind of business that held many board meetings and I was not as up to date with the day-to-day running of the company as I would have liked. I took some time out to have a look at how other shops were faring.

Wandering around Keswick in the Lake District one afternoon I drifted into one of the many mountain shops that had developed in the town. The manager was showing a new member of staff around and I sneaked along behind, listening to their conversation.

'Do we give much discount?' the new man asked.

The manager's reply was staggering. 'There are over sixty outdoor shops within a fifteen mile radius of Keswick,. he said. 'We have to give something away or we'll go out of business.'

The number seemed extraordinary; when we started the only climbing shops in the Lake District were George Fisher in Keswick and Frank Davies in Ambleside. Both men knew the majority of their customers personally and would give us as much tick as they thought we would be able to pay back. They would be horrified at the new outdoor industry and staggered at the growth in the fashion side where mountain clothing has almost become standard day-to-day dress. Technical climbing gear seemed to have become a sideline.

Later I went down to the outdoor trade show in Harrogate. I had always enjoyed these shows, which were a chance to look at new equipment, make deals, chat with old friends and socialise.

For the second time in my life I felt like Woody Allen in *Sleeper*, emerging to a changed world. Many of the original pioneer businesses had been swallowed into large conglomerates. Nevisport had been lucky to be large enough to live on as an independent company, but the small, privately run climbing shops were finding it hard to survive. A new breed of young men were setting the pace and the few older faces that I recognised had, with a few exceptions, either changed companies or stepped back for the younger generation. I wandered around the stands feeling lost and shy and a bit of a dinosaur.

It was time to make changes. Suds and I were no longer 'the new kids on the block' and the competition was fierce. Both of us were approaching sixty – it was time to let the next generation take over.

Our third disaster came sometime later with the sale of the company; the business had been our baby for over thirty years and we were immensely proud of it. After much discussion with bankers and so-called financial experts we sold Nevisport as a management buyout. From the early days of sleeping on the floor of the shop, with a spot of poaching to keep the wolf from the door, it had flourished into a national company. It was a terrible wrench but it seemed at the time it was the right decision. Sadly the banking crisis in the recession of 2007 hit the company badly and the boys were forced to sell out prematurely.

A year or so later I was still recovering but well enough to travel, so Gay and I joined a bunch of my dog sledging friends who had hired a Norwegian icebreaker to visit our old Antarctic bases. We flew to Ushuaia in Argentina, the southernmost city in the world, on the southern tip of South America. Here we picked up our boat, the *Polar Star*, and headed south down the Antarctic Peninsula visiting familiar haunts on the way.

Calling at Deception Island, which I had last seen looking like the scene of an atomic bomb exploding as it erupted, we looked over the ruins of the old British base and were able to swim in warm springs in the Antarctic Ocean. The British have never reestablished their base here but both Argentina and Chile have reconstructed theirs and it's rumoured that children have been born on the island and both countries claim that this entitles them to sovereignty. The old volcano is clearly still active so one of these days they may get a big surprise!

Stonington Island was as beautiful as ever but the base that had been my home for two years was in a terrible ruined state and almost unrecognisable. The windows were boarded up and everything was gutted from the inside. The North-East Glacier had receded and no longer poured on to the island so it could not be used as an inland route. Of all the British bases this was the one that had been the main focus in the dog sledging era and it seemed to us tragic that the British Antarctic Survey had allowed it to get into this state.

The island was full of ghosts and I felt as if we were invading its tranquillity. I was surprisingly glad to get back on board ship and leave the place that had been my home at the happiest time in my life.

Horseshoe Island was much better. The base was as we had left it and was now a sort of museum. I even recognised the books on the shelves. The generator was still working and the lovely fireplace we had built was pleasingly intact. Ian Curphey and I found the ski we had carved as a sign on the door over forty years previously, which remained in place and looked brand new.

From there we visited a new base at Rothera Point which had been a snowy beach when I sledged over it to meet Rod and Curph on the day that Neil Armstrong landed on the moon. The place was unrecognisable. There was a landing stage for the largest of ships, an airstrip and hangar, and modern office-like blocks with laboratories, workshops, a cafeteria, a bar and private bedrooms. We discovered that Rothera had the same dialling code as Cambridge! A call home is the same price as a local UK call. This was a far cry from our primitive world of wooden huts, dogs, Morse code messages home and a visit from the ships once a year. We were given a huge welcome from the young residents who must have looked upon us as visitors from the Stone Age. They had a museum of sorts with some old bits of sledging gear. Rooting through this I found an old map with 'The Huns' dog team and Ian Curphey written on it and was able to return it to its owner. We really had become museum pieces!

Driving dogs in Antarctica finished at the end of our era. A few years after I left the Survey all the dogs were shot. Some well-intentioned bureaucrats had decided that they were a non-indigenous species of Antarctica and might affect the existing wildlife; the fact that there were no land animals on the frozen continent seems to have totally eluded them. I thank God that I wasn't there at the time.

South Georgia was much changed too; Grytviken had been devastated during the Falklands War and a brand new sterile factory-like building had replaced our comfortable old base. There was a sign 'Keep off the grass' alongside the footpath up to the wreckage of the old whaling station, probably necessary because of the increase in tourist liners visiting the island. A notice at the base entrance explained to 'inmates' how to make a complaint against a senior member of staff, something that would have been contemptible in my day. We were to hear that scientists were discussing whether or not to shoot the herds of reindeer now well established on the island. These were originally introduced by the whalers in the nineteenth century. The animals are now living happily in their ideal habitat but as I write this in 2015 the cull is already under way.

At the most there are 20,000 scientists and technicians working on Antarctica at any one time, no more than the population of a small town, and in the vastness of Antarctica this is insignificant. At almost the size of Western Europe and the United States put together, man has as yet done little damage. I pray it will always be so.

The world has moved on and my journey south had been something of a disappointment. The great ice-covered continent is still to me the most beautiful place on earth. Ice had receded at the northern tip of the peninsula and on South Georgia, but further south it seemed to me that there was little change. Perhaps there is time for us to make the necessary modifications to our lifestyles and reduce the burning of fossil fuels to slow down global warming. Perhaps it was a mistake to return, but since my visit, like many of my friends, I spend a great deal of time trying to figure out a way to get back there.

22 | Discovering America

It's the 12th of September 2013. I'm sitting at a campsite at Lee Vining on the side of Mono Lake in California, one of the loveliest places I know. It's a salt lake on the edge of the desert with its back to the Sierra Mountains and the Tioga Pass, the old wagon trail that leads over into what is now the Yosemite National Park.

Yesterday Mike Simpkins and I walked out into the desert to a rocky place called Granite Basin to a local climbers' testpiece called *Hair Raiser Buttress*. Mike did most of the leading and I was pleased that he kept a good firm rope. It's steep and gnarly and a long way between bolts. Mike is sixty-eight and recently retired from Australia, and has restarted his climbing after a few years' break. He's still a very talented climber.

I'm over seventy now and as keen as ever. There are four of us camping here, all old wrinklies with more metal hips and artificial joints than we like to mention. None of us can go through customs without setting off the alarms. The California sunshine and pristine dry rock suits our aching bodies. It's a horrible thought that if my hips had packed in thirty years earlier I might have ended my days in a wheelchair.

Our little corner of the campsite is a popular meeting place, it's well known that we have an unending supply of whisky and, like the Pied Piper of Hamelin, I attract young American climbers with my crap banjo playing. Here we all are, still climbing and not that badly. Surprisingly only slightly less able than I always have been, it's just that around us everybody else's standards have soared.

Pondering this I realise that young climbers are a different breed to us. In the fifties our small groups, hitching at weekends to North Wales and the Lakes, at a time when we knew almost every climber in the country, would have been mystified by the modern climber, much as the likes of

Geoffrey Winthrop Young, a link to the past golden age of mountaineering, who was still alive and living in the Dungeon Ghyll Hotel in Langdale, must have thought about us. Numbers have multiplied a hundredfold and both places have become national parks. The broken-down walls and barns are repaired and the mountains are alive with people. A whole industry has developed from what was once an escape for a few impoverished enthusiasts.

As a schoolboy there was an unending supply of war surplus boots and clothing but the stuff was only just adequate. The Italian hemp rope and a few slings didn't allow for much error and the old adage, 'a leader must not fall', was perfectly true. Most leaders would climb roped on rock only slightly above the grade they were capable of soloing. The weekend 'crunch, crunch' of nailed boots up Langdale and the drunken stagger from the Old Dungeon Ghyll bar to Ike Myers' barn at Wall End would horrify the modern hard men. Today they exercise in the gym, cycle to work and drink orange juice by the bucket. A new, young and determined contingent of climbers has emerged with a modern and more technical approach. The ease of transport makes it conceivable to have a long weekend in the Alps. With modern equipment it's possible to fall safely and many climbers practise this as part of their training, a thought of which terrifies me.

The thing we all have in common is the great joy and adventure of the sport. It must be something to do with adrenaline, the need for that exhilarating rush one gets in extreme situations. It does not make sense that we should risk life and limb and sometimes thousands of pounds in the pursuit of a goal, which has no purpose or gain other than some kind of self-congratulation. Oddly, my great memories are not of sunshine on the perfect day swanking up impeccable rock, but are of shivering cold in appalling conditions trying to tunnel through a cornice on Ben Nevis at night with a knackered head torch or topping out on the Grépon in a thunderstorm with sparks crackling on my axe and wondering if the next flash bang would be my last.

I was never much of a hillwalker, somehow my legs have never been that good. I struggle along behind, usually a couple of hundred yards in the rear knowing that my companions will stop, wait and then set off refreshed, just as I arrive. Funnily enough, that's more or less as I like it. I seem to come into my own as things steepen up. Somehow the motion of climbing suits me better. At the same time I suffer from what I call pre-climbing nerves; I sleep badly before a big climb feeling incompetent and plagued by fear and anticipation, and hence arrive at the foot half asleep and feeling like death. But once I start to climb and the excitement kicks in I come back to life.

It was great to be involved in what I think was the beginning of the new modern era in mountaineering in the late sixties. How for a century nobody thought of curving an ice-axe pick down is incredible. Mountaineering has always been a sport of the traditionalist and I guess the Austrian straight-picked Aschenbrenner, at walking-stick length, was the implement of a gentleman. Our workshop in Nevisport spent hours bending down old ice axe picks and shortening the shafts. When Hamish MacInnes invented the Terrordactyl there was a revolution. It was possible to hang back on your tools on steep ice and relax. The lovable MOACs were replaced by an array of wired nuts and eccentrics of all shapes and sizes. Hawser ropes became woven, and the old hammer and pegs that were once a permanent part of my climbing kit were now left on a shelf in the shed … with the new stuff we were off!

I had never been to America; it felt too organised and tame. I liked the idea of big walls but somehow national parks with thousands of people didn't appeal. How wrong can you be?

In the early seventies a young American climber, Jim Donini, who worked as a shop assistant in Nevisport, had given me an idea.

'If you ever go to the States, Spike, go to Wind River Range in Wyoming, it's just like Yosemite Valley without the people,' he said.

Jim has become one of the world's finest mountaineers and his advice is well worth taking, but it was to be thirty years before I finally took it and it was not until 2006 that Suds and I finally decided to go. His wife Catherine was having none of it without her, so I decided to take Eilidh, now eleven years old, along as well. It was an odd little family group that arrived at a dude ranch in Lander, Wyoming, where we had arranged for horses to take us into the mountains. I had failed to tell the ranchers that apart from Eilidh none of us had been on a horse in our lives.

I had assumed the day's ride up to the Cirque of the Towers, the most well known venue in the Wind River Range, would be a doddle up a gentle trail. A bad mistake! We were launched into the big American saddles and set out riding up the deep, wooded valley of the Popo Agie River, which we crossed and recrossed. The horses clambered over fallen trees, slid down steep embankments and wallowed up to their flanks in the water. They seemed to know what they were doing but my horse had the habit of bending down suddenly to munch a tasty bit of grass and more than once I somersaulted over its head, much to the amusement of our guides. By the time we reached the Cirque I was in no state to look in wonder at the incredible scenery. My knees hurt so badly that I was unable to stand and I lay comatose in the grass, my only consolation being that both Suds and Catherine were in the same state and lay where the horses had dropped them.

Our guides dumped the equipment and turned back immediately promising to return in two weeks' time. They can't have relished the long ride home that night but were marvellous horsemen and probably made it back in half the time it took us.

I finally staggered to my feet. We were in a perfect Garden of Eden in a wooded glade alongside Lonesome Lake with soaring mountains reflected in its waters. Pingora Peak, Warbonnet, Shark's Nose and Lizard Head Peak. This was once the hunting ground of the Crow and Shoshone Indians and it was easy to imagine a circle of wigwams right on the spot we were standing.

As our riders vanished back down the trail we realised that we had no matches and only six teabags, but this was minor to the oncoming nightmare. Nobody had mentioned the mosquitoes – clouds of the damn things descended on us, biting out lumps and itching us like mad, they were to become our constant and hated companions during our stay. Eilidh took charge as none of the adults were in any state to organise the camp and we crawled stiffly into our sleeping bags leaving the eleven year old to sort things out.

The following morning I managed to light a fire using the sparker on my Primus stove and the smoke helped to reduce the mosquitoes, but tea became a dream of the past. Suds and I set out to climb Pingora Peak. Its north-east face is the most famous climb in the range and is listed as one of the top fifty climbs in America and we were not disappointed. We made a glorious approach over alpine meadows in a blaze of spring flowers with snow-clad peaks all around the Cirque with herds of deer grazing and a lone moose watching us suspiciously.

We scrambled up an easy sloping ramp to emerge high on the crest of the buttress where we finally roped up and began climbing a series of flake cracks. Thus began my love affair with American climbing. Pitch after pitch of superb clean rock, very exposed but never too difficult and in exquisite surroundings. We followed a series of right-facing corners to the crux of a smooth slab split by a steep crack and then a couple of hundred feet of easy climbing to the perched blocks of the north-east summit. Looking north-ward at the spectacular peak of Warbonnet I noticed that as it emerged from the shade the morning sun caught its entire summit ridge, looking like the feathers on an Indian chief's headdress. Some observant pioneer must have noticed this extraordinary phenomena that gave the mountain its name.

We basked in the sun for an hour and then began a careful series of abseils down the west face. A tricky place as there were sharp flakes of rock all the way down our line of descent, any of which could have caught our ropes as we tried to pull them down and would have been a very tricky situation had they jammed. Within a couple of hours we were back with the ladies at the campsite sitting with running eyes in a smoky fire trying to avoid the mosquitoes.

During the next two weeks we saw only two people: a couple of walkers passing through the Cirque from whom we manage to cadge a couple of tea bags. Eilidh found a flint arrowhead by our campsite, a reminder that this was still the Indian's heartland and their reservation. These lovely people now live in poor accommodation and near poverty in settlements surrounding the mountains.

Our horses arrived spot on time and we faced yet another nine hours of purgatory but arrived safe but sore back in Lander. We drove north through Buffalo to the spectacular Devil's Tower. A most extraordinary rock projecting 800 feet out of the plain. The climbing here was spectacular bridging up vertical columns with wide cracks that fitted none of our gear. A friendly pair of American climbers played 'pass the giant Friend' to give us some protection on this very exposed wall.

The tower was first climbed in 1893 by two local ranchers, William Rogers and Willard Ripley, who had wedged a log ladder running hundreds of feet up one of the corners. The remnants of this astonishing ladder can still be seen and one can only wonder at the determination of these pioneers. Its first true climbing ascent was not until 1937 by Fritz Wiessner, Bill House and Lawrence Coveney. Fritz led the entire climb free using only one piton, which he claimed to regret. We found the climbs very tough even with modern gear!

There was no sign of aliens from the extra-terrestrial spaceship in *Close Encounters of the Third Kind*, filmed here on location, but we did watch the film on an open-air screen in the campsite with the real tower rising behind the screen. My daughter claims that I snored loudly through most of the movie. We then headed over into Colorado and climbed in Eldorado Canyon and then all too soon our month was up and it was the long-haul flight back to the UK.

Since 2006 I have made an annual pilgrimage to America. Retirement is a great thing – who would have believed in the early days that it would become relatively easy and inexpensive to travel around the globe? Most of my time has been spent in Yosemite Valley or Tuolumne Meadows, which I guess is the heart of American climbing. The big walls are beginning to be beyond my reach; I never did get up the Nose on El Capitan, and as one gets older the competitive urge isn't quite so challenging, but there's still plenty of classic climbs to follow and the atmosphere is astonishing.

I always planned to get together with Toby, my schoolboy friend and original climbing companion at Wall End and on our early trips to the Alps. We had drifted into a routine of annual Christmas cards and the occasional phone calls, always vowing we would get back together. Marriage and children and life had separated us, but as we approached retirement things began to look more than possible. It had been in my mind for us to go into the Lakeland Fells above Watendlath tarn and find the spot where he, Dicko and I spent the terrifying rainy night wrapped in the remnants of a US Army bivvy tent.

Sitting in our usual corner of the campsite at Lee Vining with Stuart Gallagher, another original resident of Wall End barn in Langdale, I casually asked, 'Have you seen Toby recently?'

He looked at me in consternation. 'Haven't you heard, he's dead?'

Apparently Toby and his wife had gone out to Sri Lanka for a holiday to celebrate their fortieth wedding and had been on the beach the day that the huge tsunami had hit the island. Their bodies have never been found. Such shocks come all too frequently as one gets older and age does not make loss any easier. There is a lesson here not to leave unfinished business too late.

I remember Don Whillans once saying that he had started counting all the friends that he had known and lost and that when he got to sixty he had given up in horror. It's the kind of counting that I would not recommend. Looking at it the other way, it's surprising how many of us are still plodding the hills; our little corner of the campsite at Lee Vining is testimony to that.

Back at home it's relatively easy to escape to Europe if the Scottish weather becomes intolerable, but Scotland is a wonderful country and

I still live in the shadow of Ben Nevis. Fort William has seen better days. Little has been done to improve the roads to the west coast and islands, while Inverness and the Central Belt swallow all the money. Without decent communications the town has little chance of developing. The pulp and paper mills are gone; the aluminium factory is slowly winding down and perhaps in this lovely area it is better that an industrial heritage is replaced by tourism. A new and younger group of people are fighting to improve things and I feel that the future of the Fort lies in capable hands.

I have been incredibly lucky to live through what must have been the second golden age of mountaineering. To walk the hills at a time when there were no deeply rutted footpaths between the summits and when there were secret unclimbed crags to be found almost everywhere. Who knows what the future will bring? I have always joked that I never desired to be the world's best climber but I do aspire to be the oldest! God willing this may just be possible.

Not quite THE END.